Pueblo Warriors and Spanish Conquest

PUEBLO WARRIORS
& spanish conquest

BY OAKAH L. JONES, JR.

UNIVERSITY OF OKLAHOMA PRESS : NORMAN

LIBRARY OF CONGRESS CATALOG CARD NUMBER: 66–10291

Copyright 1966 by the University of Oklahoma Press, Publishing Division of the University. Composed and printed at Norman, Oklahoma, U.S.A., by the University of Oklahoma Press. First edition.

To My Wife, Nancy,
Whose Understanding and Patience Made This Work Possible

Preface

T HE IMPACT of European colonizing nations and the United States upon the Indians of North America has been a subject of considerable study by historians, anthropologists, and sociologists during the twentieth century. The conflict and interrelationship of these civilizations during the course of more than four centuries have been examined from many points of view. Certain phases of the contact between whites and Indians have received greater attention than others, and it is upon these more popular aspects that public attention concentrates.

For over seven years I have been attracted to one of the more neglected phases of that contact—that of the role played by the Indian auxiliary in the subjugation of North and South America by Spain, France, Great Britain, and ultimately the United States. Frequent passing references may be found in the histories of various regions of North America to Indian warrior groups accompanying small armies of the white man in the conquest and pacification of other Indians. In fact, these Indian allies or "auxiliaries" sometimes became the primary forces employed in the reduction of hostile natives. Taking advantage of the traditional lack of unity among the countless groups of Indians in North America, the conquering or colonizing nations used large numbers of these Indian auxiliaries to promote further disunity and to facilitate an early subordination of the natives to the less numerous, newly arrived whites.

Spain set the precedent for dependence upon Indian auxiliaries. Yet the very important role played by Indian allies in the expansion of New Spain northward has generally been neglected. Only Philip W. Powell's *Soldiers, Indians, and Silver: The Northward Advance of New Spain, 1550–1600* has so much as one chapter devoted exclusively to the interesting and highly involved technique of Spanish use of Indian auxiliaries in her defensive expansion from the sixteenth through the eighteenth centuries. Otherwise, casual references are all that exist in the many works relating to the northern frontier of New Spain and the gradual expansion of its perimeter.

Certainly the Indian auxiliary was not the only means Spain adopted in promoting the geographical expansion of her North American holdings. Outstanding individual leadership, well-disciplined regular troops, and extensively enlisted civilian soldiers also contributed to the cause. Moreover, the military operations were supported by the ecclesiastical mission, the civilian town, the mining camp, the cattle ranch, and the crop farm in the consolidation of Spain's hold upon particular regions. In truth, both the Hapsburg and the Bourbon kings practiced the principle of diversification in the expansion of New Spain. Likewise they both promoted the maxim of "divide and conquer," especially when dealing with the various Indian nations in frontier areas.

The purpose of this book is to examine intensively the procedures, organization, contributions, and significance of the Indian auxiliaries of one culture during a crucial century in the vital central sector of New Spain's northern frontier. The Pueblo Indians of New Mexico exemplify the disunity among the natives with whom the Spaniards came in contact. Although most of the Pueblos had united temporarily to expel the Spaniards from New Mexico in 1680, their subsequent reversion to disunity facilitated the Spanish reconquest of that province in the last decade of the seventeenth century.

Not only was there an apparent lack of unity among the sedentary Pueblos themselves, but there was a more significant and traditional rift between the Pueblos on the one hand and the *indios bárbaros*, or barbaric Indians, of the region on the other. Spanish authorities took advantage of these differences not only at the time of the reconquest, but in the century which followed, and their extensive use of Pueblo Indian auxiliaries in the defense of New Mexico during the eighteenth century gradually attracted hostile tribes to the support of Spain. By the end of the century it was no longer necessary to employ large numbers of Pueblo auxiliaries, for Utes, Jicarilla Apaches, Navahos, and even some Comanches could be used more effectively to combat the warlike Apaches. The significant contribution of the Pueblos in the century from 1692 to 1794 not only provides an important development in the local history of New Mexico but also furnishes an understanding of Spanish procedures with and dependence upon the Indian auxiliary in the defense of the entire northern frontier against hostile Indians, French incursions, and later British and North American encroachments.

To understand the nature of the conflict on the New Mexican frontier in the eighteenth century and to faciliate comprehending Spanish policies and practices there, it is necessary to recognize the various types of Indians with whom Spain came in contact. Spanish *conquistadores*, missionaries, and colonizers found two basic types of Indians in the Americas throughout the colonial period.

These consisted of, first, the highly developed, highly civilized groups such as the Aztecs, Mayas, Incas, Chibchas, Pueblos, and Tlaxcalans. Some of these people were centralized under one authoritative ruler, whereas others, such as the Mayas and Pueblos, lived in well-organized yet autonomous communities, similar in general to the Greek city-states of the Old World. The second major type of Indians encountered by Spain, and by far the most consistently troublesome, was the decentralized, highly nomadic one which continually resisted Spanish advances.

On the northern frontier of New Spain the Europeans encountered both highly developed, settled, farming nations like the Pueblos, Papagos, Pimas, and Opatas, and the nomadic, warlike, far-ranging, unsettled groups such as the Seri, Tarahumara, Apaches, Utes, and Comanches. Both types were present in New Mexico where Spain dealt with settled Pueblos, resistant village-dwelling Hopis, or Moquis as they were called by the Spaniards, and nomadic and unsettled Navahos, Apaches, Utes, and Comanches. At some times, as is apparent in this study, Spain was able to establish peace with bands of these nomads. This is particularly true early in the eighteenth century of the Jicarilla, Cuartelejo, and Sierra Blanca Apaches, and later in the same era with the Comanches, Utes, and Navahos.

Five major Indian peoples inhabit the Four Corners region today. They are the Pueblos, Hopis, Apaches, Navahos, and Utes. Many minor groups live in regions removed from this central point. These include the many Yumans, Pimans, Paiutes, and Chemehueves. Also, many of the nations that formerly roamed into New Mexico, such as the Comanches, no longer inhabit the region.

The Pueblo people live in the region of the Río Grande Valley in central New Mexico and in the western part of the state. Their name means "village" in Spanish, and was given them because of their common habit of residing in compact, multi-storied structures. They are the surviving remnants of a people who formerly in pre-Spanish times inhabited the Four Corners area. They do not constitute a single entity or tribe, but each village today, as in the Spanish period, functions as an integral yet autonomous unit. There are now five major linguistic groups among these villages, but none of these divisions reflects consistent geographic unity. These groups are the:

1. Tiwa – Taos, Picurís, Sandía, and Isleta pueblos.
2. Tewa – San Juan, Santa Clara, San Ildefonso, Tesuque, Pojoaque, and Nambé; also some Tewas live at Hano on First Mesa in the Hopi Reservation.
3. Towa – Jémez; also formerly resided at Pecos.
4. Keres – Acoma, Laguna, Zía, Santa Ana, San Felipe, Santo Domingo, and Cochití.
5. Zuñi – Zuñi or Halona

In 1960 there were about 21,500 Pueblo Indians living on nineteen grants in New Mexico. For several years their number has been growing. In 1958 there was an increase of 4,855 noted over the 1948 figures, thus reflecting an increase of about 3.11 per cent in ten years. In Spanish times there were about 10,000 to 15,000 of them, but they were more highly scattered prior to the arrival of the Spaniards. Many sites existed in the region south of Isleta and Albuquerque and in the one near present-day Bernalillo, but consolidation, assimilation, and threats of nomadic nations caused the abandonment of many of these sites. Basically a farming people, the Pueblos nevertheless developed a complicated social system, practiced an intricate religion, and were skilled in artistic work such as pottery, architecture, and weaving. Today they are also among the finest of craftsmen in the arts of silver and turquoise.

To the west of the Pueblos live another village-dwelling people, the Hopi. They reside in eleven self-governing villages on three rocky mesas in eastern Arizona, entirely surrounded by the more numerous Navahos. Their total population is about three thousand and they speak the Shoshonean language of the Uto-Aztecan family. These people fiercely resisted the Spanish efforts to conquer and control them throughout the eighteenth century, and they even welcomed Tewas from the Río Grande Valley who had fled during the reconquest period.

The Navahos who surround the Hopis are of Athabascan stock and call themselves Dinéh, meaning "the people." They originally came down from the north and entered the Southwest in bands, living by hunting and food-gathering, in the period from 1000 to 1500. They constantly plundered the more docile Pueblos and learned much from the latter about farming, weaving, silver work, and religious organization. They took up farming themselves and their name probably derives from the Tewa word *Navahúu,* meaning "cultivated field arroyo." The Navahos were, however, primarily semi-nomads and herdsmen, not house dwellers and horticulturists like the Pueblos. They also differed markedly from the Pueblos in that they were believers in individual ownership of property. There were over 85,000 of them in 1960, and they are increasing at an annual rate of about 2.25 per cent. The Navahos live in scattered communities, none of which may be considered to be very large, on a sixteen-million-acre reservation located mostly in New Mexico and Arizona. In some ways their civilization has become highly developed, particularly in their ritual and religious practices.

Perhaps the best-known Indians of New Mexico are the Apaches, but there are also many misconceptions regarding them. All Apaches are of the same Athabascan stock as the Navahos, but there are many bands in scattered locations throughout the Southwest. These include the Jicarilla and Mescalero Apaches of New Mexico as well as the western Apaches such as the White Mountain, San Carlos, and Chiricahua. Many of the names of these bands no longer reflect earlier usages, especially those of the Spanish period. Somewhat nomadic by nature, these Indians readily took to the horse and increased the range of their predatory raids. They fought essentially for self-preservation, first from the Spaniards, then from the Pueblos and their allies among the European invaders, and finally from the pressures exerted on them by the Comanches. They were originally tipi-dwellers or builders of brush structures known as wickiups, and their greatest artistic achievement is probably their skill in basketry. Today there are about 2,500 Apaches on two reservations in New Mexico and approximately 8,000 of them in Arizona.

The fifth group of Indians in the Four Corners area is the Utes. Actually there are three sub-groups of this nation, the Southern Utes, the Ute Mountain branch, and the Northern Utes. They are of Shoshonean stock and now inhabit three states (Colorado, New Mexico, and Utah). Originally there were some ten bands of them, and they ranged into northern New Mexico during Spanish times, reaching as far southward as Abiquiú and San Juan in the Chama Valley area. Their total population today is about 3,000.

Any study of New Mexico in the eighteenth century must necessarily include the Comanches, who are no longer living in that region but formerly were the "lords of the plains" and the scourge of the Pueblo country. A highly decentralized, nomadic, warlike people, the Comanches drove the Apaches southward in the early eighteenth century and alternately traded with or raided the Pueblos, especially Taos in the north. Their four bands ranged over the High Plains and approached New Mexico from two directions—from the north through the San Luis Valley of southern Colorado and northern New Mexico, and from the east through the mountain passes, especially near Taos and Pecos pueblos. They were the most accomplished horsemen of the Southwest and early in the eighteenth century acquired an advantage over their enemies by trading for firearms with other Indians of the plains to the east of their normal range.

During the eighteenth century Spain was most successful in New Mexico with the various Pueblo peoples. She established peace with these warriors early in the period and gradually attracted nomadic groups to her cause. In this way she added the Jicarillas, some Sierra Blancas, and finally some of the nomadic, raiding *indios bárbaros* themselves. Near the end of the century former enemies, such as the Navahos, Utes, and Comanches joined the Spanish cause, but the Apaches and the remote Hopis were never entirely subjugated during the Spanish occupation of North America.

Many people have contributed to the initiation and continuance of this work. Above all, I want to recognize the influence and guidance of my fellow Spanish Borderlands historian, Professor Max L. Moorhead of the University of Oklahoma. It was he who inadvertently first suggested this topic to me, and at numerous times since he has patiently listened to my findings, theories, plans, and tentative conclusions. Also, he has read each of the parts of this project at various times with an objective, inquiring attitude, offering many helpful suggestions. In addition, he has provided useful information from his own research, including points and observations relating to Spain's Indian auxiliaries on other frontiers.

Without the help and facilities provided by the University of New Mexico and the New Mexico State Records Center, the development of this work would have been impossible. All of the research in the extensive documents of the Spanish Archives of New Mexico was carried out in Albuquerque or Santa Fe. Ted J. Warner, formerly of the Coronado Room at the University of New Mexico Library and now of Brigham Young University, not only permitted me access to the photostatic copies of the Spanish Archives of New Mexico and those of the Archivo General de la Nación at Mexico City, but also offered frequent helpful suggestions from his own study of the presidio of Santa Fe. Likewise, Miss Myra E. Jenkins at the New Mexico State Records Center in Santa Fe, where the state archives are now housed, has encouraged my work among the original documents of the Spanish Archives of New Mexico, which are preserved so efficiently there. It was she who also aided in securing photographic copies of documents and illustrations for inclusion in this project.

Illustrations are an important addition to any work on Indians of the Southwest. The Department of Development, State of New Mexico, publishers of *New Mexico Magazine*, co-operated willingly and promptly with my request for photographic assistance. They provided copies of their photographs of Acoma and the mission at Pecos Pueblo, two of the significant sites in this study. Miss Ruth E. Rambo of the Historical Research Library at the Museum of New Mexico, Santa Fe, aided me also in my search for historical photographs used in the completion of this work. Likewise, my good friend, Gilbert Campbell, director of the acquisitions division of the United States Air Force Academy Library and resident of Palmer Lake, Colorado, has generously donated some of his own personal collection of photographs of the Southwest, especially of the pueblos, for inclusion in these pages.

I want also to express my sincere thanks to Johannes Malthaner, professor emeritus of modern languages in the University of Oklahoma, for his help in translating and bringing to light passages from the German work by Gottfried Hotz, *Indianische Ledermalereien*. His efforts contributed greatly to my understanding of circumstances surrounding the much-debated Valverde and Villasur expeditions northeast of New Mexico in 1719–20.

My thanks are also extended to the *New Mexico Historical*

Contents

Illustrations

Pueblo Warriors and Spanish Conquest

★1+
Introduction

THE FIRST USE OF NORTH AMERICAN INDIANS as auxiliaries for European forces in the New World was made by Hernán Cortés between 1519 and 1521 in the conquest of Aztec Mexico. Although employment of native warriors in this capacity and alliance with dissident tribes were not the only techniques utilized by that Spanish *conquistador*, these were of prime importance in facilitating Spanish domination of central Mexico. Cortés' epic campaign, with its precedent-setting use of Indian auxiliaries, served as a model for future Spanish efforts to expand in all directions from the ancient Aztec capital of Tenochtitlán. Although minor alterations were made in the specific techniques employed with each Indian tribe, the reliance upon native allies remained a fundamental characteristic of Spanish conquest and settlement for three centuries. In truth, the Indians of North America conquered themselves. Natives serving as auxiliaries for a small number of Spanish soldiers, and later for militia elements recruited from the local populace, frequently furnished the quantitative strength in the

3

campaigns against rebellious tribes. Lack of solidarity, so often noted among North American Indian nations, was fatal. Spain first recognized and exploited this weakness, but France, Britain, and the United States followed suit, and native resistance continued for four centuries to crumble before the white man's most successful stratagem—divide and conquer.

Throughout the major part of the colonial period, Spain devoted her attention to consolidating and protecting her vast holdings, acquired so rapidly at the beginning of the sixteenth century. The short early period of searching for great natural wealth, rich cities, and mythical civilizations ended in less than half a century. By the decade of the 1550's, Spanish explorers had found great silver mines, such as those of Pachuca, Guanajuato, and Zacatecas, and they had convinced themselves that further wealthy civilizations, like that of the Aztecs, did not exist in North America. Future expansion in the last two and one-half centuries of Spanish occupation was conditioned by one foremost preoccupation—protection. The need for defense was apparent whatever the motivating force—economic, social, or political. Protection of expanding mining ventures throughout the northern part of New Spain aroused repeated interest from Spanish authorities. They also desired to protect small scattered areas of settlement along the vast frontier, which gradually pushed northward. Religious establishments, such as the many *misiones* founded by the various regular orders (especially by the Jesuits and Franciscans), and separate villages of Indians also required protection. In addition to the constant threat from hostile Indians, Spain had to meet the menace presented by foreign countries. From its establishment until its dissolution, her empire was the object of much international jealousy. Britain, France, The Netherlands, and later Russia and the United States each desired to share in its wealth or to deprive Spain of its rewards. Thus, for the major portion of her occupancy, Spain

4

relied upon a policy of defensive expansion in North America to protect what she already had.[1]

The greatest continuous menace to Spanish authority in North America was that presented by the Indians of one tribe or another. To meet this recurring problem, Spain resorted to all sorts of measures in an attempt to provide a workable system of defense. Faced with constant problems in Europe as well as in the New World, her defensive program was always plagued with bureaucratic weaknesses and shortages of men, supplies, and weapons. Also, great distances, poor transportation, and inadequate communications were retarding factors. But the most important weakness was her lack of adequate finances to support full-scale warfare on all her frontiers, especially the lengthy northern border of New Spain. Unable to overcome these fundamental impediments, Spain attempted to solve her problem by improving and adapting her policy to the unfavorable conditions.

The early conquerors and their military forces were generally

[1] For a discussion of the concept of defensive expansion see Herbert E. Bolton, "Defensive Expansion and the Significance of the Borderlands," *The Trans-Mississippi West: Papers Read at a Conference Held at the University of Colorado, June 18–June 21, 1929* (ed. by James F. Willard and Colin B. Goodykoontz), 1–42, and Charles E. Chapman, *The Founding of Spanish California: The Northwestward Expansion of New Spain, 1687–1783*. The French threat is most capably presented in Henry Folmer, *Franco-Spanish Rivalry in North America, 1524–1763*. Notable studies of the British threat may be found in Herbert E. Bolton and Mary Ross, *The Debatable Land: A Sketch of the Anglo-Spanish Contest for the Georgia Country*; Herbert E. Bolton, *The Spanish Borderlands: A Chronicle of Old Florida and the Southwest* (ed. by Allen Johnson); Lawrence C. Ford, *The Triangular Struggle for Spanish Pensacola, 1689–1739*; Lawrence Kinnaird (ed.), *Spain in the Mississippi Valley, 1765–1794: Translations of Materials in the Spanish Archives in the Bancroft Library*; and Arthur P. Newton, *The European Nations in the West Indies, 1493–1688*. Newton's work is also useful on the Dutch threats to Spain's empire, particularly in the Caribbean. Various phases of the menace presented by the United States have been examined. Among the more important are Kinnaird's work noted above; John W. Caughey, *Bernardo de Gálvez in Louisiana, 1776–1783*; and, two books by Arthur P. Whitaker, *The Spanish-American Frontier, 1783–1795: The Westward Movement and the Spanish Retreat in the Mississippi Valley*, and *The Mississippi Question, 1795–1803: A Study in Trade, Politics, and Diplomacy*. Russian advances and the threats to Spain may be examined in Stuart R. Tompkins and Max L. Moorhead, "Russia's Approach to America," *The British Columbia Historical Quarterly*, Vol. XIII, Nos. 2, 3, 4 (April and July–October, 1949), 55–66, 231–55.

5

not regulars at all, but volunteer captains with indefinite royal commissions and followings of mere adventurers. Agreements known as *capitulaciones* were negotiated between the crown and the *conquistador*, and the latter or a group of adventurers generally provided the financial support for the venture. The majority of the royal troops in New Spain during the seventeenth century were concentrated in coastal towns to repel frequent attacks made by buccaneers. Before the middle of the eighteenth century, the military organization of the Kingdom of New Spain therefore amounted only to a few companies of militia and fewer of regulars.[2]

During the first two centuries of Spanish occupation the crown never attempted to maintain a regular standing army of royal troops in New Spain, relying mostly upon forces recruited from the citizenry of that region. This militia-type force involved three contingents. The first and the poorest ones, known as the *compañías sueltas*, or separate companies, were assigned to guard the coasts; the second group, provincial militia, was distributed throughout the interior; and a third unit of "crack" organizations was stationed in important cities such as Mexico, Puebla, and Veracruz.[3]

As captain-general of the kingdom, the viceroy of New Spain had supreme command over all naval and military forces, the militia of the provinces, and the police force of the capital. In wartime he was assisted by the *consejo suprema de guerra*, a council composed of military leaders, and in peacetime he administered directly those troops stationed within the province of the capital, while intendants and local officials performed the task of supervising those outside of the capital.[4]

In the second half of the sixteenth century, frontier warfare became more highly organized since a system was developed on the Chichimeca frontier north of Mexico City. The constant warfare

2 Donald E. Smith, *The Viceroy of New Spain*, 199.
3 *Ibid.*, 200, 206.
4 *Ibid.*, 105, 197.

6

against the many bands of Chichimecas necessitated the creation of the first bodies of regularly paid and systematically organized Spanish soldiery in New Spain.[5] A presidial troop came into being in the 1570's to serve as an escort on the highways and to act as a roving patrol. Sometimes the forces of these presidial units comprised only three or four soldiers under a captain or *caudillo*, but occasionally as garrisons they might number as many as fourteen. During that decade they were systematically recruited, paid, and instructed by the viceregal government. In the absence of royal troops, protection on the frontier was provided by presidial troops and, as in the past, by a mobilization of the citizenry and allied Indian tribes in time of crisis.[6]

By the 1580's a distinction was being made between soldiers serving at their own expense and those receiving regular salaries from the royal government.[7] Enlistments were usually largest in local military units. All settlers from sixteen to forty years of age had to be registered, and they were required to serve for ten consecutive years in the militia. However, after half this service, they could apply for duty in the *tropa veterana*, or regular company, under royal support.[8] According to their individual *asientos*, or enlistment contracts, the settlers were required to present themselves with arms and horses in good condition before the lieutenant captain-general within thirty days after the initial call to duty. Commanded by individual captains, who were usually either *peninsulares* (Old World Spaniards) or *criollos* (colonial-born Spaniards) and generally landholders or mine owners, these militia units were composed largely of *criollos* themselves. Recruitment rolls of the 1580's reveal that about 60 per cent of the soldiers thus obtained were

5 Philip W. Powell, *Soldiers, Indians, and Silver: The Northward Advance of New Spain, 1550–1600*, 136.

6 *Ibid.*, 130.

7 *Ibid.*, 263.

8 María del Carmén Velásquez, *El estado de la guerra en Nueva España, 1760–1808*, 94.

native to New Spain, the majority being from the Mexico district.[9]

In the eighteenth century basic changes were made in this initial military system. By 1760, troops in New Spain could be divided into two basic categories: the regulars of the *tropa veterana* and the militia. Regular units were used almost exclusively for garrison duty and at strategic points on the frontier as well as in the principal ports. Examples of these garrisons were those of the most important units at Veracruz, in the fortress of San Juan de Ulúa, and others located at San Diego de Acapulco and on the Isla del Carmén, in the Laguna de Términos. In the capital there was a company of 220 infantry and one of 103 cavalry, both organized in 1695. Their principal function was to guard the viceroy and his palace, but they also protected Spanish treasure, prisons, and public buildings, patrolled the streets, and suppressed public disorders. In case of emergency they could reinforce the Veracruz garrison. In addition to these units, the viceroy had a personal guard made up of a company of twenty-three halberdiers whose function was mainly decorative.[10]

The northern frontier from California to Texas was guarded by a system of presidios, twenty-two in number, with a total strength of only 907 men. In addition to the fixed presidial garrisons there were a number of small mobile squadrons, or *compañías volantes*, which totaled 149 men in Nuevo Santander and Nuevo León.[11] The small garrisons, sometimes called *presidios de tierra*, escorted travelers, guarded convoys, and defended against the incursions of the *indios bárbaros*, the nomadic hostiles who continued to resist

[9] Powell, *Soldiers, Indians, and Silver*, 132, 136. The average age of these soldiers was about twenty-five, but ages ranged from a minimum of nineteen to a maximum of fifty.

[10] Lyle N. McAlister, "The Reorganization of the Army of New Spain, 1763–1766," *HAHR*, Vol. XXXIII, No. 1 (February, 1953), 2–4.

[11] *Ibid.*, 3. The total of 1,056 in these two forces compares favorably with those in Table 1, Appendix One, compiled from Estado . . . de infantería, dragones, y compañías sueltas . . . de Nueva España, México, September 7, 1758, AGN, Correspondencia de los Virreyes, Vol. III, f. 419, in Lyle N. McAlister, *The "Fuero Militar" in New Spain, 1764–1800*, 93.

Spanish authority. The only offensive warfare which the presidios conducted was that which they called "defensive."[12]

The second major component of New Spain's military forces was that of the militia or citizen soldiery. Organized into military units and supposedly given periodic training, the militia was of two types: urban and provincial. A standard organizational concept had been developed in 1734, but in New Spain these units were in fact "neither organized nor disciplined."[13] In theory they were to be raised by political districts such as *alcaldías mayores, gobernaciones,* or *corregimientos,* and within these jurisdictions the municipalities—the *ciudades, villas,* and *pueblos*—were supposed to maintain companies of infantry or cavalry. By 1760 these companies had neither been assembled nor called into active service since 1741, their rosters listed men who had died or long since moved from the jurisdiction, their officers were untrained and overage, and the units themselves were without uniforms, arms, or equipment.[14] They were soldiers in name only, existing in specific local areas or scattered over the countryside without being quartered in any central location.[15]

During the mobilization undertaken by Spain for the Seven Years' War, companies of militia were found to exist mainly on paper.[16] Immediately after the war a major reorganization of the military units in New Spain was effected. The previous dependence upon fixed fortifications was to be supplemented thereafter by the creation of colonial armies, led by a nucleus of royal troops. The

---

12 Carmén Velázquez, *Estado de la guerra,* 92.

13 McAlister, "The Reorganization of the Army of New Spain, 1763–1766," *HAHR,* Vol. XXXIII, No. 1 (February, 1953) 4–5.

14 *Ibid.,* 5.

15 Carmén Velázquez, *Estado de la guerra,* 92.

16 McAlister, "The Reorganization of the Army of New Spain, 1763–1766," *HAHR,* Vol. XXXIII, No. 1 (February, 1953), 7. The author concludes on the following page that these forces were inadequate to repulse a strong expeditionary force, but were strong enough to maintain internal security and to defend against hostile Indians. This last statement may be seriously challenged in view of the critical condition of Spanish settlement on the northern frontier and the widespread Indian raids, especially in the latter half of the eighteenth century.

mass of these forces was to be recruited from the local citizenry, and there was to be an increase in number as well as an improvement of organization and discipline. Little attention was devoted to the regular components or toward the urban militias beyond standardizing their functions throughout the kingdom. The greatest part of the new program was directed at the formation of provincial militias to become the bulk of the colonial army.[17]

To popularize militia service, privileges and exemptions were granted to provincials. The complete *fuero militar* (body of military privileges) was granted for all officers, placing their involvement in litigation, civil and criminal, under military jurisdiction. Enlisted personnel were also to receive the *fuero militar* when their specific units were mobilized.[18]

This reorganization had far-reaching social, economic, and political effects. Preoccupation with military affairs increased and expenses for these activities grew, absorbing an ever increasing share of the financial expenditures of New Spain. Yet, the program brought few immediate improvements. The citizens resisted the inducements for enlistment; discipline and morale declined among the regular troops; desertion became a serious problem; and marked deficiencies of arms, uniforms, mounts, and equipment continued.[19] One of the greatest problems faced by the viceroys was the disinclination of the Spanish inhabitants to pursue a career of military service. Since New Spain was not invaded, the people developed a passive attitude towards enlistment projects undertaken by the viceroy and his officials.[20] As a result the provincial

---

17 *Ibid.*, 8–16.

18 *Ibid.*, 25.

19 *Ibid.*, 27–32. The author notes that out of the six provincial regiments only that of Mexico was completely armed and uniformed. The Puebla and Toluca regiments had rebuilt muskets but no uniforms, and the other three had neither arms nor uniforms. In the mounted units, one example of the regimental deficiencies will suffice. The Querétaro regiment was completely mounted and partially uniformed, but it lacked carbines, its basic weapon.

20 Carmén Velázquez, *Estado de la guerra*, 231.

militia was a far from effective force. When mobilized in 1781–82, during the war with Great Britain, most of its units were found to be under-strength, poorly trained, and inadequately equipped. Although mostly unfit for active duty, the militia cost 449,420 pesos a year and was a great drain upon the resources of the empire.[21]

After 1776, the northern frontier was organized as a separate military unit, independent of the viceroy of New Spain and placed under a *comandante general.* The military forces of the Provincias Internas del Norte were divided into two major services. One, involving the majority of the troops, was thinly distributed as an outer line of defense against the *indios bárbaros* while the other element, composed of various urban regiments and companies, was concentrated near the interior settlements to preserve internal order and to act as a reserve in case of foreign invasion.[22]

Yet, troops were not available in sufficient numbers and in enough locations to defend the entire frontier adequately. Their effectiveness was seriously limited by great distances between posts, poor transportation, and inefficient, inadequate supplies of powder, ammunition, and weapons. Other problems included the necessity of recruiting untrained troops and officers from the mestizo element of the population, the weaknesses of the colonial regular army, lack of discipline and training, and a practical ignorance of the strategy of war.[23]

Teodoro de Croix, *comandante general* in 1780, reported that the king spent huge sums on troops who could only defend themselves and could do nothing to protect the neighboring countryside, much less make campaigns against the hostile Indians of the region. He observed that chaos reigned within the presidios, where there was poor discipline, inefficient administration, rare payment of

---

21 McAlister, *"The Fuero Militar" in New Spain*, 55.

22 Smith, *The Viceroy of New Spain*, 211.

23 Alfred B. Thomas (trans. and ed.) *Teodoro de Croix and the Northern Frontier of New Spain, 1776–1783*, 11.

soldiers, and corruption among the paymasters. He further noted that the troops were unskilled in handling arms, knew nothing of subordination and proper discipline, lost their horses, wore out their uniforms, arms, and harnesses, and frequently went hungry. Croix recognized that the real threat to New Spain was not a foreign but an Indian menace. By the end of his administration in 1783, his efforts to strengthen the frontier had yielded some positive results. By that time he had 4,686 men (presidiaries and militia) scattered from Texas to Sonora to defend the frontier, and he had injected new life into the presidios, setting up patrols between them and creating a line of military settlements behind them. He had also organized an effective militia in Nueva Vizcaya, relocated the presidial line and improved post sites in Sonora, distributed forces more efficiently in Coahuila, and made peace with many of the formerly hostile tribes from the lower Río Grande to the Gila River.[24]

New Mexico, as a protruding salient beyond the main line of frontier military posts, posed a great defensive problem throughout the eighteenth century. As late as 1780, Croix noted that its only defense consisted of the presidio of Santa Fe and a "militia of Indians and Spaniards, ill-equipped with arms and horses and without instruction and discipline."[25] Although Croix considered the Indians as part of the militia of New Mexico, it must be noted that they were not actually an integral part of that organization. Throughout the eighteenth century they seem to have been treated as a separate force by Spanish authorities within the province. Therefore, the province had three forces with which to defend itself from hostile Indians who attacked the region from three directions. The small presidial unit at the capital, usually numbering approximately eighty soldiers, was the nucleus and the only

24 *Ibid.*, 12–13, 25, 65–67.
25 *Ibid.*, 24.

regular component in New Mexico. A local militia of unreliable *vecinos* (heads of households usually, but sometimes individual settlers) occasionally supplied help from the capital and outlying settlements such as Albuquerque, Santa Cruz de la Cañada, and Bernalillo. The third and most numerous force in the defensive pattern was the Pueblo Indian auxiliary element, which had been used on nearly every campaign since the conquest of the province was completed by Diego de Vargas in the last decade of the seventeenth century.

Perhaps the reliance upon non-Spanish auxiliaries did not begin with Hernán Cortés in 1519. The practice may have arisen from the seven-century conflict with the Moslems on the Iberian Peninsula. Mercenaries were frequently used throughout Europe in the Middle Ages, and the practice may have been transferred to the New World with the Spanish explorers and *conquistadores*. It appears as though the technique was employed in the fifteenth-century conquest of the Canary Islands, and it may have been used on a limited scale in reducing the Caribbean natives from 1493 through 1513, particularly during the conquests of Española and Cuba. Whatever its origins before reaching the North American continent, it was certainly a primary aspect of Spanish reduction of native elements after the landing near Veracruz in 1519. Cultural diversity and political fragmentation rendered the Indians of this new continent incapable of withstanding pressure from the Europeans. Indians ignored the benefits of racial solidarity in the face of threats from outside their hemisphere, for they fought on both sides in the ensuing conflict.[26] As one authority on Spanish-Indian relations has concluded:

> In a very real sense the Indians of America were the conquerors—or destroyers—of their own world, to the advantage of the

[26] William T. Hagan, *The Indian in American History*, 3. Although this work deals with the relations between the United States and the Indians, the conclusion is equally valid for the Spanish relationship as well.

European invaders. Time and again the story was repeated: Indians conquered other Indians to enable Europeans to control vast New World areas. Much, or even most, of European conquest in America was aided and abetted by the Indians' fighting their own race—a fight that was supervised by handfuls of white men who astutely profited by long-standing native rivalries or the basic enmity between nomadic and sedentary Indian peoples.[27]

Despite the significant role played by the Indian ally in the conquest, colonization, and defense of New Spain, particularly on the northern frontier, little direct attention has been devoted to the use of Indian auxiliaries. Spanish methods of inducement and recruitment, the organizational structures and composition of these contingents, the chain of command and field leadership, battle techniques, distribution of captured booty, the specific military contributions of these auxiliary forces, and their indirect services as interpreters, suppliers of food, and informants all need to be examined. The Pueblos of New Mexico, although important, were by no means the only Indian allies on the frontiers of New Spain, nor were they the first to establish such a relationship with the Spaniards.

Spain's initial use of Indian auxiliaries in North America, it should be re-emphasized, occurred in the Cortesian conquest. At the village of Cempoala, near present day Veracruz, Cortés secured active native allies who provided food, servants, and a troop of *tamenes*, or porters, to carry baggage, guns, and munitions. The cacique of the Totonacs, once he had allied with Cortés, attempted to induce the Spaniards to attack a hostile tribe in the vicinity. In truth, "hereditary feuds and intermittent warfare were the normal condition of the whole country."[28] When Cortés departed from Cempoala on August 16, 1519, with 15 horsemen and 300 foot soldiers, he took some of the natives and their chiefs, who proved

[27] Powell, *Soldiers, Indians, and Silver*, 158.
[28] F. A. Kirkpatrick, *The Spanish Conquistadores*, 74.

14

quite useful on the road.[29] He gathered recruits from other villages as he marched and made the first recorded Spanish use of auxiliaries in battle in his assault on Tlaxcala in September. Cortés noted that he used in this successful struggle his horsemen, 100 foot soldiers, 400 Indians from Cempoala, and 300 from Ixtacmaxtitlán.[30]

Although they were not the first Indian auxiliaries, the Tlaxcalans themselves now became Cortés' most important allies in the conquest of Mexico. The "high degree of independence and local authority" of the Tlaxcalan communities and their long resistance to the Aztecs effectively prepared them for the position they were soon to occupy. By the time the Spaniards arrived in their province, the Tlaxcalans had already developed a system of native warfare which would be of great assistance to them in the future reduction of the Aztec Empire. Generally, they fought in separate groups, usually numbering several thousand each, with distinctive insignias and leaders, advancing into battle to the accompaniment of musical instruments, and utilizing bows and arrows, darts, stones, lances, and macanas (war clubs) as weapons. Their military tactics usually consisted of alternating arrow barrages with close personal engagements.[31]

Tlaxcalan military aid was not given immediately, but only when Cortés determined to go to Cholula. Although thousands set out to accompany him, only about 6,000 arrived in the Valley of Mexico with the *conquistador*. Before reaching that objective they made their first direct contribution as auxiliaries at Cholula, where

29 Hernán Cortés, Second Dispatch, Segura de la Frontera, October 30, 1520, in Irwin R. Blacker and Harry M. Rosen (eds.), *Conquest: Dispatches of Cortés from the New World*, 222–23.

30 *Ibid.*, 29. William H. Prescott, *History of the Conquest of Mexico*, 228–30, states that the number of auxiliaries had reached 3,000 before the assault on Tlaxcala, but he apparently confused this number with the later quantities acquired for the subjugation of the Aztecs. Prescott does note that the allies were of "great service to the Spaniards."

31 Charles Gibson, *Tlaxcala in the Sixteenth Century*, 10, 15. Pueblo Indians also were highly independent, had a high degree of local authority, and had no central governing body.

they aided in the discovery of the native plot to entrap and execute the Spanish intruders. The newly acquired Indian allies then participated with the Spaniards in the subsequent slaughter in the streets of that city.[32]

Having convinced the Europeans of their faithfulness and having demonstrated their value in battle, the Tlaxcalans formed an integral part of the army which later entered Tenochtitlán. The splendor of the entrance into the Aztec capital has been depicted by William Hickling Prescott and other historians, but for purposes of this study the organization and placement of the Indian auxiliaries may be noted. Cortés and a small band of horsemen comprised the advance guard; the Spanish infantry followed with the baggage in the center of the column; and at the rear came the long files of native warriors. Divided into battalions, these auxiliaries carried their own banners. Four chiefs marched in the van and pages carrying their weapons followed. Then came the standard-bearers and others waving banners, followed by the warriors themselves. Prescott notes that the Tlaxcalans, particularly their leader Xicotencatl, tried to imitate their European masters not only in their tactics but in their military etiquette and behavior as well.[33]

From the initial entrance into Tenochtitlán until its final reduction in 1521, the auxiliaries from Tlaxcala participated in nearly all the Spanish military expeditions. They accompanied Cortés to the East Coast in 1520 to meet the threat presented by the arrival of the new Spanish army from Cuba under Pánfilo de Narváez. Tlaxcalans performed well on "*la noche triste*," June 30, 1520, when the Spaniards retreated from the capital. A Tlaxcalan offered to guide the defeated and disorganized Spaniards to his country,[34]

---

[32] *Ibid.*, 22; Prescott, *Conquest of Mexico*, 265, 272–73. Cortés noted that 100,000 Indian allies from Tlaxcala accompanied him, but this is apparently an exaggeration as he later observed that he descended into the Valley of Mexico with more than 4,000 Indians of Tlaxcala, Guajocingo, Cholula, and Cempoala. See Cortés, Second Dispatch, Segura de la Frontera, October 30, 1520, in Blacker and Rosen, *Conquest*, 38.

[33] Prescott, *Conquest of Mexico*, 295, 491–92.

16

and the Europeans were harbored there while they recuperated and reorganized for a second assault on the Valley of Mexico. The faithful allies participated in the construction of the brigantines, which were built initially in their province, then disassembled, carried to Texcoco, and reassembled for launching on the lake.[35] More than 20,000 were reported to have joined in the final siege and attack on Tenochtitlán along with Texcocans, Huejotzingans, and other natives in 1521.[36] During this attack, Cortés was unhorsed on one occasion and immediately a Tlaxcalan Indian rushed to help him, aiding a servant of the conqueror to raise the horse and permitting the Spanish leader to remount.[37] During the course of the battle, however, Cortés noted that his greatest difficulty with the Indian allies was preventing their desertion and restraining them during ferocious attacks upon their enemies.[38]

After the conquest of Mexico, Tlaxcalans accompanied the principal land expeditions conducted during the next decade. They participated in Pedro de Alvarado's march to Guatemala in 1524, and six years later aided Nuño de Guzmán in western Mexico.[39] Three thousand allies, including the Aztec leaders of Tacuba and Mexico, joined Cortés in his march to Honduras in 1524, building bridges to cross rivers where the Spaniards refused to perform such a task.[40] The precedent set by the Totonacs and Tlaxcalans was already bearing fruit for the Spanish *conquistadores* in the third decade of the sixteenth century. New allies were recruited among groups of Mayas in the Yucatán country after 1527. Francisco de Montejo's expedition into that region used friendly Mayas, receiv-

34 Hernán Cortés, Second Dispatch, Segura de la Frontera, October 30, 1520, in Blacker and Rosen, *Conquest*, 76.

35 Gibson, *Tlaxcala in the Sixteenth Century*, 22; C. Harvey Gardiner, *Naval Power in the Conquest of Mexico*, 92–102, 115–16.

36 Gibson, *Tlaxcala in the Sixteenth Century*, 22–23.

37 Hernán Cortés, Third Dispatch, Cuyoacan, May 15, 1522, in Blacker and Rosen, *Conquest*, 110.

38 *Ibid.*, 142–44.

39 Gibson, *Tlaxcala in the Sixteenth Century*, 23.

40 Prescott, *Conquest of Mexico*, 644–46.

ing them as vassals of His Majesty, and requiring them to aid in warfare, to furnish supplies, and to act as guides or scouts.[41]

As a reward for the extensive services provided by the aborigines, the Spanish Crown granted them many privileges, especially the Tlaxcalans. These special dispensations were made also to serve as an inducement to other Indians for their co-operation. Tlaxcala received its *fueros*, or privileges, in the period between the conquest of Mexico and the colonization projects undertaken in the north by them, at royal request, after 1591. One authority has observed that the Tlaxcalan experience closely paralleled that of the Canary Islands. The subjugation of natives followed a similar pattern, beginning with the initial conquest by the Spaniards. Then the natives were used for further conquests and were finally accorded the privileged treatment.[42]

In this manner during the sixteenth century, Charles I and Philip II authorized the creation of such *fueros* for Tlaxcala. The viceroy of New Spain was directed to honor and favor the Indians of that city and republic.[43] All laws published by that native province in 1545 were confirmed by royal authority, and a governorship was recognized there, "having particular memory of the good zeal and fidelity that the Tlaxcalan Indians had for our service in the past."[44] Aborigines of this region were not to be forced to serve elsewhere; they were permitted to correspond directly with the king if they had important business or complaints to present; and, in such cases, the viceroy, *audiencia*, and judges could not prevent such appeal.[45] The natives also were given permission to carry swords, wear Spanish clothing, and ride horses.[46] The crown be-

---

41 Robert S. Chamberlain,*The Conquest and Colonization of Yucatán, 1517–1550,* 43.

42 Gibson, *Tlaxcala in the Sixteenth Century,* 161–62.

43 *Recopilación de leyes de los reynos de las indias,* Tomo II, Libro VI, Título I, Ley *xxxviiii.*

44 *Ibid.,* Tomo II, Libro VI, Título I, Leyes *xxxx, xxxxi.*

45 *Ibid.,* Tomo II, Libro VI, Título I, Leyes *xxxxiii, xxxxv.*

46 Gibson, *Tlaxcala in the Sixteenth Century,* 163.

stowed a royal coat of arms upon Tlaxcala, awarded it the title of *"La Leal Ciudad de Tlaxcala"* in 1535, and upgraded it to *"Muy Noble y Muy Leal Ciudad,"* in 1563. The city was promised perpetual control of the province of Tlaxcala, and subsequently the crown prohibited any interference with its native markets. Most important of all, in 1585 the Tlaxcalans were exempted from tributary payments.[47]

Although the Tlaxcalans were neither the first nor the only Indians to serve as allies of the Spaniards in the early decades, they were the most loyal and most numerous supporters of Spanish expansion in all directions from Mexico City. The general pattern developed by Cortés, involving initial conquest and then alliance with and military assistance from the vanquished natives, was common to most of the Indian peoples encountered by that *conquistador* and those who followed him. It was true even for the mighty Aztecs, who, once conquered, aided in the subjugation of other regions, such as that of western New Spain after the Mixtón War in 1541–42.[48]

On the expanding frontier north of the capital, particularly in the region of the Gran Chichimeca north of Zacatecas in the second half of the sixteenth century, native auxiliaries formed the bulk of the fighting forces employed by Spanish authorities. Used as burden-bearers, warriors, interpreters, scouts, and emissaries, they occupied a significant role in the civilization and pacification of the country roamed by the various Chichimeca tribes. Tarascans and Otomies were employed primarily in these campaigns. Occasionally armies composed exclusively of native warriors, especially of the ever-faithful Otomí nation, roamed the *tierra de guerra* to search for, defeat, and help Christianize the hostile nomads of the

---

47 *Ibid.,* 164–67. An excellent summary of the royal privileges granted to the Tlaxcalan Republic may be found in Appendix VII of this work, 229–34.

48 *Ibid.,* 158–59. A force of 450 Spaniards and 30,000 Tlaxcalan and Aztec allies is reported in J. Lloyd Mecham, *Francisco de Ibarra and Nueva Vizcaya,* 33.

north. In some regions, defense was completely entrusted to these aborigines.[49]

By the end of the Mixtón War in Nueva Galicia, Spanish laws prohibiting the use of European weapons and horses by the natives of New Spain had been fairly well broken down under the necessity of maintaining Indian fighting forces as buffers against widespread Chichimeca raids.[50] Since Tarascans and Otomíes had been indoctrinated in the methods and practices of Spanish warfare during the Mixtón War, it was quite natural that they should become the first important auxiliaries in the *entradas* carried out against the Chichimecas. They played a major role as interpreters and negotiators both in the war and in the arrangement of peace treaties.[51] Indian interpreters were allowed to ride Spanish horses and carry Spanish weapons for protection during these expeditions.[52]

Three important developments are notable in the use of Indian auxiliaries during this period. None were original, but all were extensions and refinements of past policies pursued by the Spaniards. First, the power of attraction possessed by the auxiliaries was everywhere apparent. Soon after 1548 some of the Chichimecas themselves, on the southern edge of the *tierra de guerra*, became allies of the white men, and, later, the more northerly Guachichiles served the Spaniards against the rebellious natives, acting particularly well as informers.[53]

The second and third developments were products of the vice-regal administration of the first Luis de Velasco. He sent friendly natives into the war zone to form defensive colonies and to encourage the hostile tribes to make peace. Also, he established an Otomí militia, under the command of the cacique of Tula. On May 1,

[49] Powell, *Soldiers, Indians, and Silver*, 158.
[50] Arthur S. Aiton, *Antonio de Mendoza: First Viceroy of New Spain*, 152, 177–78; Powell, *Soldiers, Indians, and Silver*, 159.
[51] Powell, *Soldiers, Indians, and Silver*, 166.
[52] *Ibid.*, 167.
[53] *Ibid.*, 167–69.

20

1557, this eminent warrior, now known as Don Nicolás de San Luis Montañez, was cloaked with the title of hidalgo and the rank of captain in the Chichimeca region. He was allowed full use of Spanish military equipment and command over his own warriors but was subject to the orders of the *alcalde mayor* of Jilotepec and required to be accompanied by a Spaniard on all campaigns. Other native leaders, such as Juan Bautista Valerio de la Cruz and Hernando de Tapia, were also commissioned to lead auxiliary forces in the defense of Spanish colonies within the Gran Chichimeca.[54]

By 1600, as a result of the policy established by Cortés and continued in the Mixtón and Chichimeca wars, the Spaniards had come to rely heavily on the military employment of friendly Indians. By that time, the principal inducements offered to attach the natives to the Spanish cause included distributing gifts, granting titles of nobility and military commissions to chieftains, permitting the use of horses, arms, and other Spanish military equipment ordinarily denied the natives, extending Spanish military protection to villages exposed to attack by hostiles, and exempting from tribute and personal service those who assumed especially hazardous assignments.[55]

Exploratory expeditions, such as those of Francisco de Ibarra northward from Guadalajara into Nueva Vizcaya and Sinaloa after 1546, also employed Indian auxiliaries. In these operations the natives were particularly valuable as interpreters, informants, and negotiators. As the frontier advanced from Zacatecas to Santa Bárbara, on the Río Conchos, and from Culiacán to San Juan de Sinaloa, in the west, by the 1570's, Indian allies contributed to this movement, thus making possible further advances by Spain into

[54] *Ibid.*, 70–71. Note that Spanish policy and law prohibiting Indians from riding horses and carrying firearms had been broken within the first century after Cortés' landing at Veracruz.

[55] *Ibid.*, 170–71. Some of these characteristics are also noted by Edward H. Spicer, *Cycles of Conquest: The Impact of Spain, Mexico, and the United States on the Indians of the Southwest, 1533–1960*, 16, 281–85, 571–72.

the present southwestern part of the United States. Although most of these auxiliaries were drawn from western New Spain, some Aztecs were included in the founding of Nueva Vizcaya, and other warriors from newly encountered tribes, such as those along the Río Sinaloa, were voluntarily recruited.[56]

One of the most unique uses of Indian allies on the northern frontier of New Spain was as defensive colonists. As early as 1560, Viceroy Velasco established Jilotepec Indians on the Mexico-Zacatecas road. Philip II recommended the colonizing of Tlaxcalans in the Chichimeca country in 1566, and Spanish officials in Durango later requested that 1,000 of them be brought northward.[57] However, nothing came of these plans until Viceroy Luis de Velasco II undertook the most extensive colonization project of all on the northern frontier.

In 1591, Velasco proposed that 400 Tlaxcalan families "volunteer" to settle the hostile frontier and teach to the Chichimecas by their example the blessings of Spanish civilization.[58] As inducements, the Viceroy authorized the Tlaxcalan settlers titles of hidalgo, freedom from tribute and personal service, segregation from other peoples, and provision of food for a minimum of two years. All privileges previously granted to Tlaxcala itself would be preserved for these settlers, and they would be allowed to ride horses and bear arms.[59]

Although six settlements were initially planned for the northern frontier, the most important were San Estéban de Tlaxcala (pres-

---

56 Mecham, *Francisco de Ibarra*, 113, 135, 237.

57 Gibson, *Tlaxcala in the Sixteenth Century*, 182–83; Charles W. Hackett (ed.), *Historical Documents Relating to New Mexico, Nueva Vizcaya, and Approaches Thereto, to 1773*, I, 154–57; Mecham, *Francisco de Ibarra*, 231. There is also an excellent unpublished seminar paper on the subject of Tlaxcalan colonization. See David Adams, "Tlaxcalan Colonization in Northern New Spain, 1550–1777" (University of Texas, 1963). This paper concentrates upon the settlement of Parras, Saltillo, and Monclova; it draws on Gibson's *Tlaxcala in the Sixteen Century*, Powell's *Soldiers, Indians, and Silver*, and many Mexican works as source material.

58 Gibson, *Tlaxcala in the Sixteenth Century*, 183.

59 *Ibid.*, 184.

ent-day Saltillo) in 1591, and Parras in 1598, under the leadership of Francisco de Urdiñola.[60] The Nueva Tlaxcala (San Estéban) settlement became the mother colony from which numerous other colonization projects occurred.[61] No other expeditions apparently were sent after 1591 from the old city of Tlaxcala, but all future projects for planned settlement northward used settlers from the original colony near Saltillo. By 1714, Tlaxcalans had conducted a punitive expedition against rebellious Indians in Coahuila, and by 1720 they were aiding Spanish troops in Texas.[62] After 1757 a small colony from Saltillo assisted in the repression of Apache raids on the San Saba River in Texas, and twenty years later a settlement of Tlaxcalans was proposed among the Taovayas Indians on the upper Red River.[63] Settlers from the Tlaxcalan colony near Saltillo may have been introduced into New Mexico during the eighteenth century.[64]

On the northwestern frontier of New Spain, Diego de Hurdaide obtained the assistance of a large number of Mayos and Lower Pimas in the reduction of the Yaquis in 1609–10.[65] In his first unsuccessful campaign he employed 2,000 of these auxiliaries with his 40 Spanish soldiers. After he had reorganized, Hurdaide recruited the largest army ever placed in the field in northwestern New Spain prior to 1610, when he increased the number of Indian

[60] *Ibid.*, 185–86.
[61] Herbert E. Bolton, *Texas in the Middle Eighteenth Century: Studies in Spanish Colonial History and Administration*, 345.
[62] Gibson, *Tlaxcala in the Sixteenth Century*, 187–88.
[63] Bolton, *Texas in the Middle Eighteenth Century*, 345; Gibson, *Tlaxcala in the Sixteenth Century*, 188, reports that nine families were designated as teachers in the Apache missions near San Antonio.
[64] Although there is no documentary evidence to prove this statement, it has been noted by many prominent authorities. See Gibson, *Tlaxcala in the Sixteenth Century*, 189; Ralph E. Twitchell, *The Spanish Archives of New Mexico*, I, 36. Twitchell records a request for revalidation of a grant made by Juan de León Brito in the Analco district of Santa Fe near the chapel of San Miguel. Twitchell states that the "Britos" were Tlaxcalan Indians but the document itself notes that León Brito was a "Mexican, and settler of the ward of Analco, in this town of Santa Fe." This is not conclusive proof that Tlaxcalans settled in New Mexico. Perhaps only one family may have been the source of the generalization that Tlaxcalans moved there.
[65] Spicer, *Cycles of Conquest*, 87.

auxiliaries to 4,000 to accompany his 50 soldiers.[66] Although two unfriendly Indians from Sinaloa tried to induce the Mayos to defect from the Spaniards, their efforts were in vain.[67] The Lower Pimas, also reputedly very good soldiers, frequently were employed in the presidial companies that were created to campaign against the northern hostiles.

When the Yaquis were conquered and became auxiliaries, they too conformed to the general pattern of subjugated tribes' joining the ranks of the Spaniards and their allies in future expansionist efforts. Once armed, however, new problems were encountered with the Yaquis since they were considered a menace to public security. The disarmament of this Yaqui force was ordered carried out with "tact and prudence" so as not to lose their confidence since they were of a bellicose spirit and could be dangerous if disarmed violently.[68]

In Sonora the Spaniards found and organized one of the most effective auxiliary forces on the entire northern frontier. The Opatas of that province constantly demonstrated their loyalty to the newly arrived Spaniards, and they were a powerful force in the pacification of rebellious Indians, especially in the eastern part of the region.[69] Spanish authorities began to make use of the Opatas in campaigns against the Jocomes and Apaches in the present areas of northern Sonora and Chihuahua between 1694 and 1696. In the earlier year, when subjected to attack by the Apaches, the Opatas proved extremely able in defending themselves, thus justifying their use as a regular part of the Spanish fighting force when the presidios extended westward to include Terrenate, Tubac, and Altar.[70]

---

66 *Ibid.*, 47.
67 Eduardo W. Villa, *Historia del estado de Sonora*, 82.
68 *Ibid.*, 49, 135.
69 *Ibid.*, 40.
70 Spicer, *Cycles of Conquest*, 98. It is interesting to note that as the presidios extended in a given direction, the Apache raids followed the same path. This would lead

Spanish employment of the Opatas bears a marked similarity to the use of the Pueblo Indians in New Mexico. In both cases the natives were distinguished by their peaceful character, their intense hatred for the surrounding hostiles, and dedication to their work. Opatas and Pueblos were primarily sedentary peoples, congregated in separate, autonomous villages, and living generally by farming. Although employed in different areas of Spanish expansion, their loyalty was unquestioned, their services widely recognized, and they performed as auxiliaries in the same period of Spanish activity on the northern frontier—essentially the last decade of the seventeenth through the first two decades of the nineteenth centuries. Minor differences of technique and practices existed until the formation of an official organization of Opatas into regularly constituted military units occurred in the last quarter of the eighteenth century. This was a major difference between the Pueblos and Opatas, for the former never were officially enlisted into the Spanish regular service. The loyalty of the Opatas of Sonora and their effectiveness in warfare continued into the early independence period in Mexico. In 1811 the Governor of Sonora, Alejo García Conde, marched from Arizpe with a "great number of Opatas" accompanying his royalist force to defeat the insurgents at San Ignacio de Piaxtla in Sinaloa.[71]

Throughout the eighteenth century Opata communities bore the brunt of continuous raids by the Apaches on the northwestern frontier. As allies of the Spaniards, these warriors had the twofold task of defending their own as well as the Spanish settlements. The compatibility of the Spanish and Opata cultures, together with the working alliance between them, speeded the process of intermin-

to the obvious conclusion that the *indios bárbaros* followed the Spaniard rather than avoided him, thus sustaining themselves on crops, stock, and slaves captured regularly from the Iberians.

71 Villa, *Historia del estado de Sonora*, 42. Pueblo Indians had no occasion to support Spanish forces in the suppression of insurgent uprisings in New Mexico during the independence period, since there were none.

gling and co-operation rather than that of separation and hostility. The common interest found in their efforts to protect their villages and peoples led to rapid cultural assimilation through military contacts, increased Spanish infiltration of miners and settlers into the Indian region, and also intermarriage.[72] In 1763 Father Juan Nentuig commented:

> Among all of these [Indians] they are the best Christians; they are the most loyal vassals of our Lord the King, never having rebelled against him or his ministers. They are the most inclined to work, to till their lands, and to raise cattle; they are the truest and bravest in war and many times have shown their courage, both by aiding the Royal troops, and, on their own account, in various campaigns at the expense of the Missions.[73]

After 1756, when 140 Opatas were engaged in the pursuit of Apaches as far north as the Gila River, companies were enlisted to reinforce the regular presidial forces.[74] Spanish defense of Sonora by 1786 consisted of six presidial companies, three companies of Opatas and Upper Pimas, and a picket of dragoons (*Piqueta de Dragones*).[75]

The organization and utilization of the companies of Opatas and Upper Pimas is of unusual significance in the Spanish use of Indian auxiliaries on the frontiers of New Spain. An inspection of 1785–86, conducted by Lieutenant Colonel Roque de Medina, assistant inspector of presidios, ordered by Josef Antonio Rengel, the interim comandant general of the Provincias Internas del Norte, reveals many of the details concerning these companies.

At San Rafael de Buenavista, on the twenty-second and twenty-third of November, 1785, Medina found a company completely

72 Spicer, *Cycles of Conquest*, 98–99, 101.
73 Quoted in *ibid.*, 319.
74 *Ibid.*, 98.
75 Jacobo Ugarte y Loyola to Marqués de Sonora, Chihuahua, June 1, 1786, Archivo General de Indias, Audiencia Guadalajara 521 (104–6–23). (I am indebted to Professor Max L. Moorhead for making this and the two subsequent documents from the same collection available for inclusion in this study.)

manned by Upper and Lower Pimas except for four Opatas and the Spanish officers. He noted that there were seventy-eight Indians in this unit, commanded by four officers, including a regular lieutenant, a second lieutenant, and two sergeants. Both of the lieutenants evidently had a peculiar genius for managing the Indians of the company. Especially notable was the second lieutenant, Nicolás de la Herrán, who understood the native language and used it in communicating with his troops. Observing the Indians closely, Medina reported that they were strong and rugged individuals capable of campaigning on foot. They were of normal disposition, were well disciplined, and were sustained by weekly rations of wheat and corn, and of beans whenever available. Medina further observed from witnessing their marksmanship exercises that the auxiliaries were capable of firing "on the white" with both firearms and bows and arrows, although they preferred to use the former.[76]

These Indian soldiers had no particular uniform, dressing generally as they pleased, but usually wearing leather jackets when on campaign. Some old and relatively useless muskets were furnished the troops, but each man had a bow and arrows, a lance, and an oval shield. Nineteen mules carried supplies and equipment during expeditionary ventures. This Indian company had the dual function of guarding the presidio of San Carlos de Buenavista and accompanying regular troops on defensive and punitive expeditions against the rebellious Seri Indians.[77]

On January 16, 1786, Medina, continuing his inspection tour in Sonora at San Miguel de Bavispe, reviewed a company of Opatas. This unit totaled eighty-five men, including a regular lieutenant, two sergeants, and eighty-one Opata Indians. However, since only

---

[76] Roque de Medina, Extracto de la Revista de Inspeccion . . . , San Rafael de Buenavista, November 26, 1785, AGI, Audiencia Guadalajara 521 (104–5–23). Note the use of firearms by Indians, a practice which was supposedly prohibited, but which was unquestionably authorized by royal authority for friendly Indians. Firing "on the white" appears to be a reversal of the current pattern in target practice since bull's-eyes of the twentieth century usually have a black center.

[77] *Ibid.*

27

eighty of these were considered effective, the company was eight short of its authorized strength, a deficiency which Medina stated would be corrected immediately by recruiting Opatas from among those who volunteered for the task. Although the inspector noted that the *comandante* set a good example for his subordinates, he was especially impressed with Sergeant Antonio Beltrán, who was an Opata. Beltrán knew Castilian as well as his native tongue, displayed exemplary conduct within his unit, applied himself well to the service, complied immediately with orders, and was very useful as a spy on the enemy. Again Medina noted the lack of a common uniform among the native troops, the same fine qualities of the Indian soldiers as he had previously observed at San Rafael de Buenavista, and their excellent marksmanship. Their ability to fire "on the white" with muskets and "carbines" in his presence led him to conclude that as marksmen they were "better than the presidial companies."[78]

The Opatas also dressed as they pleased and were furnished muskets and so-called carbines, many of which were in need of repair. Also, they had thirty mules, only half of them being useful, to carry supplies during their campaigns. This company, situated three leagues from the mission of Santa María Baserac, although advantageously located for pursuing and punishing hostile warriors, had been employed in campaigns with troops from Nueva Vizcaya as far north as the Gila River in April and May, 1784.[79]

Opata Indian auxiliaries thus reached a stage not attained by other natives in their alliance with the Spaniards. This Sonoran tribe was formally incorporated and organized within the Spanish military defensive system during the latter half of the eighteenth

[78] Roque de Medina, Extracto de la revista de inspeccion . . . , San Miguel de Bavispe, January 21, 1786, AGI, Audiencia Guadalajara 521 (104–5–23). Medina also listed Chaplain Friar Georje Loreto in his report but apparently did not include him in the total of eighty-five for the company. Otherwise the total would have been eighty-six (five officers and eighty-one Opatas.)

[79] *Ibid.*

century, after it had supplied continual auxiliary service in the conventional manner. Thus, Opatas reached a plateau never achieved by the Pueblos of New Mexico. The companies created by royal authority among these natives had a total strength very similar to that of the presidio of Santa Fe in the same period, but no Indian company was ever established by the Spanish in the New Mexican capital. Generally, Opatas were commanded and supervised by regular Spanish officers of the *tropa veterana*, although it was apparently possible for Indians to obtain the rank of sergeant. At least one subordinate officer in each unit was thoroughly familiar with the language, customs, and habits of the Indians employed in that company, whether they were Opatas or Pimas. Troops of these companies were furnished rations, supplied with firearms, and became a reliable unit in the defense of one sector of northern New Spain.

Although there is an obvious parallel between the Opatas in Sonora and the Pueblos in New Mexico, particularly in the objectives for which they were employed, there are significant differences. In addition to those already noted, it may be added that the various Pueblos in the Río Grande region were at all times led by their own native chieftains and governors, although they were recruited by Spanish officials according to a quota system, and expeditionary forces were under the over-all jurisdiction of a Spaniard. Their equipment, methods of fighting, and the numerous other functions performed were indeed quite similar to those of the Opatas.

In the area within the present boundaries of the United States, Spain made frequent use of Indian auxiliaries. Upper Pimas, after the time of Father Eusebio Francisco Kino, allied themselves with the Spaniards in the Pimería Alta region against the increasing threats from the northeast.[80] In Texas, the raids of Lipán, Natagé,

80 Spicer, *Cycles of Conquest*, 124. These Upper Pimas included the Papagos of

29

and Mescalero Apaches, after Spain reoccupied the province, encouraged the missionaries to furnish Indians from their jurisdictions to aid the soldiery in defending that province. Thirty mission Indians and an equal number of soldiers comprised the first formal punitive expedition into Apache country in 1723; nine years later 60 friendly Indians served as auxiliaries with 157 Spaniards on a similar campaign.[81] In a general expedition undertaken against hostile Tonkawas and Taovayas, 90 mission Indians and 30 Tlaxcalans who accompanied the expedition were paid one-half of one peso a day while Spaniards received double that amount.[82] Indian alliances became standard policy in Spanish Florida, Guale, and, particularly during the latter half of the eighteenth century, in the new province of Louisiana. There Spain even adopted French methods to gain the allegiance of the natives since her own military forces were inadequate to protect such a vast frontier.[83]

By the end of the seventeenth century Spain had developed a program for the pacification of hostile tribes on the northern frontier. This flexible plan included five major points, not always employed in their entirety in a given region and usually bringing varied results. The principal aspects of this program were:

1. Diplomacy to attract nomadic tribes to peaceful sedentary life.
2. Missionary efforts to integrate the Indians into Spanish civilization.

---

present southern Arizona. Both the Pimas and Papagos became auxiliaries of the United States' forces in Arizona during the 1860's.

[81] Bolton, *Texas in the Middle Eighteenth Century*, 27–28.

[82] *Ibid.*, 89. This expedition also recruited 134 friendly Apaches to serve as auxiliaries against the Nations of the North. Twenty years later, it was recommended that one thousand Indian allies be assembled at the Taovayas villages, joining three hundred Spanish troops at the Colorado River to march toward Coahuila, crushing the Eastern Apaches between two divisions en route. See Bolton, *Texas in the Middle Eighteenth Century*, 125.

[83] For discussions of Spanish Indian policy see note 1 references in this chapter and Elizabeth H. West, "The Indian Policy of Bernardo de Gálvez," *Proceedings of the Mississippi Valley Historical Association for the Year 1914–1915*, 95–101.

3. Colonization with pacified sedentary Indians to attract the hostiles to peace by example.

4. Subsidization of both sedentary and nomadic Indians from royal funds.

5. Recruitment of and major dependence on Indian auxiliaries for the defense of the frontier.[84]

All except the third of these provisions were employed by Spain in dealing with the natives of New Mexico. It was, of course, not necessary to transplant sedentary Indians in that province since village-dwelling, farming natives already existed in the Río Grande region. The major problem facing Spain in New Mexico at the end of the seventeenth century was the reconquest and pacification of the Pueblo Indians, who had expelled all Spanish settlers from the province in the famous Pueblo revolt of 1680.[85] Once this had been achieved, Spanish authorities could concentrate on applying the full program for establishing peace throughout the area.

Spain's greatest continual problem on the northern frontier during the eighteenth century was that of defense against the widespread raids of the *indios bárbaros*. By 1710 it was apparent that forces had been unleashed along this line which Spanish armies were unable to control. Colonization not only failed to advance northward, but even receded as mining settlements and villages were abandoned. Apache bands, pushed southward by the pressure of Utes and Comanches, increased the frequency and devastation of their attacks from 1730 to 1750, striking south of Arizpe and as far west as the Yaqui River in Sonora. The situation grew even worse after 1750, and Spanish authorities admitted the failure of their century-long effort to control the Apaches. In the last three

84 Powell, *Soldiers, Indians, and Silver*, 204. Powell lists only the first four aspects of this program, whereas the author would add the fifth one as an overlooked general part of the over-all Spanish policy.

85 The best account of the Pueblo revolt, its origins, leaders, events, and effects is Charles W. Hackett (ed.), *Revolt of the Pueblo Indians of New Mexico and Otermín's Attempted Reconquest, 1680–1682*.

decades of the eighteenth century Spain made a conscientious and finally successful effort to overcome this resistance. By 1800 raiding had greatly diminished and the immediate threat to continued Spanish occupation of the northern frontier had been dissolved.[86]

Settlers, military forces, and Christianized Indians in New Mexico faced a common threat from hostile tribes, which enclosed the province from at least three directions at all times. Occasionally they were completely surrounded and cut off from the rest of New Spain, especially when Apache raids severed the supply route from Chihuahua. The menace presented by raiding warriors was perhaps greater in New Mexico than in any other province on the frontier. There the Apaches, who constituted a threat to the entire northern region, were reinforced by marauding Utes, Comanches, and Navahos. Gradually, by forcing the hostile natives into a dependent status and by continuing to employ Pueblo Indian auxiliaries, the Spaniards succeeded in defending their establishments in that remote province and in creating a relatively peaceful condition there by the end of the century. Yet, the process was not a sudden one. It evolved over nearly a century of experimentation and consolidation, of fostering disunity among rebellious Indians and unity among those at peace with Spain. The nucleus of this unified policy in New Mexico was the Spanish-Pueblo "alliance" which was achieved after the Pueblo revolt of 1680–92.

[86] Spicer, *Cycles of Conquest*, 236–40. For an excellent account of the changing Spanish alliances and relations with the Indians of New Mexico, emphasizing the change in royal policy which brought about a unified front against the Apaches in the late eighteenth century, see Elizabeth Ann Harper John, "Spanish Relations with the *Indios Bárbaros* on the Northern Frontier of New Spain in the Eighteenth Century" (unpublished Ph.D. dissertation, University of Oklahoma, 1957).

★ 2 ✛

Pueblo Assistance in the Reconquest of New Mexico, 1692–1704

THE RECONQUEST OF NEW MEXICO by Diego de Vargas Zapata y Luján in the last decade of the seventeenth century was one of the crucial events in the long period of Spanish colonial history. It restored that Iberian nation's control, authority, and prestige in an area where a damaging blow had been struck in 1680 by the Indians themselves. It re-established Spain on the northern frontier of New Spain and secured an important strategic site in support of that country's basic policy of defending its widespread holdings on the North American continent.

Yet this advance and military achievement were not the only gains of the last years of Charles II's reign. Beginning with the administration of the Conde de Galve as viceroy of New Spain (1688–96), there was intense activity on the distant frontiers, reminiscent of sixteenth century explorations, discoveries, and expansion. The Tarahumara Indian uprising in Nueva Vizcaya was suppressed, Father Eusebio Francisco Kino extended Jesuit missions among the Upper Pimas, Father Juan María Salvatierra

33

solidified the missions in Baja California, soldiers and missionaries temporarily held Texas, and Spain's strategists planned to occupy Pensacola Bay in Florida.[1] The reconquest of New Mexico was, therefore, only a part of the renewed activity in the north, but it was a highly important one, since New Mexico was the keystone in the frontier arch recently shaken loose by the Pueblo Revolt. If this region could not be reoccupied, the warlike tribes in all of the border provinces might continue to resist the Spanish advance.

Since Spanish military forces had failed to hold the province in 1680, they could hardly subjugate its rebels without reinforcements. Once more Spain looked to her Indian allies. There were the Mexican Indian auxiliaries, particularly the ever faithful Tlaxcalans, but they were already occupied at Saltillo and other defensive settlements to the south.[2] There were friendly tribes in the Paso del Norte district, but their numbers were limited and they were comfortably settled. And there were the Pueblos themselves who might be divided and conquered piecemeal, converted to peace and collaboration, and turned against their brothers who were still in rebellion. Although some few allies from the Paso del Norte region were employed in the first *entrada* during 1692, Spain in the long run adopted the third alternative in regaining and consolidating her control over New Mexico. The reconquest marks the beginning of a century-long dependence on Pueblo Indian auxiliaries for the pacification and defense of New Spain's northernmost interior frontier.

During the seventeenth century, prior to the Pueblo Revolt of 1680, Spain had already established many of her institutions in New Mexico. There were provincial governors, municipal *cabildos*, religious missions, tribute-collecting encomiendas, and military

[1] Irving A. Leonard (trans. and ed.), *The Mercurio Volante of Don Carlos Sigüenza y Góngora: An Account of the First Expedition of Diego de Vargas into New Mexico, 1692,* 29–30.

[2] Fray Francisco Atanasio Domínguez, *The Missions of New Mexico, 1776* (trans. by Eleanor B. Adams and Fray Angelico Chávez), 304.

forces in this era. Certainly the most powerful officer was the provincial governor. In his dual role as head of the civil government and captain-general of the military establishment, his authority was virtually absolute.[3] Among the many duties with which he was charged was the defense of the province from internal and external attack and of the Pueblo Indians from abuse and exploitation.[4] To protect the Spanish towns, ranches, and missions from possible Indian revolt or hostile invasion, the governor was responsible for the direction of military campaigns, distribution of arms and equipment, supply of ammunition, assignment of soldiers for escort and garrison duty, and the maintenance of discipline within the province.[5]

The nucleus of the military force at the governor's disposal prior to 1680 was a group of feudal citizen-soldiers who served without salary but were compensated with the tribute and service from encomiendas. Their number was usually set at thirty-five, and they were expected in times of crisis to defend the province by taking command of fighting units composed of both Indians and Spaniards.[6] There was no presidio in the area, and none was established prior to Vargas' reconquest in the last decade of the seventeenth century.[7]

Santa Fe was both the center of the non-Indian population, which never exceeded 3,000 in the seventeenth century,[8] and of civil and military authority. Pueblo Indians were allowed to remain in their villages and to organize their own government according

---

[3] J. Manuel Espinosa, *First Expedition of Vargas into New Mexico, 1692,* 9.

[4] France V. Scholes, "Civil Government and Society in New Mexico in the Seventeenth Century," *NMHR,* Vol. X, No. 2 (April, 1935), 75.

[5] *Ibid.,* 77–78.

[6] *Ibid.,* 79. For the encomienda system, see Lesley B. Simpson, *The Encomienda in New Spain: The Beginning of Spanish Mexico.*

[7] For a thorough investigation of early presidial activity at Santa Fe, see Ted J. Warner, "The Career of Don Félix Martínez de Torrelaguna, Soldier, Presidio Captain, and Governor of New Mexico, 1693–1726," (unpublished Ph.D. dissertation, University of New Mexico, 1963).

[8] Espinosa, *First Expedition of Vargas,* 10.

35

to the Spanish model. They elected their governors, lieutenant governors, caciques, alcaldes, sergeants, church officials, and captains of war. Usually a Spanish *alcalde mayor* resided in each district as the personal representative of the royal governor of all civil and military matters.[9] The Indian governors of each pueblo were responsible directly to this official.

Warfare in the seventeenth century against the nomadic Apaches and Navahos was sporadic. Periods of peace alternated with others of hostilities. Occasional successes resulted in the resettlement of conquered bands in *genízaro* towns throughout the province. Although they frequently ran away, these *genízaros* were employed usually as servants, and they were Christianized, but they also served effectively as scouts and auxiliaries on Indian campaigns, hence the name.[10]

Pueblo Indians were not used extensively by the Spaniards for early campaigns against the raiding tribes. In contrast to the surrounding nomads, they were initially considered unwarlike, and it was assumed that they would be no match for the ferocity of the Apaches. However, their defensive attitude, concealment of their true feelings, hostility toward aliens, and their apparent talent for appraising the relative strength of the belligerents—all would be of future use.[11]

The Pueblo revolt of 1680 resulted in the complete expulsion of Europeans from New Mexico. Abortive attempts to restore Spanish authority began with Governor Antonio de Otermín's campaign in 1681,[12] but Indian disturbances and internal disunity among the Spaniards continued to wreck any hopes of a consistent advance

9 *Ibid.*, 8.

10 Bolton, *The Spanish Borderlands*, 184. These resettlements were, however, more common in the eighteenth century than in the seventeenth. Abiquiú, on the Chama River, is a good example.

11 Cleve Hallenbeck, *Land of the Conquistadores*, 4.

12 For the Pueblo revolt and Governor Otermín's attempted reconquest, see Hackett, *Revolt of the Pueblo Indians.*

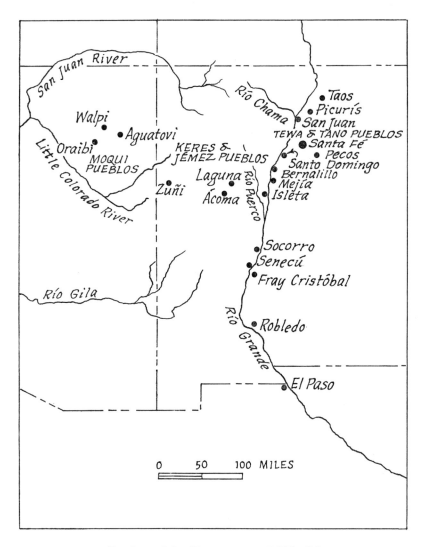

Region of the Reconquest, 1692–96

Adapted from J. Manuel Espinosa, *Crusaders of the Río Grande* (Chicago, Institute of Jesuit History, 1942), 55.

during the ensuing decade. Apparently in these years the Europeans on occasion did experience friendly relations with the Utes, but the Pueblos and Apaches remained hostile. Concerning the latter, Fray Alonso de Posadas wrote in 1686:

> There is one nation that possesses and is the owner of all the plains of Cíbola [and] that they call the Apache. The Indians of this nation are so proud and so arrogant and warlike that they are the common enemy of all the nations they are beneath.[13]

Fray Posadas noted that the mountains of New Mexico were full of Apaches, and that they frequently ambushed the Indian pueblos, killing animals and carrying off the Pueblo women and children whom they secured in their raids to become their slaves, and that they robbed the Spanish horse herds and destroyed the cornfields.[14]

Captain Roque de Madrid's departure from the El Paso district on August 16, 1692, launched the official recovery of New Mexico. Diego de Vargas, who had proposed to complete the reconquest at his own expense, was authorized to take three squads of soldiers from the presidio of El Paso del Norte and 50 soldiers from that of Parral, both fully armed and mounted, for this venture.[15] After considerable delay in awaiting the soldiers from the south, the reconqueror and newly appointed Governor decided to begin the advance without them. However, 100 picked Indian warriors

13 Informe del Padre Fray Alonso de Posadas sobres [sic] las tierras del Nuevo México, AGN, Historia 3. This document tends to offset the conclusion of Jack D. Forbes, *Apache, Navaho, and Spaniard*, 282, that in the period 1680–92 "there is no basis for the thesis that the Athapascans [Apaches] and the settled peoples of the Southwest were basically enemies." That the Pueblos were divided into factions by 1692 is indeed quite true, but the assistance of Apache allies for each of these groups is not clear in Vargas' diary of 1692. Forbes notes this himself on pages 238–39. In addition, the Vargas correspondence does not reflect Spanish warfare in the reconquest period against allied groups of Pueblos and Apaches. Published evidence to refute Forbes' thesis of a natural friendship between Apaches and Pueblos in the period preceding the revolt may be found in Hackett, *Historical Documents* and in *Revolt of the Pueblo Indians*; Spicer, *Cycles of Conquest*; and Frederick W. Hodge, George P. Hammond, and Agapito Rey (trans. and eds.), *Fray Alonso de Benavides Revised Memorial of 1634*.

14 Informe del Padre Fray Alonso de Posadas, AGN, Historia 3.

15 Conde de Galve to Diego de Vargas, May 28, 1692, AGN, Historia 38, Expediente 1.

were recruited from the nearby refugee pueblos of Ysleta del Sur, Socorro, and Senecú. These Pueblos had retreated from their villages in New Mexico with the general Spanish exodus a dozen years earlier.[16]

Captain Madrid departed at two o'clock on the afternoon of August 16, proceeding northward with the presidiaries, pack animals, wagons, livestock, and Pueblo auxiliaries and making camp at Robledo, where he awaited the arrival of his commander. Five days later Vargas reached the encampment with the rest of the force, and the combined expedition headed for Santa Fe.[17] According to Vargas' plans, the first *entrada* was to reconnoiter and determine the state of affairs in the province while actual resettlement would come in the following year with a second, more completely organized and better-equipped expedition.

Accompanying the force was a very important Pueblo Indian, Bartolomé de Ojeda. Fray Silvestre Vélez de Escalante later noted that this Zía warrior had previously fought very well against Spanish soldiers who had attacked his pueblo. He then had come voluntarily to El Paso to join the *conquistador*. Ojeda was *"muy ladino,"*[18] spoke Castilian well, and knew how to read and write.[19]

16 J. Manuel Espinosa, *Crusaders of the Río Grande*, 49. This work and the same author's *First Expedition of Vargas* are the best studies of the reconquest. The former embraces the period from 1692 through 1696 whereas the latter deals entirely with the first *entrada*. The author's research encompassed the extensive Vargas correspondence found in the SANM, Documento 55, and the AGN, Provincias Internas 139, 140, and 141, all of which have been consulted in the completion of this study. Less complete and less accurate is Jesse B. Bailey, *Diego de Vargas and the Reconquest of New Mexico*.

17 Espinosa, *First Expedition of Vargas*, 58.

18 This term was used by the Spaniards to refer to those Indians who were particularly accomplished in the Castilian tongue. In some regions it was used to designate those Indians who had embraced the Spanish way of life. It is still used in some parts of Hispanic America today, particularly in Guatemala, where it is applied to almost the entire non-Indian population according to Richard N. Adams, "Social Change in Guatemala and U. S. Policy," *Social Change in Latin America Today*, 240. Ojeda's achievement in mastering Castilian is a significant product of the Spanish missionary activity prior to 1680.

19 Fray Silvestre de Escalante, Noticias de . . . la custodia . . . de Nuevo México . . . , BNM, Legajo 3, Documento 2. This important document is largely based upon the Vargas correspondence cited above in note 16. An incomplete copy exists in AGN, Historia 2, and another incomplete one was published in *Documentos para la historia de México* (3d serie; México, 1856), 113–208.

Not only was he invaluable as an interpreter for the Spaniards, but he was at all times a reliable informant concerning the state of affairs among the Indians.

Ojeda reported that the province of New Mexico was torn by anarchy and civil strife among the natives. The Keres of Zía, Santa Ana, San Felipe, Cochití, and Santo Domingo, together with the Jémez, Pecos, and Taos Indians, feared the Tewa, Picurís, and Acoma Pueblos. In addition, the Zuñis and Moquis (Hopis) were at war with the Keres, and the Apaches were causing considerable fear and devastation among the Pueblos in general.[20] This disunity, accurately reported by a Pueblo Indian, made the situation opportune for the reconquest, since Vargas could now take advantage of the existing factionalism to employ the technique of "divide and conquer" in the re-establishment of royal authority in New Mexico.[21]

The expedition moved northward, roughly following the course of the Río Grande. During most of the march the friendly Indian warriors went ahead of the main expedition,[22] acting as scouts to determine the presence and strength of expected resistance. Vargas stopped on September 9 at the abandoned ranch house of Mexía, about sixty-six miles south of Santa Fe and in the vicinity of present-day Albuquerque. There he established his base camp, leaving most of his supplies and a garrison force of fourteen Spaniards and fifty Indian allies under the command of Captain Rafael Telles

20 Escalante, Noticias, BNM, Legajo 3.

21 Forbes, *Apache, Navaho, and Spaniard*, 237. The author analyzes completely and accurately the factions which existed at that time. His study on pages 237–38 concludes that there were five groups at war with one another. First, there were Luis Tupatú and the Picurís, Tewas, and Tanos of Tesuque, Nambé, Cuyamunque, Pojoaque, Jacona, Santa Clara, San Ildefonso, San Juan, San Cristóbal, San Lázaro, Santa Fe, and Picurís Pueblos; second, there were the Pueblos of Taos and Pecos and the Apaches of the east; third, there were the Keres of Cochití, San Marcos, San Felipe, Santo Domingo, Santa Ana, and Zía; fourth, there were the Jémez and Acoma Pueblos as well as the Moquis, Navahos, and western Apaches; and fifth there were the Zuñi Pueblos.

22 Espinosa, *First Expedition of Vargas*, 62.

40

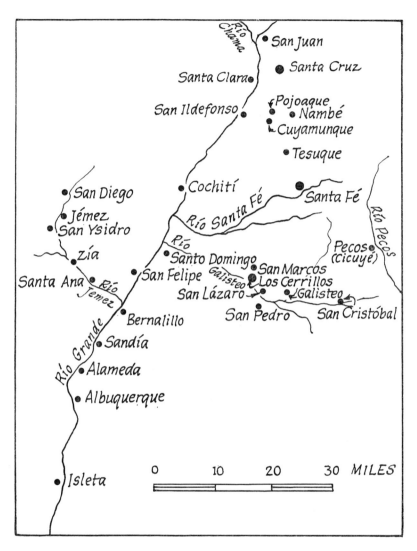

The Río Grande Valley, 1692–1704

Adapted from Cleve Hallenbeck, *Land of the Conquistadores* (Caldwell, Idaho, Caxton Printers, 1950), 156.

41

Jirón. The following day he continued northward with forty soldiers and the remaining fifty Indian auxiliaries.[23]

Although the primary objective of the advancing expedition was the reduction of the reported resistance at Cochití, Vargas dispatched scouts to reconnoiter the surrounding countryside. Cochití was to be surrounded and a siege conducted to prevent the escape of anyone found there. Vargas, upon arrival, relayed through his interpreter that there would be no firing until he gave the order, but he found the pueblo abandoned and entered it unopposed on September 11.[24]

The small expedition reached Santa Fe a few days later after establishing contact with a faction of the Keres Indians at San Felipe. There Vargas learned of their warfare against the Tewas and Tanos and of their desire to aid him in bringing "death to the Tewas."[25] In Santa Fe, Vargas received his first formal offer of assistance from the rebelled Pueblos. On September 16, Luis Tupatú and his brother Lorenzo, both of Picurís Pueblo and the former one of the principal rebels in the great uprising of 1680, arrived with 300 Indian warriors from their villages.[26]

Luis Tupatú, the Picurís chieftain, dismounted from his horse and was welcomed by Vargas and the missionary father over cups of chocolate.[27] The Pueblo leader offered to render obedience to the Spaniards, and Vargas exacted as proof of his allegiance a promise of military service in the proposed campaign against Pecos Pueblo. Although the Spanish commander desired to leave immediately, Tupatú begged for a six-day delay to get his men supplied and equipped so that he could participate in the expedition.[28]

[23] *Ibid.*, 70; Sigüenza y Góngora, *Mercurio Volante*, 59; Escalante, Noticias, BNM, Legajo 3.
[24] Espinosa, *First Expedition of Vargas*, 72–74.
[25] *Ibid.*, 76.
[26] Bailey, *Diego de Vargas*, 53. Luis Tupatú was described in Vargas' journal and in Sigüenza y Góngora's *Mercurio Volante* as "Luis del Picurí."
[27] Escalante, Noticias, BNM, Legajo 3; Bailey, *Diego de Vargas*, 53.
[28] Sigüenza y Góngora, *Mercurio Volante*, 69.

This permission was apparently granted, for Tupatú returned with 300 well-armed warriors in time for the departure of the campaign force on September 21.[29] Some of the newly acquired allies were used as scouts. They advanced on foot ahead of the main body to examine the route through Galisteo to Pecos, to determine the location of water holes, and to ascertain the whereabouts of any potential enemies.[30] Although nothing was found at Galisteo, an Indian scout named Nicolás, of the Tano-speaking Pueblos, reported that he had found tracks which he attributed to two Apache spies who had apparently observed the Spanish advance and the first night's encampment. Nicolás also found an abandoned enemy horse, which Vargas presented to him after shaking his hand and embracing him to impress the other Indian warriors with the Spaniard's sincerity and to encourage them in their own efforts.[31] The scouts also reported that the Pecos Indians were en route to meet Vargas[32] and subsequently a peaceful entry was made into their village.

After a short stay at Pecos, Vargas returned to Santa Fe. There he made plans for the future. Since the expedition had not been intended for permanent colonization, Vargas, with winter rapidly approaching, decided to withdraw again to El Paso. He provided for an interim native government during his absence and ordered his artillery captain, Roque de Madrid, to take the Indian allies who had accompanied the force from El Paso, first to Santo Domingo and then to the base camp at Mexía.[33] Since they were reportedly crippled and their horses exhausted, they were to be sent home.[34]

---

29 *Ibid.*

30 Espinosa, *First Expedition of Vargas*, 115–16, and *Crusaders of the Río Grande*, 72.

31 Espinosa, *First Expedition of Vargas*, 119.

32 Espinosa, *Crusaders of the Río Grande*, 73.

33 Diego de Vargas, Diario de operaciones, SANM, Documento 53.

34 Espinosa, *First Expedition of Vargas*, 182–83.

43

As for the newly acquired Indian allies from the pueblos, Vargas advised Luis Tupatú and Lorenzo to collect their most agile, valiant, and best-equipped young men with their arms and horses. They were to accompany him on a western foray, through the Keresan pueblos of Cochití, Santo Domingo, and San Felipe, then to Acoma, Jémez, Zuñi, and the Moqui villages, to bring them all to obedience.[35] However, the friendly natives were unable to comply with this request because they had not been able to gather their harvests due to unfavorable weather. Vargas, therefore, decided to appoint Luis Tupatú as governor of the *reducciones* (reduced pueblos) while the Spaniards departed westward.[36]

The western expedition left Santa Fe on October 30. It consisted of eighty-nine soldiers and only thirty Indian allies, whom Vargas admitted "were the only ones I was able to take."[37] At Pecos, the first stop on an indirect march, the Spanish commander installed newly elected officers of the pueblo, including two war captains for the control of the auxiliaries.[38] Traveling with a large reserve of horses to assure speed and mobility, the force reached Acoma after only four days of marching, Zuñi on November 14, and the Moqui country five days later.[39] There Indian interpreters named Miguel and Francisco, employed to communicate with the Moquis, reported a conspiracy against the Spaniards.[40]

Although this expedition was imperiled a number of times, especially at the Moqui villages, Vargas did not have to wage a single battle. On December 8, he summoned the Indian guide and three natives from Zuñi, thanked them, and paid them for their services with buffalo hides. He then furnished them with provisions

---

[35] Vargas, Diario de operaciones, SANM, Documento 53.

[36] Espinosa, *First Expedition of Vargas*, 68.

[37] *Ibid.*, 186.

[38] *Ibid.*, 170.

[39] Espinosa, *Crusaders of the Río Grande*, 88.

[40] Espinosa, *First Expedition of Vargas*, 207, 214. The interpreters were undoubtedly Zuñis.

for the return journey to their pueblo.[41] With the remainder of his command, the *conquistador* returned to Mexía and thence to El Paso to begin preparations for the colonizing expedition of the following year.

In terms of the objective of the first *entrada*—to determine the state of affairs in New Mexico—the operation was a complete success, although the small force had been in jeopardy on at least three occasions. In four months, twenty-three pueblos of ten Indian nations had been "restored" to the Spanish Empire without using an ounce of powder or shedding a drop of blood, except in conflicts with the Apaches. Seventy-four captives were freed, 2,214 Indians were baptized, and the Spanish language was found to be yet alive.[42]

Still, the reconquest was incomplete. The Europeans had neither subjugated the entire region nor continuously maintained their authority over the province. Vargas himself realized this when he reported to the viceroy that "until five hundred families and one hundred presidial soldiers enter this kingdom it will be as casting a grain of salt into the sea."[43]

Nevertheless, the success of the expedition rested upon many factors. Careful preparation, courage, and decisiveness aided Vargas, as did the dissensions among the Indians.[44] There were other factors, however, such as the willingness of the Pueblo allies to cooperate with the small Iberian expeditionary force. Without their aid as soldiers, interpreters, scouts, informants, and provisioners, it is doubtful that such a small handful of men could have succeeded at all. Certainly, Vargas and his followers learned a great deal from this preliminary reconnaissance. These lessons proved invaluable to them in the reconquest and colonization which followed in 1693.

Early in that year, Vargas was granted the right to solicit col-

[41] *Ibid.*, 245.
[42] *Ibid.*, 30–32.
[43] Diego de Vargas to Viceroy Conde de Galve, Santa Fé, October 16, 1692, in Espinosa, *First Expedition of Vargas*, 162.
[44] Sigüenza y Góngora, *Mercurio Volante*, 41.

onists for New Mexico and to enlist 100 soldiers for the establishment of a presidio at Santa Fe. Forty thousand pesos were set aside by the Viceroy of New Spain to finance the enlistment of the soldiers and to help meet the costs of the colonization venture.[45] However, after weeks of preparation, personal visits, and the resolution of numerous miscellaneous problems, Vargas reported that only 42 enlistees had been obtained and that 200 horses had been purchased. By mid-June, however, he had spent the 40,000 pesos, successfully recruited 100 soldiers, and had obtained an unspecified number of families and a quantity of supplies for the expedition. To meet expenses, however, he requested that an additional 15,000 pesos be provided for his use.[46]

Finally, after many delays, the colonizing expedition of over 800 persons, including soldiers and Indian auxiliaries (presumably Pueblos from the El Paso jurisdiction), about 900 cattle, 2,000 horses, and 1,000 mules was ready. It began the long trek northward on October 4, 1693, crossing the Río Grande the following day with the aid of the Indian allies.[47]

The Indian situation in New Mexico had changed considerably from that which had existed when the Spaniards had departed ten months previously. Vargas made extensive use of native interpreters and informants, a technique which he had learned well during the first *entrada*. Bartolomé de Ojeda again accompanied the force as did other friendly Keres and Tano Indians. Near present-day Los Lunas, New Mexico, a Pueblo Indian from Zía named Lorenzo assisted the expedition by reconnoitering the Keres pueblos along the Río Grande and the villages of the Jémez. He had also delivered to Cochití a letter written by Vargas, announcing the arrival of the Spaniards and requiring the Cochiteños to render obedience to His

---

45 Espinosa, *First Expedition of Vargas*, 33.

46 Espinosa, *Crusaders of the Río Grande*, 120–23.

47 *Ibid.*, 129–30. Hubert H. Bancroft, *History of Arizona and New Mexico, 1530–1888*, 202, states erroneously that the departure was on October 13.

Catholic Majesty Charles II. However, he reported that most of the Pueblos had turned against the Europeans since they suspected that they were to be punished for their past resistance. Only Santa Ana and San Felipe were ready to aid the *conquistador*, while Ojeda's own pueblo of Zía was undecided.[48]

Farther up the river, at the hacienda of Anaya, near present Bernalillo, Vargas ordered all the friendly Keres in his company, under the leadership of their captain Bartolomé de Ojeda, to depart for Zía. There they were to remain and, in return for establishing Spanish authority at that pueblo, they were to be provided with a beef each Sunday and Wednesday.[49] The only other Pueblo Indians whom Vargas found loyal to their promises of the previous year were those of Pecos to the east.

The Spanish Governor, remembering the friendship of Luis Tupatú and the Tewa and Tano Indians of the region north of Santa Fe, dispatched two friendly Tanos (probably from Pecos) who had been in charge of transporting a field gun during the advance, to visit Tesuque, San Juan, San Lázaro, and other villages north of the capital.[50] These natives, however, were reluctant to accept the offer of friendship because they had received an erroneous report that extensive punishment would be inflicted upon them for their leadership in the rebellion of 1680.

Resistance to the advancing Spanish column was concentrated in Santa Fe. Vargas requested and received a contingent of 140 Pecos Indian allies to aid in an assault on the city, and this was begun December 29. With the battle cry "Santiago! Santiago! Death to the rebels!" the city was stormed and won by the following day. The Spaniards lost one man while the Pecos auxiliaries had 5 killed. Eighty-one of the rebels perished—9 in battle, 2 by suicide,

48 Espinosa, *Crusaders of the Río Grande*, 134–35.
49 Vargas, Diario, AGN, Historia 38.
50 Bailey, *Diego de Vargas*, 97.

and 70 by execution after the battle was concluded.[51] Although the capital and chief objective had been secured, the reconquest was far from complete. Military campaigns had just begun, and Vargas needed all the Indian allies he could acquire before pacifying the province. The year 1694 was one of constant warfare against various rebellious Pueblo groups as well as some Apache bands.[52] In addition, there was a serious shortage of grain and food supplies which imperiled the newly arrived Spanish settlers.

Although the principal resistance continued both above and below the capital, Vargas elected first to reduce the opposition in the former direction by assaulting the pueblo and mesa of San Ildefonso. With sixty fully armed soldiers, thirty militia, and some Pecos allies, he attacked the mesa in early March, 1694, but heavy snow and rain prevented a successful siege. San Ildefonso held out, twenty of Vargas' troops were wounded,[53] and Spanish prestige suffered a damaging blow.

Vargas next struck southward at La Cieneguilla de Cochití, where the Indians of Santo Domingo and Cochití were concentrated and fortified. With the aid of Keresan natives from Santa Ana, Zía, and San Felipe, commanded by Ojeda, Vargas conducted a successful assault with three major columns on April 17. Captain Roque de Madrid and Bartolomé de Ojeda led the principal contingent of 40 Spaniards and 100 Indian auxiliaries along the main road approaching the enemy's position. A smaller force of 40 Spaniards was led by Vargas' brother along a second road, while the Governor himself led the third force along the road facing the Río Grande to complete the envelopment. The three columns

---

51 An all-inclusive account of the events of 1693 may be found in Testimonio de los autos de guerra de la reconquista . . . de la Nueva México, AGN, Historia 38, Expediente 2. See also Espinosa, *Crusaders of the Río Grande*, 158–62, and Bancroft, *History of Arizona and New Mexico*, 205.

52 For the activities of 1694–96, see Testimonio de los autos de guerra de la reconquista . . . de la Nueva México, AGN, Historia 39, Expedientes 1–3.

53 Espinosa, *Crusaders of the Río Grande*, 170–73.

closed in upon the mesa with complete surprise. After its capture, the Indian fortress was pillaged, and the loot was distributed among the victors.[54] As a partial payment for their services, Vargas promised 200 head of cattle to the pueblos of Pecos, San Felipe, Zía, and Santa Ana. An Indian named Serbín from Santa Ana was placed in charge of the distribution.[55]

Vargas wisely did not try to return immediately to the scene of his earlier failure at San Ildefonso. Instead, he consolidated his position at Santa Fe, made efforts to improve the precarious economic status of the colony, and planned a long-range campaign in two stages: first, a strike to the west to obtain more Indian allies; and, second, a combined assault on the the fortified mesa north of San Ildefonso.

On May 27, 1694, Ojeda and the Indian war captains of Zía and Santa Ana came to Santa Fe to report on their own campaign in the west against the rebels at Jémez Pueblo. They had heard of an Indian plan to ambush Zía and had decided to surprise the Jémez by taking the offensive first. Their successful assault caused the latter to withdraw temporarily from their villages with a loss of three killed, and five prisoners, whom Ojeda had brought with him to Santa Fe. The Pueblo leader and the war captain of San Felipe returned to the capital on June 14, however, to report that new threats from the Jémez existed in their area and to request aid from the Spanish Governor to protect the loyal Keresans.[56]

The food shortage in the province was more critical than was the Indian threat at this stage, so Vargas led a small foraging expedition northward from the capital on June 30. With him went Juan de Ye of Pecos Pueblo, fifty soldiers, an equal number of militiamen, and an army of Pecos Indian auxiliaries. The native chieftain

54 *Ibid.*, 179–80; Bailey, *Diego de Vargas*, 133–38; Bancroft, *History of Arizona and New Mexico*, 208.

55 Bailey, *Diego de Vargas*, 139.

56 *Ibid.*, 144–46. The author errs in stating Ojeda's pueblo as Santa Ana.

49

and his allies marched in the vanguard, while the soldiers and militia comprised the main column, and the pack train brought up the rear.[57]

Proceeding by way of the abandoned pueblo of Picurís, the expedition reached Taos Pueblo but found it also deserted. The Indians were hiding in Taos Canyon, east of the pueblo, but could not be persuaded to return to their village. Juan de Ye, leaving behind his spurs, powder pouch, cloak, shield, arquebus, and mule, went to the mountain canyon to talk with the enemy in an effort to get them to return.[58] The Spaniards never saw him again.

Having failed in his repeated attempts to negotiate with the Taos Indians, Vargas decided to break them economically while simultaneously aiding the Spanish settlers. He confiscated the pueblo's store of maize, and what his auxiliaries could not load on the mules of the expedition, he burned before departing.[59]

Since the route from the capital to Taos had been very difficult and was expected to be even more so now with the loaded mule train, Vargas returned by a most unusual route. He proceeded northward into the present San Luis County of southern Colorado as far as the Culebra River, followed it westward to the Río Grande, and then turned south to Santa Fe by way of Ojo Caliente and the Chama River Valley. Although he was attacked by Utes on July 12, and lost eight men, he succeeded in reaching San Juan Pueblo and Santa Fe with the much-needed supply of maize.[60]

Upon returning to the capital, the Governor heard from his loyal Keresan auxiliary chieftain, Bartolomé de Ojeda. Demonstrating his ability to write Castilian as well as speak it, Ojeda advised

[57] J. Manuel Espinosa, "Governor Vargas in Colorado," *NMHR*, Vol. XI, No. 2 (April, 1936), 181.

[58] Espinosa, *Crusaders of the Río Grande*, 192. This is, incidentally, one of the better descriptions of the equipment possessed by the Indian auxiliary in this early period.

[59] Espinosa, "Governor Vargas in Colorado," *NMHR*, Vol. XI, No. 2 (April, 1936), 183.

[60] *Ibid.*, 184–85. There is also an account of this expedition in Ralph E. Twitchell, *The Leading Facts of New Mexican History*, I, 402.

Vargas that the rebels at Jémez had made a new agreement in which they resolved not to lay down their arms until they had killed all the Spaniards or had expelled them from the province. He further advised that the Acomas, Zuñis, Moquis, and Coninas [Apaches] were helping the rebels.[61] Vargas consequently resolved to strike at the Jémez villages without delay to sever this new confederation.

The campaign in the west against these towns opened on July 21, 1694. Vargas left Santa Fe on that date with 120 Spaniards[62] and marched along the Río Grande, meeting Ojeda at San Felipe Pueblo. The Keresan leader returned to Zía to organize the auxiliary forces, and on July 23, the Spanish force joined the Indians there.[63] The latter group was composed of Keresans from Ojeda's pueblo of Zía and from Santa Ana and San Felipe. The combined expedition then proceeded to Jémez, where a surprise assault was carried out on the twenty-fourth of July.[64]

Two parties were formed to conduct the attack on the rebellious pueblo. One group, consisting of twenty-five Spanish soldiers and most of the Indian allies, climbed the rear of the mesa overlooking the enemy's village, while the main body assaulted frontally. The attack of both divisions occurred simultaneously at dawn, and resistance collapsed by mid-afternoon after a bloody engagement.[65]

Eighty-four Jémez Indians lost their lives in this encounter, and over 300 women and children were taken prisoner.[66] In addition, 175 head of cattle were seized, 106 of them being given to Father Juan de Alpuente for his use in establishing a new mission at Zía. There were no deaths among the Spanish forces or their Indian

---

61 Escalante, Noticias, BNM, Legajo 3.

62 *Ibid.*

63 Espinosa, *Crusaders of the Río Grande*, 199–200.

64 Twitchell, *Leading Facts*, I, 404.

65 Escalante, Noticias, BNM, Legajo 3. Espinosa in his *First Expedition of Vargas*, 37, calls this engagement "short," but the terminal hour indicates that the battle lasted at least ten hours, which would hardly meet such a description.

66 Espinosa, *Crusaders of the Río Grande*, 200, specifies that there were 346 prisoners, but Escalante's Noticias reflect 361.

allies, but many were wounded.[67] The remainder of the Jémez warriors fled to the mountains.

Vargas ordered the maize and food supply confiscated and had the pueblo sacked. Of the nearly 500 bushels[68] of maize acquired, the majority was distributed to the friendly Keresan Indians for transportation to their individual pueblos.[69] Once the plunder had been completed, Vargas set fire to both of the Indian towns in the area, and withdrew to Santa Fe.[70]

Still preoccupied with the reduction of the fortified Tewas at San Ildefonso, the governor now turned his undivided attention and full resources to that objective. Since the Jémez warriors who had escaped the surprise of July 24 were now scattered in the mountains, he struck a bargain with emissaries whom they sent to the capital to plead for the restoration of their women and children, whom Vargas held as prisoners. The Spanish Governor promised the Jémez men that if they would come down from the mountains to their ancient pueblo and would assist him in the war against the Tewas, he would grant their request, returning all of the prisoners immediately.[71]

The last major campaign of the reconquest began on September 4, 1694. With every available soldier and 150 Indians from Jémez, Pecos, and the three friendly Keres pueblos of Zía, Santa Ana, and San Felipe, Vargas marched northward to Tesuque. Here he ordered Sergeant Juan Ruíz to detach 40 soldiers to reconnoiter Cuyamunque, Jacona, and San Ildefonso Pueblo;[72] then he proceeded to the mesa north of San Ildefonso.

[67] Escalante, Noticias, BNM, Legajo 3.

[68] Three hundred *fanegas* were reported as confiscated. Since a *fanega* is approximately equivalent to 1.58 bushels, there were actually about 474 bushels taken. For English measurements of Spanish terms, see J. Villasana Haggard and Malcolm D. McLean, *Handbook for Translators of Spanish Historical Documents*.

[69] Escalante, Noticias, BNM, Legajo 3.

[70] Twitchell, *Leading Facts*, I, 405.

[71] Escalante, Noticias, BNM, Legajo 3.

[72] Reconquista del Reyno de Nuevo México, AGN, Historia 39, Expediente 3. Accounts of the battle of San Ildefonso appear herein as well as in Espinosa, *Crusaders*

An improperly planned and ineptly conducted attack that day on the rebels of the nine pueblos who had gathered at the *peñol* north of San Ildefonso failed. Even the Indian allies were ineffective during this operation, for they fled when surrounded by the enemy.[73] The Indian units also attacked on the following day in company with three soldiers and an *arriero*, but they were again put to flight;[74] Vargas thereafter settled down to besiege the fortified mesa.

Severely hurt by the siege and facing a critical shortage of food, the Tewas attacked the Spaniards and their allies on September 7, but were repulsed. One of Vargas' Indians scalped an enemy warrior and was reported to have celebrated his feat with his companions in a war dance, accompanied by song, around the victim's body. The following day the Tewas sued for peace and were ordered to reoccupy their old pueblos within eight days.[75] On September 11, Vargas recognized the punctual and unqualified assistance of the Jémez warriors by returning their women and children, whom he had held as prisoners since late July.[76]

This was the last major military expedition of 1694. Constant warfare and extensive use of Pueblo Indian auxiliaries had been characteristic of the period between February and September of that year. The remainder of that and the entire following year were spent in the consolidation of earlier military gains, re-establishment of colonial government, inspections for the security of the realm, and strengthening of the colonists' position in New Mexico. Missions were refounded, political jurisdictions were re-established,

---

of the Río Grande, 205ff.; Escalante, Noticias, BNM Legajo 3; Twitchell, *Leading Facts*, I, 406–407; and, Ralph E. Twitchell, *Old Santa Fe: The Story of New Mexico's Ancient Capital*, 134–35.

73 Bailey, *Diego de Vargas*, 170.

74 Bancroft, *History of Arizona and New Mexico*, 211. The significance of using a mule driver (*arriero*) is not clear. Perhaps he was acquainted with the trails to the top of the mesa.

75 Espinosa, *Crusaders of the Río Grande*, 206–207.

76 Reconquista del Reyno de Nuevo México, AGN, Historia 39, Expediente 3.

Indian pueblos were reoccupied, local Indian officials were elected in each pueblo,[77] and the region concentrated upon replenishing its depleted food supply.[78]

The traditional encomienda right to collect tribute from an allotted number of subjugated Pueblo Indians was not restored. Thereafter, all tribute went directly to the Royal Treasury. No further encomiendas were granted except one for the reconqueror, Diego de Vargas, and his was not implemented.[79]

From the latter part of September through December, 1694, Governor Vargas visited each pueblo in the province. Although these visits were made under the pretext of investing newly elected native officials with their offices, it is probable that there was another motive. While inspecting the pueblos, the governor could observe the degree to which pacification had been completed; he could also ascertain whether the Indians had returned to their pueblos, as instructed, and he could locate any areas where resistance to Spanish authority still continued.

The election and investment of officers at each of the pueblos is an interesting and informative aspect of the reconquest, for it reveals the civil and military organization of the Pueblo Indian auxiliaries. Local governors, such as Bartolomé de Ojeda, now of Santa Ana, were elected in each pueblo, but the position of war captain reveals more exactly the organization of the auxiliary forces. There were five Indians elected to this office and confirmed by Vargas at Santa Ana, seven at Zía, and five at San Felipe.[80]

In some pueblos a *capitán-mayor de la guerra*, or war major, was chosen by the Indians and confirmed by the governor. As of September 28, Jémez had one man in this capacity along with six war captains of the conventional type, and San Felipe had two

---

[77] Espinosa, *First Expedition of Vargas*, 37.
[78] Forbes, *Apache, Navaho, and Spaniard*, 262.
[79] Espinosa, *First Expedition of Vargas*, 38.
[80] Bailey, *Diego de Vargas*, 177–78. Ojeda apparently had moved from Zía to Santa Ana. The Vargas journal also associates him with the latter village hereafter.

capitanes-mayores supervising five war captains.[81] Although Pecos was without a major officer, Vargas appointed nine war captains there. At Santa Ana, Bartolomé de Ojeda was the one exception to Vargas' rule of appointing separate civil and military officers. He was made the governor of his pueblo, captain general of all the Pueblo auxiliaries, and *capitán-mayor* for the Keres-speaking natives.[82]

In general, Vargas, who made all of these inspections himself, found the Indians "content and happy." He checked conditions in all the pueblos he visited, inspected crops and buildings, and required that the natives recognize their vassalage to His Majesty. As exemplified by the procedure employed at San Felipe, this act consisted of ringing the bells of the mission, taking the Holy Sacrament, and proclaiming three times "God protect Charles II, King of Spain."[83] Vargas' visits in this period reached Pecos, San Felipe, Zía, Santa Ana, Jémez, Cochití, Santo Domingo, Tesuque, Santa Clara, San Juan, San Lázaro, San Cristóbal, Cuyamunque, and San Ildefonso. When the Governor submitted his *auto de remisión* on January 10, 1695, the reconquest was considered to be completed.[84]

The subjugation, organization, and return of the Pueblo Indians to their villages did not, however, conclude the Spanish difficulties with them. Although 1695 was not a year of extensive warfare, it was one of continued problems not only with the friendly Indians and the *indios bárbaros*, but with the colonists as well. There were also serious economic problems.

Apparently the people of Santa Fe, especially the merchants and even some of the soldiers of the presidio, were selling arms to the Indians to ransom captives and to enrich themselves. The Gover-

81 *Ibid.*, 179.
82 Vargas, Diario después de veinte de Septiembre, Año de 1694, AGN, Historia 39, Expediente 3.
83 *Ibid.*
84 Bailey, *Diego de Vargas*, 186.

nor, being advised of this practice, which was in direct opposition to the king's orders to deny firearms to the rebellious Indians, decreed that henceforth settlers could not sell their weapons to the Indians but must strive to preserve all that they possessed.[85] This order was intended solely to stop the arms traffic with the *indios bárbaros* and had nothing to do with the arming of the Pueblos.

During the year, the Governor re-established the Spanish farming community at Santa Cruz de la Cañada, north of Santa Fe, colonizing it with settlers after forcing the Indians to move out of the area.[86] Since the province was experiencing great difficulty in sustaining itself, Vargas believed that some impetus must be given to agricultural development to overcome the economic strife of the colony. Crop failure during the winter of 1695–96, combined with the renewed hostility of the Indians, led to another Pueblo uprising in early June of the latter year.[87]

On the fourth of June, Taos, Picurís, Cochití, Santo Domingo, Jémez, and the Tewas rose in rebellion, killing five missionaries and twenty-one soldiers and settlers.[88] The insurrection did not occur without some warning, however, for various missionaries had reported conspiracies earlier and had been advised by the governor to move to the capital for their own safety.

Vargas received news of the rebellion, not from a Spaniard, but from a Pueblo Indian of San Felipe, who sent the Governor a letter advising him that the rebellious Keresans of the nearby pueblos had gone to the mountains, taking with them the sacred re-

[85] Diego de Vargas, Bando, Santa Fé, May 31, 1695. SANM, Documento 57.

[86] Bailey, *Diego de Vargas*, 186. This area had been settled in the seventeenth century and was a prosperous farming community prior to the Pueblo Revolt of 1680. It is still an agricultural area today, now known as the Española Valley. Vargas' action, however, was later criticized severely for contributing to the unrest of the natives who subsequently rebelled in 1696.

[87] Bancroft, *History of Arizona and New Mexico*, 216 .

[88] *Ibid.*; Bailey, *Diego de Vargas*, 226. However, the most comprehensive study of this rebellion appears in Ralph E. Twitchell, "The Pueblo Revolt of 1696—Extracts from the Journal of General de Vargas," *Old Santa Fé*, Vol. III, No. 2 (October, 1916), 333–73.

ligious vessels of their villages.[89] Only Pecos, Tesuque, San Felipe, Santa Ana, and Zía remained faithful during this uprising.[90] Bartolomé de Ojeda, the loyal auxiliary leader from the Keres pueblos, made an independent foray against the Jémez, took one prisoner, and returned to his pueblo. He then dispatched a letter to Vargas, requesting aid and stating: "As you know we are on the frontier, and I beg of you to send me firearms, powder, and bullets for you know well that we are very loyal vassals of His Majesty."[91]

The Spanish Governor received reports from all sectors of the settled area and adopted a policy of carefully weighing the scope and nature of the revolt before acting—a policy of "watchful waiting." Instead of striking instantly in all directions with his inadequate force and perhaps jeopardizing his position in the province, Vargas adopted a long-range, defensive-offensive strategy. The first phase occurred during the early days of the revolt when he urged the settlers and *"indios cristianos"* to withdraw to the fortified communities such as Santa Fe. He also instructed the native governor at Pecos to furnish "friendly Indians of war" to assist him in the field, and Governor Felipe of that pueblo arrived on June 7 with a force of 100 mounted Indian auxiliaries.[92]

For the offensive phase of his strategy, Vargas adopted a policy of wearing down the morale of the enemy through a war of attrition,[93] concentrating upon the economic life of the rebellious pueblos. Although he dispatched Indian scouts to locate the insurrectionary natives and their allies among the *indios bárbaros*, and personally led a reconnoitering expedition to Tesuque, Nambé,

[89] Diego de Vargas, Diario, Año de 1696, SANM, Documento 60a.

[90] Espinosa, *Crusaders of the Río, Grande*, 244. Domingo Tobina, alcalde of Tesuque, SANM, Documento 60d, clearly demonstrates the loyalty of that pueblo by informing the Spanish governor of rebellious tribes north of Santa Fe.

[91] Bartolomé de Ojeda to Governor Diego de Vargas, Zía, June 8, 1696, quoted in Espinosa, *Crusaders of the Río Grande*, 249.

[92] Diego de Vargas, Diario, Año de 1696, SANM, Documento 60c.

[93] Espinosa, *Crusaders of the Río Grande*, 256. The Spanish general's understanding of total war is unusual for this period.

San Ildefonso, and Jacona on June 7, he made no major effort to attack until twenty days later, almost a month after the initial uprising. This apparent inaction had its indirect effects upon the Indians. Since they had abandoned their villages and had gone to the mountains their crops were left untended, and each day their food shortage increased, magnifying their economic plight.

Departing from Santa Fe on June 29 with a small regular force and sixty Pecos auxiliaries, Vargas marched to Santa Cruz de la Cañada, where he established his field headquarters, to insure that the Tewa and Tano rebels stayed in their mountain retreats. There, facing starvation, the Pueblos would have either to surrender or abandon their settlements and flee northward.[94]

Without a major engagement in the north, the general campaign shifted to the west in July. Pitched battles occurred with the Jémez on the twenty-third and twenty-ninth, costing the rebels thirty men, while their allies, the Acomas and Zuñis, lost eight more.[95] For this offensive the Spanish general had at his disposal a small cavalry force, forty-five Pecos warriors, and eleven Indians from Tesuque under the leadership of a faithful governor named Domingo.[96] The defeat of the Jémez, Acomas, and Zuñis although it was by no means devastating, was decisive since it forced the dissolution of that confederation, caused the Jémez to flee to the mountains again,[97] and impressed all of the western pueblos enough so that they were no longer considered to be a serious threat.[98]

In the first two months of the rebellion the casualties on the Spanish side had been very light—one killed and four captured—while the hostile Indians suffered serious losses—ninety-three killed

---

94 *Ibid.*, 257. The Picurís are a good example. They fled northward and were captured by the Cuartelejo Apaches. Not until 1706 were they rescued and returned to their pueblo by a Spanish expedition. See Chapter III below.

95 Bailey, *Diego de Vargas*, 243.

96 Espinosa, *Crusaders of the Río Grande*, 261.

97 Twitchell, *Leading Facts*, I, 410.

98 Espinosa, *Crusaders of the Río Grande*, 272.

and forty-eight prisoners. The lack of maize among the rebellious Pueblos made their position in the mountains untenable. The economic pressure applied by Vargas, which he gradually increased, had borne good results from the Spanish point of view.[99]

In early August, the Governor led a campaign of Spanish soldiers and Indian auxiliaries from Zía, Santa Ana, and San Felipe Pueblos for an attack on Acoma. Twelve Indians were sent ahead to spy on the enemy, while Vargas organized his force into two groups, one of which he led personally and the other of which was commanded by Ojeda, to assault the 357-foot mesa from opposite sides. Although the attack of August 14–15 did not succeed in obtaining the summit, Vargas did manage to confiscate the crops and burn the fields surrounding the *peñol* before returning to Zía.[100]

With the western area mostly pacified and its crops destroyed, Vargas returned to Santa Fe and made plans for an extensive northern campaign. While the Spanish Governor was organizing this expedition, he received an interesting report from one of his most important auxiliary leaders, Felipe, the governor of Pecos Pueblo. It reveals the ferocity and intense hatred for the enemy displayed by the native allies. Felipe reported that he had surprised a rebel Indian outside of the pueblo and had shot the marauder through the temple. The loyal Pueblo chieftain, as proof of his deed, sent Vargas the victim's head, one hand, and a foot.[101]

On September 21, with the aid of soldiers from the presidio of Santa Fe and Indian auxiliaries from Pecos and Tesuque (probably commanded by Felipe and Domingo, respectively), the Spanish conqueror re-established his headquarters at Santa Cruz and opened his northern campaign. In his subsequent march beyond Santa Cruz he found Picurís and Taos Pueblos abandoned. His

[99] *Ibid.*, 266, 272.
[100] *Ibid.*, 274–77; Bancroft, *History of Arizona and New Mexico*, 217.
[101] Journal of Diego de Vargas, August 30, 1696, quoted in Espinosa, *Crusaders of the Río Grande*, 279.

plea for the Taos to come down from their mountain retreat was greeted by a volley of arrows, to which the Indian auxiliaries replied with musket fire. Pursuing his usual military tactic of converging forces, but this time in a very restricted area, Vargas formed three tiny divisions to assault the canyon (probably Taos Canyon, east of the present town), to obtain the food and supplies of the Indians, to burn their log huts, and to devastate their fields. By September 26, the majority of the enemy had surrendered, and Vargas shifted his attention to the reported mass flight of the Picurís toward the northeast. He pursued them onto the eastern plains and secured some prisoners, but the others, including Lorenzo Tupatú, escaped to the north where they either joined or were captured by the Apaches.[102]

By the end of 1696, the submission of the Pueblo Indians was again complete except for those who had fled to join the various Apache bands and the Navahos.[103] Some pueblos, including Acoma, Zuñi, and the Moqui villages of present-day Arizona, had not been subdued militaristically, but by the end of the year they were no longer a serious threat to the province. Governor Vargas' application of economic warfare, striking at the crops, food, and dwellings of the sedentary Pueblo Indians, had been a much more effective technique in bringing an end to the rebellion than a more extensive military campaign of the conventional type would have been.

Although the military subjugation of the pueblos was not finally completed until after the expiration of Vargas' term of office, the province was no longer imperiled by Pueblo resistance. Conspiracies were reported and investigated thereafter, but never again would these Indians rise in a concerted effort against the Spaniards.

---

102 Espinosa, *Crusaders of the Río Grande*, 280–88. These Picurís were the ones whom Juan de Ulibarri was dispatched to rescue, in 1706, and who were subsequently returned to their pueblo. See note 94, this chapter, and Chapter III below.

103 *Ibid.*, 297.

The diminution of the Indian population during the reconquest, caused by the abandonment of the pueblos and the loss of life in warfare, exposure, and sickness, in addition to the subsequent flight of many to join the Apaches and Navahos, was a significant factor in reducing Pueblo opposition to the Spaniards.[104] With the increased Spanish population and the economic prostration of the Pueblos during the four years of the reconquest, there was an appreciable change in the role of the Indians of the Río Grande region. Exhausted by years of warfare and famine, they now concentrated upon the re-establishment of their agrarian economy. While so doing, they were exposed continually to the Spanish system of government, the teachings of the Franciscan missionaries, and trade within the province. They became an integral part of the organized population, although they dwelled apart from the rest, and they could no longer afford to rebel.

Pueblo Indian auxiliaries had been a vital factor in the reconquest of New Mexico. Antipathies and hatreds among the various pueblos had been repeatedly exploited by Diego de Vargas in facilitating the re-establishment of Spanish control in the province. Indian interpreters such as Ojeda, Felipe, and Domingo had been a most important asset for the general. Reliable Pueblo Indians were his "eyes and ears" in determining the presence, strength, and disposition of enemy forces. His wise policy of recognizing local elections within the pueblos and allowing Indians to retain their own way of life and their own officials aided the reconquest. Had Spain attempted to mix the tribes or impose her leaders upon the Indian pueblos, the results would have been different.

Although Spanish law forbade the use of firearms or horses by Indians,[105] Governor Vargas wisely saw fit to provide the Pueblos with both. These elements of superiority served not only to attract

---

104 Twitchell, *Leading Facts*, I, 412.
105 *Recopilación de leyes*, Tomo II, Libro VI, Título I, Leyes *xxi, xxiii,* and *xiv.*

rebellious Indians but also to strengthen his Indian allies in their warfare against both the insurrectionists and the *indios bárbaros*. Every effort was made to demonstrate that a peaceful acquisition of the province was intended, but Vargas carefully organized his military forces, including the Indian auxiliary troops, because he did not want to repeat the mistake of unpreparedness which former Governor Antonio de Otermín had committed in 1680.

Without the military assistance, information, food, other supplies, and continued loyalty of some of the Pueblo Indians, Diego de Vargas could not have completed the reconquest and colonization of New Mexico. The small regular force with which he had been provided, the inadequacy of supplies and food, and the isolated position of the colony undoubtedly would have spelled failure. Had not the Pueblos—at least a part of them—been friendly, the Spanish settlement would have been entirely surrounded by hostile tribes. In this situation the Europeans could have been very quickly overwhelmed and forced to retreat again to El Paso.

New Mexico was well on its way toward economic recovery by the spring of 1697, when clothing, food, and other supplies arrived from New Spain to insure the permanence of the province. In that year Vargas was replaced by Pedro Rodríguez Cubero, who remained as governor until 1703.[106]

Rodríguez Cubero concentrated upon subduing the still rebellious western pueblos, especially those of Acoma, Zuñi, and the Moqui. Since the Keresans of Cieneguilla, Santo Domingo, and Cochití had taken refuge on the *peñol* at Acoma, the new Governor led a force of soldiers and other Keresan auxiliaries (probably from Zía, Santa Ana, and San Felipe) there in June, 1698. Without a major engagement, he succeeded in persuading them to descend,

106 Espinosa, *Crusaders of the Río Grande*, 304. Rodríguez Cubero was appointed by Charles II, and immediately upon arrival in Santa Fe he imprisoned Vargas, charging him with mistreating the Indians and causing the rebellion of 1696. Although exonerated later, Vargas served three years in prison and he and Rodríguez Cubero understandably became bitter enemies.

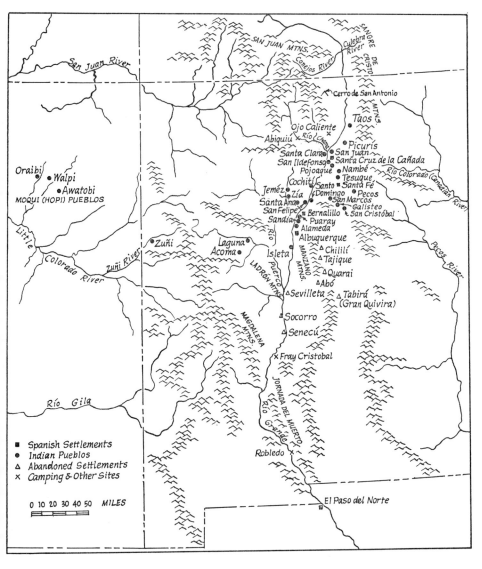

New Mexico in the Eighteenth Century

Adapted from G. P. Hammond and A. Rey, *Juan de Oñate* (Albuquerque, University of New Mexico, 1953).

make peace, and establish themselves in the new pueblo of San José de Laguna, north of Acoma, on July 2, 1698.[107]

Two years later the Governor turned his attention to the Moquis of present northeastern Arizona. Although their war captains came to Santa Fe in May, 1700, to sue for peace and to ask to return to the Christian way of life, they later changed their minds. Moreover, when Rodríguez Cubero personally conducted an expedition against them, supported by thirty friendly Indians, it was without success. The Moquis remained independent throughout the rest of the eighteenth century as an Indian Gibraltar in an otherwise Spanish-controlled province.[108]

By the early years of the eighteenth century the submission of the Pueblos was relatively complete. Except in the Moqui area, the power of the Spaniard was apparent everywhere, and the Pueblos were tired of revolts which seemingly ended in disaster.[109] Then, and for the remainder of the century, the Apache problem became of paramount interest.[110]

An alleged uprising of the western pueblos (Acoma, Zuñi, and Laguna) created a temporary flurry of activity in 1702. The Governor dispatched Sergeant Juan de Ulibarri to conduct an investigation at these pueblos in March of that year. Ulibarri found all "quiet and obedient" at Laguna and Acoma on March 4–5, and proceeded to Zuñi. There, in an interview with Father Juan de Garíacochea, the alcalde Joseph Naranjo, and the garrison force of twelve soldiers, he discovered an apparent misunderstanding concerning what had actually occurred.[111] Naranjo informed him

107 Escalante, Noticias, BNM, Legajo 3.

108 Espinosa, *Crusaders of the Río Grande*, 348–49. Other expeditions occurred at intervals after the administration of Rodríguez Cubero, but no continuous concentrated efforts were made to recover the distant Hopi pueblos.

109 Twitchell, *Leading Facts*, I, 419.

110 Forbes, *Apache, Navaho, and Spaniard*, 280.

111 Investigación del levantamiento de indios, SANM, Documento 84. The garrison of twelve soldiers was reduced to three in 1703, but they behaved "scandalously," since they lived in public with the native women, including even the governor's wife. They were killed by the Zuñi in the same year. See Twitchell, *Leading Facts*, I, 419–20.

that a meeting of the Zuñi, Acoma, and Laguna natives had indeed been called, but that it was to discuss reprisals against the Apache intruders and Navaho marauders who had allied with the Moqui in an effort to kill the Spanish missionary and the military escort garrison assigned at Zuñi.[112] For the false report and inflamed conditions created by an Indian named Ytacae, Governor Rodríguez Cubero ordered that the people of his pueblo punish him by delivering fifty lashes.[113]

Campaigns against the Faraón Apaches and the Navahos conducted by Governor Rodríguez Cubero were generally fruitless. The Governor's projected expedition against the former never took place, and the latter, planned to include 100 soldiers and 125 Indian allies, was abortive.[114] In 1703 Cubero was replaced by Diego de Vargas, now the recipient of the title Marqués de la Nava Brazinas.

During late March and early April, 1704, Vargas led an expedition in the Sandía Mountains against the Faraón Apaches. This campaign[115] was of singular importance, for it marked the beginning of a new era when Spanish and Pueblo Indian forces were united to combat the incursions and the growing threat of the Apaches. No longer would there be Pueblo disunity and resistance to the Spaniard. Henceforth, all of the pueblos would render support in the Governor's military campaigns.

On March 27, having heard of numerous Faraón Apache livestock raids in the vicinity of Cieneguilla and Bernalillo, Vargas

112 Investigación del levantamiento de indios, SANM, Documento 84. The "Apaches" mentioned here were probably Navahos, whom the Spaniards considered to be of the same nation. They frequently applied the term "Apaches-Navajos" to these natives.

113 Juan de Ulibarri to Governor Pedro Rodríguez Cubero, Zuñi Pueblo, March 8, 1702, SAMN, Documento 85.

114 Escalante, Noticias, BNM, Legajo 3.

115 The best sources for the study of this campaign are the Autos de guerra de la primera campaña . . . a los Apaches Faraones . . . , Año de 1704, SANM, Documento 99, and Ralph E. Twitchell, "The Last Campaign of General de Vargas, 1704" *Old Santa Fé*, Vol. II, No. 1 (July, 1914), 66–72.

decided to honor the requests of the alcaldes of that region to "make offensive warfare by blood and fire."[116] He ordered the presidial captain, Félix Martínez, to compose a list of fifty soldiers with some officers on half-pay to join him for the campaign. In addition, he ordered the alcaldes and governors of the Tewas, Keres, and Pecos Pueblos to select well-armed *gente de armas*, dispatching them to join his force at the rendezvous point (*plaza de armas*) of Bernalillo of March 29.[117]

In a general review of forces provided for the expedition, Vargas, at Bernalillo on March 30, noted the following Indian auxiliaries:[118]

From Pecos
    Don Felipe (Governor)
    Four war captains (Miguel, Diego, Pedro, and Agustín)
    Joseph de Naranjo (Captain of the scouts)
    Forty-two men

From San Felipe
    Three war captains (Cristóbal, Juan, and Miguel)[119]
    Fourteen men

From Santo Domingo
    Four war captains
    Four men

From Cochití
    Three war captains (Lorenzo, Alonso, and Francisco)
    Twelve men

From Nambé
    Two war captains (Cristóbal and Lorenzo)
    Three men

116 Autos de guerra, SANM, Documento 99.

117 *Ibid.*

118 *Ibid.* Naranjo's original pueblo is somewhat obscure since he is associated at various times with Zuñi, Santo Domingo, the Tewas, and here with Pecos. The figures appearing in this table have been compared favorably with those in the Twitchell article cited in note 115, this chapter.

119 Twitchell, "The Last Campaign of General de Vargas, 1704," *Old Santa Fé,* Vol. II, No. 1 (July, 1914), 68, errs in combining Juan and Miguel into one name.

From Tesuque
　　One war captain (Martín)
　　Eleven men
From San Ildefonso
　　One war captain (Juan)
　　Three men
From Santa Clara
　　One war captain (Juan Roque)
　　Four men
From San Juan
　　One war captain (Lorenzo)
　　Five men
From Jémez, Zía, and Santa Ana
　　Alcalde mayor Diego de Montoya
　　Numbers of men not specified

Combined with 47 Spaniards (both soldiers and settlers), these auxiliaries, drawn from twelve separate pueblos, amounted to at least 120 Indians, not including the representatives of the three villages whose numbers were not enumerated. Joseph Naranjo and 30 of the auxiliaries were detached and sent ahead to serve as scouts, reconnoitering the Sandía Mountains, presumably to locate the enemy. On March 31, 2 Tewas from this group reported a skirmish between the scouts and the hostiles, and that the Apaches had thereafter retreated to well-fortified positions in the sierra. Naranjo himself returned later the same day with reports of the Apache position. Although the pursuit was begun the following day and Vargas again sent Naranjo with 40 Indians to find the enemy and discover his watering places in the mountains,[120] the campaign collapsed after April 2, when the Marqués was stricken with a fatal illness. He was taken to Bernalillo, where he died on April 8, 1704.[121]

120 Autos de guerra, SANM, Documento 99.
121 Espinosa, *First Expedition of Vargas*, 41.

Despite the fact that the last campaign of Diego de Vargas was a failure, it was a most significant forecast of the nature of Indian warfare, which was to be almost characteristic of the entire eighteenth century. The Apache would continue to be the dominant menace until the Comanches arrived on the northern and eastern frontiers. As a result, the conflict hereafter would center around the Spanish-Pueblo unity on the one hand and the *indios bárbaros,* whether they were Comanches, Apaches, Utes, or Navahos, on the other.

The period from 1692 to 1704 had been one of conquest, directed primarily against the rebellious Pueblo Indians. The Pueblo unity in the revolt of 1680 had been shattered by 1692. The Spaniards made use of the new disunity to facilitate the reconquest and colonization of New Mexico. By 1704 they had restored unity among the Pueblos, but it was then in support of Spanish civilization rather than opposed to it.

Hereafter Spanish military forces would no longer enlist Pueblos to combat other Pueblo armies. A new era had begun with a long-term Spanish policy in this portion of the northern frontier of gradually subduing hostile tribes and of obtaining their support against the dwindling number of remaining enemy tribes. The example of the Pueblo auxiliaries eventually inspired the Ute, Comanche, Navaho, and even some Apache bands to accept peace and to unite against the Apache nation at large.

★ 3 ✦

Organization and Unification, 1704–1729

Within a decade after the reconquest of New Mexico and the suppression of the last Pueblo uprising of 1696, the Indian problem in the province began to acquire new characteristics. No longer was the principal enemy a band, town, or nation of Pueblos. Various groups of Apaches, Navahos, Utes, and the newly-arrived Comanches became more serious threats to the isolated northern region. Thus, the presence of so many enemies helped to draw the Spaniards and Pueblos together, cementing the uncertain "alliance" which had been achieved earlier.

The campaigns of Diego de Vargas between 1692 and 1696 had taken advantage of Pueblo disunity. Practicing such techniques as "divide and conquer," an economic war of attrition, and offensive warfare by "blood and fire," the Spanish *conquistador* had completed the subjugation of most of the New Mexican region. However, the conquest could not have been completed without the assistance of friendly Pueblo Indian forces. These native allies had furnished Vargas with interpreters, supplies, foodstuffs, and military elements to support his numerous campaigns against other rebellious groups of Pueblos.

By 1704 a notable change had occurred. Although there were still some rebels among the Pueblos, especially at Acoma, Zuñi, and the Moqui towns, Spanish operations against the Indians of the province had begun to change. Most indicative of this alteration was the unsuccessful campaign of March and April in that year against the hostile Faraón Apaches in the Sandía Mountains, east of present-day Bernalillo. Although Governor Vargas was stricken with a fatal illness, the formation, composition, and basic practices of this expedition were illustrative of the new type of warfare and the campaigns undertaken during the eighteenth century.

For this military venture, as has been noted earlier, Vargas employed Indians from twelve of the Pueblo villages. Some of these natives came from towns such as Zía and Santa Ana, which had been friendly throughout the reconquest. Others were from newly subjugated pueblos, such as San Juan and San Ildefonso.[1] However, this campaign illustrated that warfare in New Mexico was no longer a question of Spaniard and Pueblo versus another Pueblo, but Pueblo and Spaniard versus non-Pueblo. Hereafter the Spanish-Pueblo tie would form the nucleus in defending the province from, and occasionally taking the offensive against, the growing menace of the *indios bárbaros*.

During the interim governorship of Juan Páez Hurtado, from 1704 to 1705, there were many unfounded reports of Pueblo uprisings. Conspiracies seemed to center around San Juan Pueblo and it appeared at one time as though an alliance between the Indians there and the Navahos was in the formative stages. Interrogation of friendly natives, including some from Santa Clara, revealed that the possibility existed of a loose alliance among the

---

[1] Autos de guerra, SANM, Documento 99. See Chapter II above for the composition of this expedition.

Utes, Navahos, Jicarilla Apaches, and San Juan and Jémez pueblos,[2] but no subsequent rebellion occurred.

With the appointment and arrival of Francisco Cuervo y Valdés as the new provincial governor in 1705, Indian affairs acquired increased attention and importance. Desirous of defending the already-pacified pueblos and strengthening the area of Spanish settlement, Cuervo wasted no time in concentrating upon the Indian problems of the realm. He called a *junta de guerra*, or war council, on April 16, 1705, in Santa Fe to organize a campaign against the Navahos. Settlers were mustered for the expedition, and Indian allies from the pueblos of Picurís, Santa Clara, Cochití, Jémez, and Zuñi accompanied the force westward.[3]

In the following month the new Spanish official, reviewing the entire frontier situation, concluded that the "forces of this realm do not have sufficient strength to punish the mentioned enemies."[4] Since the rebellious tribes were aware of this weakness, they frequently challenged the authorities by raiding the settled region, including such Spanish towns as Bernalillo, where eighty head of cattle were taken in one bold effort. The Governor concluded that what the province most needed was thirty additional presidials from Nueva Vizcaya,[5] but it is doubtful that had they been furnished they could have ended the frontier war with the nomadic tribes.

Extensive Indian campaigns occupied the summer months, and Pueblo allies were used for all efforts against threatening tribes. In June, Cuervo struck against the Gila Apaches and in July he dispatched a large force of soldiers, settlers, and Pueblos under the

---

2 Juan Páez Hurtado, Relación de una conspiración . . . , December, 1704, SANM, Documento 104.

3 Francisco Cuervo y Valdés, Autos en campaña contra los Apaches, Santa Fé, April, 1705, SANM, Documento 110. Although the title of this document indicates that the threat was from "Apaches," the text specifies "Navajo Apaches," which means Navahos. See Chapter II, note 112 above.

4 Cuervo y Valdés to Viceroy Duque de Alburquerque, Santa Fé, May 18, 1705, AGN, Provincias Internas 36, Expediente 5.

5 *Ibid.*

command of his *maestre del campo*, Roque de Madrid, against the Jémez and Navahos. The latter campaign extended into August and September, and some success was experienced against the Navahos. However, the Indian allies occasionally got out of control. One member of the expedition relates an incident of this nature in which he found the Pueblo auxiliaries killing an old woman. He stopped them, and she promptly begged to be baptized. After the chaplain performed this act, the native allies killed her.[6]

Within a year after Cuervo's arrival, his vigorous Indian policy had begun to reap dividends. The most serious threat from the hostiles—that of the Navahos—had apparently been overcome, and a state of relative tranquility had been reached. The Governor reported by mid-summer of 1706 that the Navahos had sent emissaries to the Christian Indians to learn "about the kindness and affection" and the "good treatment" which Cuervo had shown toward them.[7]

Since the region now enjoyed an unusual period of relative peace, Cuervo concentrated upon strengthening Spanish settlements along the Río Grande. First, he resettled the vicinity of present Galisteo, establishing the Indian town of Santa María de Gracia de Galisteo with 150 families of 630 persons, principally Christianized Tano Indians who had been scattered over the province since 1702. A new church was built there, and fields were soon cultivated and planted in corn.[8] Cuervo also established the new Spanish *villa* of Albuquerque with 30 families comprising 252 persons.[9] Not satisfied with these two efforts, the Governor desired to extend further the area of Spanish military authority by creating

6 Escalante, Noticias, BNM, Legajo 3.
7 Cuervo y Valdés, Informe, August 18, 1706, in Hackett, *Historical Documents*, III, 382.
8 Cuervo y Valdés to His Majesty [Philip V], Santa Fé, July 13, 1706, AGI, Guadalajara 116, Number 260. Also discussed in Cuervo y Valdés to the King, Santa Fé, April 23, 1706, in Hackett, *Historical Documents*, III, 22, 379.
9 Cuervo y Valdés to the King, April 23, 1706, in Hackett, *Historical Documents*, III, 22, 379.

a new presidio at either Zía or Socorro,[10] but such a project was never accomplished.

The best illustration of Cuervo's interest in uniting and defending the Pueblos is his dispatch of a military expedition in 1706 to recover the Picurís Indians, who had been living among the Apaches since their flight during the revolt of 1696. Undoubtedly, this was the most memorable event of Cuervo's administration. This rescue campaign indicates the Spanish official's desire to restore all of the friendly Indians (principally Pueblos) to their former villages and to establish firm, binding ties with these groups to achieve unity within New Mexico against outside threats. Simultaneously, the event provides an excellent example of the combined Spanish and Pueblo forces so often used during the eighteenth century.

Although the fugitive Pueblos from Picurís[11] often had asked for help from the Spaniards, and it was apparent that they were now being held as slaves by the Apaches in the region of present Pueblo, Colorado,[12] the Spanish authorities had been unable to maintain peace in the province long enough to provide the requested assistance. Instructions were issued by the governor to Sergeant Juan de Ulibarri,[13] in command of the expedition, to proceed to the "*tierra incognita,*" on the plains where the Picurís were held captive. Mention was made of Don Lorenzo Tupatú's (the son of Luis Tupatú, who had been one of the instigators of the Pueblo uprising of 1680) being the "principal Indian and head chief" of the nation requesting aid.[14] It was he who had led the flight from his village in

10 Cuervo y Valdés to His Majesty, Santa Fé, July 13, 1706, AGI, Guadalajara 116, Number 260.

11 Hallenbeck, *Land of the Conquistadores*, 200, states erroneously that the Indians were from Taos.

12 Cuervo y Valdés to His Majesty, Santa Fé, October 18, 1706, in Hackett, *Historical Documents*, III, 383.

13 Ulibarri's name is occasionally rendered as "Uribarri" but the original records show the former spelling.

14 Diario y derrotero que hizo el Sargento Mayor Juan de Ulibarri . . . , Año de 1706, AGN, Provincias Internas 36, Expediente 4.

1696 when Diego de Vargas led the northern campaign against Picurís and Taos.

Authorized to enlist 50 soldiers and settlers and 100 Christian Indians from the pueblos, Ulibarri actually departed on July 13, 1706, with only 40 Spaniards—28 soldiers from the presidio and 12 citizens from the local militia—and the required number of natives.[15] The allied force marched through San Juan Pueblo to Taos, then followed the route through Taos and Cimarron canyons to the vicinity of present Cimarron, New Mexico, on the eastern slope of the mountains. Apparently moving northeastward over Ratón Pass, Ulibarri proceeded by present Trinidad and the Purgatoire River to its junction with the Arkansas River (then called the Napestle), about forty-five miles downriver from the modern Pueblo, Colorado. From that point he moved eastward and encountered the fugitive Picurís among the Cuartelejo Apaches.[16]

15 *Ibid.* The account of this expedition is also contained in Cuervo y Valdés to His Majesty, Santa Fé, October 18, 1706, in Hackett, *Historical Documents*, III, 383–84. The best secondary work on the subject is Alfred B. Thomas (ed.), *After Coronado: Spanish Exploration Northeast of New Mexico, 1696–1727.* See also the heretofore neglected skin paintings analyzed in Gottfried Hotz, *Indianische Ledermalereien.* The author of this work maintains on pages 330–32 that the runaway Pueblos were enslaved by the Cuartelejos after 1696, that the Christian Indians had initiated the request to be rescued, that Ulibarri had 20 soldiers, 12 settlers, and 100 natives enlisted from various pueblos along with him, and that the Cuartelejos were located in eastern Colorado. In this late contention he has followed Thomas, not the evidence presented in the note below.

16 Thomas, *After Coronado*, 16–20; Waldo R. Wedel, *An Introduction to Kansas Archeology*, 467–68. There has been considerable debate concerning the proper location of Cuartelejo. This uncertainty centers upon two sites—one in Otero or Kiowa county in eastern Colorado, and the other in Scott County in western Kansas. Thomas adopts the former, but the archeologist Wedel, after intensive investigation of the latter site and failing to find any such village in eastern Colorado, noted that "no shred of archeological evidence" exists to support the conclusion that eastern Colorado is correct. Wedel agrees with the historian Hackett. In this study the Scott County location has been adopted because there is as yet no such site found in Colorado and because archeological evidence indicates the definite presence of a unique puebloan structure in the midst of a Plains Apache cultural area, together with Pueblo-type artifacts and practices at the Kansas site. However, the historian must recognize that such acceptance must be tentative, as a similar site in Colorado may be discovered. In addition, the Scott County ruin is approximately 120 miles northeast of the junction of the Arkansas and Purgatoire rivers in eastern Colorado, near the location of Thomas' Cuartelejo. It may, therefore, be the *ranchería* of Sanasesli, 40 leagues (104–20 miles) northeast of Cuartelejo, where a detachment of Ulibarri's force rounded up eighteen additional persons for the return to New Mexico.

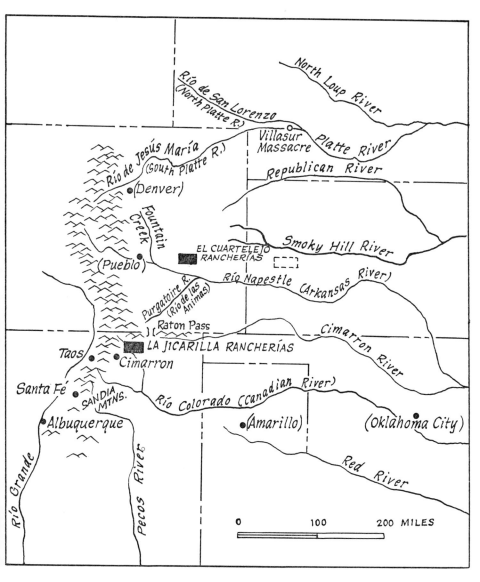

Territory Northeast of Santa Fe in the Eighteenth Century

Adapted from Alfred B. Thomas (ed.), *After Coronado: Spanish Exploration Northeast of New Mexico, 1696–1727* (Norman, University of Oklahoma Press, 1932), 261.

75

Here the commander found the Pueblos scattered in different *rancherías*. Using his two principal scouts, José Naranjo, the Indian who had served Vargas well in the Sandía Mountain campaign of 1704, and Juan de l'Archévèque, a French survivor of the La Salle adventure who had lived in New Mexico since 1691,[17] Ulibarri rounded up the Picurís for the return journey. The rescued Indians had no horses and were described as destitute, so that the Spaniards provided the natives supplies and loaned them horses, particularly the two chiefs, Don Lorenzo and Don Juan Tupatú, for the return trip to Santa Fe.[18]

The joint venture of Pueblos and Spaniards arrived in the capital with sixty-two Picurís Indians, including the chiefs.[19] Undoubtedly the expedition must have strengthened Spanish-Pueblo relations during the governorship of Cuervo, and it must have contributed greatly to the continual improvement noted in Indian affairs within the province prior to 1707. Not only had additional Pueblos been "rescued" and returned to their former village, but the technique of joint Spanish-Pueblo expeditions had been improved upon, extended to the northeastern frontier, far-removed from the scene of earlier co-operative ventures, and organizational patterns for such expeditions had been developed. The campaign also served to further Spanish knowledge of the numerous nations to the north. Cuervo described them as the *"rancherías de indios infieles,"* and he specifically named the Utes, Carlana Apaches, and Comanches as being classified with this group.[20] Pueblo Indians furnished experienced scouts such as Naranjo, supplies such as those obtained at Taos, and military strength, if only in numbers, with

17 Thomas (ed.), *After Coronado*, 16.
18 Juan de Ulibarri, Diario, AGN, Provincias Internas 36, Expediente 4.
19 *Ibid.* However, note that the number is increased to sixty-four in Cuervo y Valdés to Viceroy Duque de Alburquerque, Santa Fé, September 23, 1706, AGN, Provincias Internas, Number 4, Fojas 149–50. Subsequently Cuervo raised this number to seventy-four in his letter to His Majesty, Santa Fé, October 18, 1706, in Hackett, *Historical Documents*, III, 384.
20 Cuervo y Valdés to His Majesty, Santa Fé, AGI, Guadalajara 116, Number 261.

which to confront the Apaches. In addition, they gained experience on an expedition which was not punitive in nature as the earlier campaigns with the Spaniards had been.

In his report on the expedition, Cuervo reviewed the aid received from the Christian Indians since his arrival. He cited in particular the services rendered by the pueblos of San Juan, Santa Clara, San Ildefonso, Cochití, San Felipe, Santa Ana, Zía, and Picurís, and of the jurisdiction of Chimayo (near Santa Cruz), Taos, Bernalillo, Albuquerque, Jémez, Laguna, Acoma, Zuñi, and Moqui—all of which he exaggerated to add up to over 300 Indian languages within the province. He further complimented the Pueblo auxiliaries by stating that when they were on campaign he had observed that they were motivated by great enthusiasm and always pursued the war vigorously. However, he recognized that their battles were bloody operations in which he believed that they were not meeting all of their Catholic obligations.[21]

Indicative of the relatively peaceful situation which confronted the Governor by 1707 was his withdrawal of Spanish garrisons stationed at Santa Clara, Cochití, Jémez, and Laguna, which he considered no longer necessary.[22] More significant, however, is the fact that Cuervo was actually complying with the policies and instructions of the viceroy. Except for that official's interest in prosecuting a war against the Moquis to provide better security for the already pacified region, the Governor was instructed to resort to war only to maintain all that had been acquired previously. He was to refrain from offensive warfare and apply "suave and bland" methods in dealing with hostile tribes, avoiding the shedding of blood in their reduction.[23]

Of unusual interest in this period was the definite appearance in

---

[21] *Ibid.*

[22] Hallenbeck, *Land of the Conquistadores*, 201.

[23] Duque de Alburquerque, Mandamiento, México, July 30, 1706, SANM, Documento 124.

New Mexico of a purportedly new authority, the position of "protector general" of the Indians. Actually this was an extension of an office used elsewhere, since it was apparently created in New Mexico during the year 1706 and had been introduced into other Spanish colonies prior to this time. A former captain, Alfonso Rael de Aguilar, occupied this position during Cuervo's administration.[24] Although the office and the title were not new to Spanish civilization, and official protectors of the Indians had been in existence since Bartolomé de las Casas had achieved such an appointment for the Indies in the sixteenth century, there is no record of their presence in New Mexico before 1706.

On January 6, 1707, Governor Cuervo held an important council in Santa Fe for the Indians of the realm.[25] The purpose of the meeting was to confirm the newly elected officials of the pueblos, and the conference included the "protector general" Rael de Aguilar, Indian governors, caciques, war captains, and other judicial officers from Zuñi, Jémez, Pecos, Picurís, and Taos Pueblos, as well as the Keres, Tewa, Tano, and Tiwa-speaking nations. This council merits unusual attention, for it illustrates in detail the Indian organizational system, the degree of Spanish control over the Pueblos, the extent to which the natives accepted such authority, and Indian satisfaction with Cuervo as governor. When all had

24 For proof that this position was officially in existence in 1706, see Alfonso Rael de Aguilar, Protector General, Certificate, Santa Fé, January 10, 1706, AGN, Provincias Internas 36, Expediente 5. This same document appears in translation in Hackett, *Historical Documents*, III, 366–69. For further verification, see Rael de Aguilar, Protector General de los indios naturales y de sus pueblos, Santa Fé, January 6, 1707, AGN, Provincias Internas 36, Expediente 1.

25 The date of this council is not absolutely clear from a close examination of the sources mentioned in note 24 above. Both the certificates of 1706 and 1707 are in agreement that the date was January 6, but the year is confused. The first document clearly states that the year was 1706 and Hackett so renders it in his translation. But the second certificate clearly indicates 1707. Since both documents cover the same subject matter, cite the same Indians in attendance, and reflect the same order of speaking, it seems that they are one and the same certificate, with an error in transcribing the date of the first. The year 1707 seems more appropriate than 1706 since the discussion involves the Indian desire to retain Cuervo as governor, although the natives were advised of the coming of a new governor, the Marqués de la Peñuela. Furthermore, a scribe recording in January would more likely err in recording the year just past than one not yet arrived.

gathered in front of the Spanish official and had been seated, the Pueblo governor of Tesuque, Domingo Romero, who was also the *capitán mayor de la guerra* for all of the Christian Indians, spoke first in good Castilian, declaring his satisfaction with Cuervo. He reviewed the past military expeditions of the Governor and concluded with a statement that he desired Cuervo to retain his present position, principally because he had established tranquility on the frontier. Other Indian governors who were *"muy ladino"* (accomplished in the Castilian language) followed with similar statements, and those who could not use the tongue of the Spaniards spoke through their interpreters or their protector general.[26]

The Spanish Governor rewarded the Indians with gifts of ribbons, bundles of tobacco, hats, needles, beads, and other trifles. He provided shoes and suits of fine Mexican cloth for the Indian governors as well as cloth for shirts and stockings. However, he was unable to comply with their request that he be continued in office, and he informed the natives of the expected arrival of his replacement, the newly appointed Marqués de la Peñuela. The conference concluded after some discussion on reports that there were many apostates among the Zuñi, Moqui, and Navaho.[27]

José Chacón Medina Salazar y Villaseñor, better known as the Marqués de la Peñuela, the new governor of New Mexico, continued and extended many of the Indian policies begun by his predecessor. Difficulties with various Apache bands and incessant warfare with the Navahos necessitated frequent military campaigns which employed Pueblo auxiliaries. In 1709, for example, five separate campaigns were conducted against the Navahos who had been raiding Santa Clara and Jémez. One of these forays under

26 Alfonso Rael de Aguilar, Protector General de los indios naturales y de sus pueblos, Santa Fé, January 6, 1707, AGN, Provincias Internas 36, Expediente 1.

27 *Ibid.* This document summarizing the conference may have been prepared at the request of Governor Cuervo to strengthen his position with the king. There is no doubt that he wished to be appointed, but he was unsuccessful in his efforts.

Roque de Madrid was even ordered for the middle of winter.[28] Extensive efforts were made also to insure that the Christian Indians received proper treatment and payment for their services.

During the first year of the Marqués' administration, Apache hostilities and raids against the Pueblos resulted in many deaths among both Spaniards and their loyal Indian allies. The marauders stole small livestock and frequently robbed horse herds, according to Juan Páez Hurtado, the lieutenant governor of the province. He suggested that two squadrons be formed, each consisting of thirty soldiers supplemented by an equal number of Christian Indians. The two units would alternate in pursuit of raiding Apaches, insuring that they were properly punished for their misdeeds.[29] Continued incursions, however, were reported throughout the province, including El Paso, Zuñi, Albuquerque, and the Sandía Mountain region. This widespread activity of the Apaches, apparently in the south and west, may have been the immediate result of the Comanche pressures applied against them, since the latter arrived in New Mexico from the Great Plains about 1705. The fidelity of the Pueblos was again demonstrated by the assistance of auxiliaries under the leadership of two Indian *capitanes mayores de la guerra*, Domingo Romero of Tesuque and Don Felipe of Pecos.[30]

Apparently successful in temporarily quieting the Apache menace by November, 1708, Governor La Peñuela confirmed Pueblo elections in that month. The natives of San Juan, Santa Clara, San Ildefonso, Nambé, Pojoaque, and Tesuque, together with their governors, caciques, and war captains, presented themselves in Santa Fe on November 7, and were endorsed in their newly elected

---

[28] Marqués de la Peñuela to Roque de Madrid, Santa Fé, December 8, 1709, SANM, Documento 157. Also summarized in Frank D. Reeve, "Navaho-Spanish Wars, 1680–1720," *NMHR*, Vol. XXXIII, No. 3 (July, 1958), 225.

[29] Juan Páez Hurtado to the Governor and Captain General [Marqués de la Peñuela], Santa Fé, October, 1707, in Diligencias hechas por el sargento mayor Juan de Ulibarri . . . , Año de 1708, AGN, Provincias Internas 36, Expediente 2.

[30] Diligencias hechas por el sargento mayor Juan de Ulibarri . . . , Año de 1708, AGN, Provincias Internas 36, Expediente 2.

offices by the Spanish Governor. La Peñuela acted through two Indian interpreters, including José Naranjo, who had assisted Ulibarri in the recovery of the Picurís two years earlier. Three days later the Marqués, acting through the protector of the Indians, Alfonso Rael de Aguilar, performed a similar task for the pueblos of Cochití, Santo Domingo, San Felipe, Santa Ana, Zía, Jémez, and Pecos. The following day he completed the installations by receiving the Picurís and Taos Indians.[31]

Although the record is incomplete, one of the campaigns of 1708 against the Apaches, perhaps in the vicinity of the Sandías, must have created a temporary rift between the Spaniards and at least a portion of the Pueblos. Apparently a soldier from the Santa Fe presidio mistreated an Indian of the new pueblo of Santa María de Galisteo.[32] At any rate, the Viceroy of New Spain, the Duke of Alburquerque, saw fit on two occasions to admonish Governor La Peñuela. In the first instance, he told the provincial administrator to protect the Indians and prevent the soldiers from molesting them, reminding the Governor of royal ordinances which reflected the crown's desire for the continued good treatment of the natives.[33] In the second, the Viceroy reiterated that the Marqués was to act sagaciously in maintaining the Indians and bringing them to the "vassalage of His Majesty."[34]

At the end of 1708, the Navahos broke the peace which they had maintained for over two years. They killed, robbed, and took many captives on raids which occurred in a period of slightly less than one year thereafter. On June 8, 1709, the Navahos raided the pueblo of Jémez, sacking not only the houses of the community, but even the church, from which they carried away the ornaments

[31] *Ibid.*

[32] Duque de Alburquerque to Marqués de la Peñuela, November, 1710, SANM, Documento 161.

[33] Virrey Duque de Alburquerque to Marqués de la Peñuela, México, July 8, 1708, SANM, Documento 143.

[34] Duque de Alburquerque to the Governor and Captain General Peñuela, México, December 4, 1708, SANM, Documento 152.

and sacred vessels. Two squads of soldiers were sent to follow the marauders, but they were only partially successful in recovering the stolen property and punishing the offenders.[35]

Throughout 1709, the Marqués ordered numerous expeditions against the Navahos. Three of them are particularly important in this study, for they provide an opportunity to examine the leadership and composition of Pueblo assistance. Early in the year, after an Indian from Santa Clara Pueblo had informed the Spanish captain in the Santa Cruz jurisdiction of a Navaho raid which had taken cows and horses from his pueblo, the Governor ordered Roque de Madrid to conduct a punitive expedition. The campaign force for this foray included José Naranjo as interpreter and scout, with auxiliaries from San Ildefonso, San Juan, and Santa Clara, as well as settlers from the Santa Cruz district.[36]

This expedition and the two which followed during the year clearly indicate that by 1709, Spanish authorities in New Mexico had organized an orderly system for conducting joint expeditions against the hostile tribes. It is also evident that settlers and Pueblo Indians were expected to participate in such punitive forays throughout the province. Likewise, they were equally obligated to join expeditions dispatched to rescue Pueblos who had been captured by the Navahos. When the Governor himself could not lead the campaign element, he generally assigned this task to his Lieutenant Governor, Juan Páez Hurtado,[37] or to his *Maestre del Campo*, Roque de Madrid.[38]

Soldiers from the presidio and the citizen militia were always

35 Escalante, Noticias, BNM, Legajo 3.

36 Marqués de la Peñuela to Roque de Madrid, Orden, Santa Fé, February 21, 1709, SANM, Documento 154.

37 Marqués de la Peñuela to Juan de Ulibarri, Santa Fé, September 6, 1709, AGN, Provincias Internas 36, Expediente 3.

38 Marqués de la Peñuela to Roque de Madrid, Santa Fé, December 8, 1709, SANM, Documento 157. Another copy exists in AGN, Orden, Provincias Internas 36, Expediente 3.

assigned to these forces by the Governor. In fact, he usually provided the expeditionary commander with a list of them, naming each and specifying the equipment and animals he possessed. *Alcaldes mayores* of the Pueblo districts were instructed simply to provide a designated number of auxiliaries, having them report to the campaign captain at the *plaza de armas*. This site was usually an Indian pueblo such as Jémez in the early summer expedition,[39] or San Juan in the foray at the end of the year.[40] Although these Navaho campaigns enlisted Pueblos, principally from the villages of Santa Clara, Cochití, and Jémez (undoubtedly because of the route selected and their nearness to the Navahos),[41] everyone in the province was reminded of his obligation to serve His Majesty.[42]

Before leaving office in 1712, the Marqués de la Peñuela made a three-year effort to stamp out some of the ancient practices of the Pueblos, and he endeavored to have these natives embrace Christianity more thoroughly. Two of the basic features of Spanish Indian policy throughout the Americas after the sixteenth century were the conversion of the subjects to Christianity and the suppression of their supposedly heathen practices. The Governor of New Mexico attempted to apply these policies more diligently to the Pueblo Indians before 1712. Particularly emphasizing the ceremonies of the natives which he concluded were repugnant and opposed to Christianity, the Marqués explained:

> They keep the scalps taken from their enemies, the unfaithful enemies whom they kill in battle, bring them and dance publicly, introducing many superstitions and scandalous acts in these dances, and they use as [illegible] many subterranean places that

39 La Peñuela to Ulibarri, September 6, 1709, AGN, Provincias Internas 36, Expediente 3.

40 La Peñuela to Roque de Madrid, December 8, 1709, SANM, Documento 157.

41 La Peñuela to Ulibarri, September 6, 1709, AGN, Provincias Internas 36, Expediente 3.

42 La Peñuela to Roque de Madrid, December 8, 1709, SANM, Documento 157.

are called *estufas*, places in which they invoke the devil, and in his company and with his advice and suggestion they exhort one thousand errors.[43]

In the last year of his administration, Governor La Peñuela conducted an interrogation of all of the pueblos. The *cabildo* of Santa Fe executed the inquiry, directing fifteen questions to the Indians, largely concerning their treatment and payment for their services. Although answers were received from almost all of the native villages, especially those of Santa Ana, Cochití, Santa Clara, Nambé, and Pojoaque, the response from Santo Domingo most clearly illustrates the nature of the answers provided. The governor of that Keresan pueblo stated that La Peñuela had not aggravated the Indians, that they had been paid satisfactorily for their services, that individuals had not been forcibly taken away from their pueblo, that the Governor had helped to defend the Christian Indians from their hereditary enemies, the "Apaches" [Navahos?], and that the Marqués had even returned a Jémez woman whom the Apaches had held as a slave. He further explained that frequent Faraón Apache incursions had secured beef and cattle from his pueblo of Santo Domingo, that the campaigns made by the people of that village with Sergeant Juan de Ulibarri had been made to punish their enemies, and that the Christian Indians had always been treated well.[44]

Although the reply of Santo Domingo's governor indicated that the Indians were "not sorry at having been made to quit their *estufas*, dances, and scalp dances because they are Christians," this

---

[43] Marqués de la Peñuela to Virrey, Santa Fé, January 26, 1710, AGN, Provincias Internas 36, Expediente 3. The estufas (literally meaning "ovens") were in reality the typical Indian kivas of the Pueblos still in use today as ceremonial chambers.

[44] See Interrogatorio de 1711–1712 y respuestas de indios, Año de 1711, BNM, Legajo 6, Documento 4, for this interrogation and the responses received. Such a procedure may have been followed and this investigation conducted as part of Governor La Peñuela's *residencia*, before he had been replaced in the office of governor. Undoubtedly the discussion of "Apaches" in this testimony refers to the Navahos until the subject of the Faraón Apaches was introduced.

feeling was apparently not widely held. An examination of San Ildefonso's reply indicates that there was some dissatisfaction with the lack of ceremonies, and San Juan regretted the loss of the estufas and ceremonials, as well as scalp dances.[45]

By 1712 the Marqués had consolidated the gains of his predecessor and had strengthened the Spanish position in New Mexico. Likewise, he had improved the relationship between the Pueblos and the Spaniards, although his efforts to stamp out Pueblo religious practices led him into dangerous ground, particularly into an area which had contributed greatly to the Pueblo revolt late in the preceding century. He had regularized the system of joint military campaigns, and on many occasions had responded to the pleas of the Indian governors for help against the predatory raids of the *indios bárbaros*. The general population increase of the pueblos, except in frontier areas such as Pecos, noted later by Fray Juan Agustín de Morfi,[46] apparently began in the governorship of La Peñuela.

The relatively peaceful condition of the province provided

45 *Ibid.* Since there was considerable dissatisfaction with the governor's attempt to eradicate the ancient Pueblo practices, it is suspected that there were probably many secret ceremonies conducted throughout the province near the end of his term. Pueblo ceremonies have withstood various attempts to stamp them out down through the present day.

46 Fray Juan Agustín de Morfi, Descripción geográfica del Nuevo México, Año de 1782, AGN, Historia 25, Expediente 6. A few representative figures from this document illustrate this increase:

Pueblo	1707	1717	Comments
San Juan	400	1,014	
Picurís	300	464	
Taos	700	784	(Included some Spaniards)
Santa Ana	340	112	families (about 560 persons)
Santo Domingo	240	78	families (about 390 persons)
Cochití	500	116	families (about 580 persons)
Jémez	300	132	families (about 660 persons)

Population figures for the eighteenth century are subject to much question. Since most of them were given in families, it is necessary to multiply each by the generally accepted figure of five persons per family. It must be noted on balance that there were losses cited at Tesuque, Pecos, and Zía, but, contrary to the previously accepted views, it is apparent that the population at the pueblos seems to have increased.

the setting for extensive unlicensed trade between the civilized groups—Spaniards and Pueblos—and some bands of Apaches. The new Governor, Juan Ignacio Flores Mogollón, addressed himself to this problem soon after his arrival in 1712. To bring a sudden halt to this practice of dealing with the "Apaches Gentiles," who lived at La Jicarilla and Cuartelejo, as well as among the Utes to the north, the new official ordered that no one of any "quality or status" was to enter these regions and *rancherías* to make exchanges of any kind. Punishment for future offenses would be four months in jail. Indians were to receive the same sentence, and *alcaldes mayores* were warned that they risked loss of office and two months in jail should they tolerate such activities within their jurisdictions. This order was to be published throughout the province, so that no one could pretend ignorance of its provisions, and it was subsequently disseminated at Santa Fe, La Cañada, Pecos, Albuquerque, and Bernalillo.[47]

Difficulties with the *indios bárbaros*, principally with the Utes and Navahos, occurred during 1713 and 1714. Many campaigns involving the use of Pueblo allies were made, and the Zuñis were used unsuccessfully to approach the Moquis to see if they might restore peace with the Pueblos, if not with the Spaniards.[48] In October, 1713, a joint expedition of Spaniards and Pueblos was sent to punish the Navahos for a raid upon San Ildefonso in which they took all the cows and oxen from the Christian Indians. Fifty soldiers, 20 settlers, and 150 Pueblo Indians, the last-named contingent led by *Capitán Mayor* José Naranjo, were ordered to meet at the rendezvous point of San Diego de Jémez for an expedition to punish the marauders.[49]

[47] Juan Ignacio Flores Mogollón, Bando, Santa Fé, December 16, 1712, SANM, Documento 185.

[48] Escalante, Noticias, BNM, Legajo 3.

[49] Autos y junta de guerra sobre un robo que hicieron los indios Apaches del Navajo . . . , Santa Fé, October 30, 1713, SANM, Documento 199. Also noted in Escalante, Noticias, BNM, Legajo 3, and Reeve, "Navaho-Spanish Wars, 1680–1720," *NMHR*, Vol. XXXIII, No. 3 (July, 1958), 227.

Reports of Ute activity were also prevalent in late 1713. Raids against Taos, where twenty-six horses were taken, and San Juan resulted in a joint punitive campaign which recovered fourteen of the horses and killed three Utes.[50] This short foray also resulted in the restoration of the Utes to their former status as "our friends" by the end of the year.[51] A second Navaho expedition, commanded by Roque de Madrid and composed of 50 soldiers and 212 Pueblo warriors, was conducted in March, 1714, to retaliate for a raid upon Jémez in which the leader of that pueblo had been killed. This campaign force followed the Chama River Valley, attacked the Navahos on several *peñoles*, killed 30 of them, captured 7, and carried off some 316 bushels of corn, 11 cattle, and 110 sheep before returning to Jémez Pueblo.[52]

One of the oustanding illustrations of the relations between the Spaniards and the Pueblos and of the problems facing the two civilizations during the Flores Mogollón administration was the *junta de guerra* regarding Pueblo Indian practices, which was held in Santa Fe during July, 1714[53] It is particularly important in an intensive examination of the use of Pueblo Indian auxiliaries, for it emphasizes the equipment possessed by these natives, their methods of warfare, and the resultant problems arising from the Spanish use of Indians to defend the frontier.

Three basic issues were examined in detail during this meeting—the right of the Christian Indians to bear arms, their strange practices while on campaigns, and their continued trade with the enemies of the province. The junta was called by the Governor on July 5, 1714, to consider whether or not the ancient practices of

---

50 Escalante, Noticias, BNM, Legajo 3.
51 Juan Ignacio Flores Mogollón, Santa Fé, January, 1713[?], AGN, Provincias Internas 36, Expediente 3.
52 Escalante, Noticias, BNM, Legajo 3. Also noted in Reeve, "Navaho-Spanish Wars, 1680–1720," *NMHR*, Vol. XXXIII, No. 3 (July, 1958), 229. The report indicated that 200 *fanegas* of corn were taken.
53 Hallenbeck, *Land of the Conquistadores*, 204, states that 1715 was the date of this council, but the documentary evidence proves that the correct year was 1714.

the natives should be abolished and if arms should be taken away from the Pueblo auxiliaries.[54] Flores Mogollón stated that the reason for calling the junta was that he suspected that the Pueblos themselves, under the cloak of peace, were creating some of the numerous raids on the horse herds and cattle, which had been attributed to the enemies of the realm. He also desired that the Christian Indians be required to wear a different dress when on campaigns so that they might be recognized as Christians and therefore be distinguished from the enemy.[55]

The question of taking arms away from the Indians was first considered at length. The military representatives of the junta favored doing so before the Pueblos sold them to the unfaithful natives with whom they were already known to trade for horses and cattle. In addition, the removal of arms from the custody of the Christian Indian auxiliaries would prevent a general uprising, although no suspicion or evidence of such an occurrence was presented during the council. The religious members of the junta, led by Fray Juan de Tagle, opposed taking arms away from the Indians, stating that they needed their firearms because the province was surrounded by enemies who frequently invaded the pueblos and such weapons were the only means of defense the friendly natives possessed to defend themselves from these raids.[56]

Turning to the next item, the ancient practices of the Pueblos, especially that of painting themselves, the junta again expressed a divided opinion. Governor Flores Mogollón, most of the settlers present, and some of the religious leaders opposed the continuance of the Indian practice of painting themselves. One of the group

---

[54] Flores Mogollón, Auto, Santa Fé, July 5, 1714, BNM, Legajo 6, Documento 16. Another useful copy exists in the SANM as Testimonio . . . , Año de 1714, Documento 207. Both Escalante, Noticias, BNM, Legajo 3, and Bancroft, *History of Arizona and New Mexico* are derived from this source.

[55] Flores Mogollón, Auto, BNM, Legajo 6, Documento 16; Testimonio, Año de 1714, SANM, Documento 207.

[56] Testimonio, Año de 1714, SANM, Documento 207; Escalante, Noticias, BNM, Legajo 3.

recommended that such an ancient custom be abolished because "no one could say certainly if he [the Indian ally] was a Christian or a Gentile" when on campaign. Another added the opinion that since the Pueblos were Christians and vassals of His Majesty, they should not be allowed to paint themselves, and he concurred with his predecessor that when painted and therefore in disguise, the Pueblos themselves were suspected of robbing horses and cattle. Tomás Holguín added that the Pueblos should not be allowed to enter churches of the province with feathers on their heads, and subsequent opinions voiced in opposition to the Indian habits were advanced by Roque de Madrid, Alfonso Rael de Aguilar (supposedly the Protector General of the Indians only eight years earlier), Antonio de Valverde, Cristóbal de la Serna, Juan de l'Archévèque, and others.[57]

A most interesting rebuttal and dissenting opinion was given by the *custodio* Fray Juan de Tagle on behalf of the majority of the religious persons present. The noted father stated that the Indians were simple folk who had only recently been conquered and that the proposed *auto* was beyond their comprehension. Priests from Pecos, Santo Domingo, Cochití, Santa Clara, Taos, Jémez, and Laguna supported his viewpoint that arms should not be taken from the friendly Indians and that they should not be denied the use of firearms in the future. Also, the friars believed that the Pueblos should not be required to discontinue the practice of painting themselves since it was not done to hide their crimes. Both Fray Tagle and Fray Antonio de Miranda concurred that the Indian custom was no worse than that of Europe. They pointed out that the Spaniards often painted themselves and that it was not a "bad thing among the Spanish" to put feathers in their hats and wear them to church.[58]

---

57 Testimonio, Año de 1714, SANM, Documento 207.
58 *Ibid.*

The Governor reviewed the various opinions presented by the junta but decided to enforce the provisions of his *auto*, taking away the arms of the Christian Indians and forbidding the practice of painting themselves in the future. However, he referred the entire matter to the Viceroy, the Duke of Linares, for review and the promulgation of the final decision.[59] The latter, apparently not concurring in the action taken by Flores Mogollón, supported the views of the friars and reversed the Governor's earlier decision.[60]

Perhaps one of the most outstanding campaigns of the eighteenth century occurred in the summer of 1715 against the Faraón Apaches. The expedition was not particularly notable for its achievements, which indeed were scanty, but it is worthy of intensive investigation for the role played by Pueblo Indian auxiliaries. Although there had been earlier campaigns against the same enemy, such as the one in the previous year with 89 men from the presidio and the *villa* of Santa Fe and 100 Indian allies,[61] this foray of 1715 may be examined as an early indication of the close Spanish-Pueblo relationship and the organizational patterns established for the defense of the province.

Depredations of the Faraón Apaches were reported by Don Gerónimo of Taos and Don Lorenzo Tupatú of Picurís from information acquired by the now famous scout and interpreter José Naranjo. These reports were submitted to a special council of war held July 20, 1715, at Santa Fe. An August retaliatory campaign was decided upon to recover the horse herd stolen from Picurís and to chastise the marauders. Don Gerónimo of Taos recommended that neither Pecos nor Keresan allies be taken along for the campaign. He distrusted the former, saying that they would inform the

---

59 *Ibid.*

60 Hallenbeck, *Land of the Conquistadores*, 205. Escalante's Noticias, BNM, Legajo 3, reveals that some of the arms were actually recovered from the Indians.

61 Autos y junta de guerra sobre si se le debe hacer la guerra a los indios gentiles de la nación Faraona, Año de 1714, SANM, Documento 206.

Acoma Pueblo, New Mexico, atop its 357-foot mesa, as it appeared about 1960; Enchanted Mesa at top center; mission of San Esteban Rey in foreground.

Circular Kiva, South Plaza, San Ildefonso Pueblo, New Mexico, in 1946; Tunyo, or Black Mesa, in right rear.

enemy of the expedition since the Faraones had fled from the Pecos vicinity at the time of the reconquest. Further, the Taos Governor explained, the Keres should not go either, for they "make a great noise when spies go out and thus advise the enemy to flee."[62]

Captain Félix Martínez, commandant of the presidio and *alcalde mayor* of Santa Fe, concurred with Don Gerónimo, suggesting in addition that both the Pecos and the Keres were needed to defend other frontiers. Governor Flores Mogollón, accepting their arguments, ordered that none of the Pecos or Keres were to accompany the expedition since the frontier "must be guarded by settlers and Indians." Only the Tiwas, Taos, and Picurís were permitted to accompany the Spanish force.[63]

Before the campaign could be organized and dispatched, it was necessary to conduct a limited punitive expedition southward in July of the same year. Apaches in the Albuquerque and Isleta areas were reported to have killed two Tewas and destroyed crops and homes before taking refuge in the Ladrón Mountains. A council of war held at the capital determined that a combined expedition of 50 Spaniards and 300 Indians, mostly from Galisteo and Pecos, be dispatched under Alonso García of Albuquerque to punish the Apaches at their *rancherías* in the Sandía and Ladrón Mountains.[64]

The threat to the south having been met, attention once more turned to the Faraón campaign decided upon in late July. Juan Páez Hurtado was appointed to command the expedition. On August 20, when the appointment occurred, he was authorized to assemble 40 soldiers, 20 settlers, and 150 Indians from Taos, Picurís, the Tiwa pueblos, and Pecos at the *plaza de armas* of Picurís, on August 30. The Governor further ordered that the

---

62 Autos y junta de guerra sobre la campaña . . . que el general Juan Páez Hurtado hizo, Año de 1715, in Thomas (ed.), *After Coronado*, 80–98.

63 *Ibid.*, 85.

64 Testimonio de las juntas de guerra que se formaron para hazarla campaña a la sierra de los ladrones, Año de 1715, SANM, Documento 224.

alcaldes mayores of the various jurisdictions designated have their Indians at the assigned pueblo by the date specified.[65]

Páez Hurtado's comprehensive review of his forces and equipment at Picurís is most revealing of the composition of a typical early eighteenth century campaign in New Mexico. The commander had previously compiled a list of soldiers and settlers accompanying him from Santa Fe, a list which included Roque de Madrid as the second in command, as of the twenty-eighth of August. This compilation also included 151 friendly Indian allies from the pueblos designated in the Governor's initial instructions, although these natives were not named individually as the Spaniards were.[66]

However, minor alterations occurred by the time the final review and muster was made at Picurís. Thirty-six soldiers and fifty-two settlers were listed by name in addition to the commander. Most of the settlers were from Albuquerque, Santa Fe, and Santa Cruz, some having as many as eleven horses and others with as many as eight mules and six horses. Many, however, lacked the leather jackets generally valued for their protection against arrows. The designated deputy commander, Roque de Madrid, was not included on this final muster, and three soldiers, described as ill, were not included in the final count.[67]

Completing the composition of the force was the band of Indian warriors, a total of 149 being finally provided from the following locations:

Pueblo	Leaders	Number of Indians
Pecos	Don Felipe and Don Juan	30
Taos	Don Gerónimo	36
Nambé		10

[65] Autos y junta de guerra sobre la campaña . . . que el general Juan Páez Hurtado hizo, Año de 1715, in Thomas (ed.), *After Coronado*, 86
[66] *Ibid.*, 87–88.
[67] *Ibid.*, 89–93.

Pojoaque	6
Tesuque	11
San Juan	17
Santa Clara	12
San Ildefonso	16
Picurís	11
Total	149[68]

Certain characteristics of this Pueblo auxiliary force are worthy of mention. The roster reveals that one Christian Indian from Tesuque was left behind because he was ill and that only seventeen from an original quota of twenty were taken from San Juan, three having hidden, for which the Spaniards would hold the *alcalde mayor* of that particular jurisdiction accountable. The presence of Indian auxiliaries from Pecos is of peculiar interest when it is realized that the Governor had decided that they should not accompany the expedition at all. Apparently the earlier decision to exclude them had been rescinded. The use of the leather jackets among the Indians as well as the presence of firearms is unusual for two reasons. First, many of the Spaniards themselves did not possess leather jackets for defensive purposes, so that the Pueblos in general were better protected than the settlers. Second, the appearance of firearms in the Pueblo units, as in earlier expeditions, illustrates the Spanish practice of arming friendly Indians. Likewise, it also reflects quite clearly that Governor Flores Mogollón's efforts of the previous year to disarm the Pueblos had been unsuccessful.[69]

With a total of 238 individuals, over 60 per cent of whom were Pueblo auxiliaries led by the loyal scout José Naranjo, the expedition proceeded northward to Taos and through Taos Canyon to

[68] *Ibid.*, 93. Hotz, *Indianische Ledermalereien*, 331, states that there were only 146 Indians on this expedition, but that they came from the same nine pueblos. Seventy-six of these auxiliaries carried firearms, according to this same authority.

[69] These observations are based upon the review of forces and equipment at Picurís on August 30, 1715, which may be found in *Autos y junta de guerra sobre la campaña . . . que el general Juan Páez Hurtado hizo, Año de 1715*, in Thomas (ed.), *After Coronado*, 93.

93

the Great Plains, where 30 Jicarilla Apaches and one Cuartelejo Apache were added to the auxiliary force.[70] Although frequently losing its direction and achieving only a very limited success, since the Apache *rancherías*, as usual, were scattered, the campaign reached the vicinity of present-day Amarillo, Texas, before returning to the capital at the end of September.[71]

Although there were sporadic outbreaks among the Apaches thereafter, the four years following 1715 were principally concerned with relations with the Moqui to the west, and the Comanches and Utes in the north.

In 1716, interim Governor Félix Martínez carried out an extensive campaign, using numerous Pueblo Indian auxiliaries against the renegade Moquis. He hoped to establish peace with them and perhaps secure their return to the Río Grande Valley, which some of them had inhabited prior to the Pueblo revolt of 1680. To augment the seventy soldiers from the presidio of Santa Fe and a quota of settlers from Santa Cruz, Santa Fe, and Albuquerque, the Governor ordered the *alcaldes mayores* in the neighboring Indian pueblo districts to send the following numbers of natives to the *plaza de armas* of Albuquerque on August 18:

Nation	*No.*	*Nation*	*No.*
Pueblo		*Pueblo*	
Taos	15	Keres	
Picurís	10	Cochití	20
Tewas		Santo Domingo	10
San Juan	10	San Felipe	20
Santa Clara	6	Jémez	

70 This is one of the earliest uses made of friendly Apaches, such as the Jicarillas, in conjunction with the Spaniards and Pueblos against a common enemy. Such a unity became the general pattern by the end of the century.

71 Autos y junta de guerra sobre la campaña . . . que el general Juan Páez Hurtado hizo, Año de 1715, in Thomas (ed.), *After Coronado*, 94–98, 266. Hotz, *Indianische Ledermalereien*, 332, agrees that the Indian guide misled the expeditionary force near present-day Amarillo, Texas, and received as punishment for this error fifty lashes.

San Ildefonso	10	Santa Ana	12
Pojoaque	5	Zía	25
Nambé	5	Jémez	20
Tesuque	10	Isleta	5
Pecos	30	Acoma	
Galisteo	4	Laguna	10
		Acoma	25
		Halona (Zuñi)	20
		Total	282[72]

With this force, including nearly 75 per cent Pueblo Indians, Martínez marched westward, the Indians carrying only bows and arrows and war clubs as weapons.[73] At the Moqui pueblos, high on their mesas in present northeastern Arizona, Martínez endeavored to obtain the submission of the rebels by using the services of his friendly Pueblos. He first arranged for the leaders of the auxiliary force to select a total of sixteen of their Indians for a peace mission to lure the Moquis and the captive Tanos down from their *peñoles*. To these Pueblos he gave a large cross, allowing Cristóbal Caiquiro of Zía to carry it, and some handfuls of tobacco. Although the Moquis returned the gesture of friendship and promised to accept the peace offered by the Spaniards, they did not descend from their mesa pueblos.[74]

Next, Martínez sent Don Felipe of the Tano nation to invite the

[72] Félix Martínez, Gobernador Interino, Diario . . . las operaciones, SANM, Documento 250. An excellent published account of this journal is available in Lansing B. Bloom, "A Campaign against the Moqui Pueblos under Governor Phelix [sic] Martínez, 1716," *NMHR*, Vol. VI, No. 2 (April, 1931), 158–226. Bloom, however, errs in citing the number of Indians from Pojoaque as six (on page 174 of his article). Note also that Zía and Santa Ana, both of which are Keresan pueblos, are included with Jémez, which is not Keresan.

[73] Martínez, Diario . . . las operaciones, SANM, Documento 250; Bloom, "A Campaign against the Moqui Pueblos under Governor Phelix [sic] Martínez, 1716," *NMHR*, Vol. VI, No. 2 (April, 1931), 185–86. Perhaps this indicates that Martínez, who had favored taking away arms from the Indians in the junta of 1714, had accomplished the task.

[74] Martínez, Diario . . . las operaciones, SANM, Documento 250; Bloom, "A Campaign against the Moqui Pueblos under Governor Phelix [sic] Martínez, 1716," *NMHR*, Vol. VI, No. 2 (April, 1931), 192–94.

renegade Tanos to come down from their heights. Felipe made two unsuccessful trips, the latter being conducted to advise the Indians that if obedience were not rendered, war would be made upon them.[75] Failing in these efforts, Martínez held a council of war in which it was unanimously agreed to attack the rebels. When final demands for obedience were turned down by the Moquis and a short engagement occurred, resulting in the deaths of eight of the hostiles while only three Spaniards were wounded, Martínez initiated an economic war reminiscent of Vargas' reconquest in 1693–94. Destruction of the fields and crops surrounding the mesas included "pulling up everything by the roots" and running off the Moqui livestock. Nothing, however, forced the submission of the Moquis and hostile Tanos, the latter having said that they "got along very well without the irreligious Spaniards."[76] With no apparent success and lacking water for his own forces, Martínez broke camp after sixteen days of negotiations and destruction,[77] and marched back to the Río Grande.

In the same year, because of Ute and Comanche attacks on the Tewa pueblos, mostly in the vicinity of Taos, and on some of the *estancias* of the Spaniards in the area, Martínez held a *junta de guerra* in Santa Fe. He then ordered that an expedition composed of fifty solders, twelve settlers, and fifty friendly Indians, all under the command of Cristóbal de la Serna, be launched in October.[78] A unique recommendation for this campaign was the Governor's

75 Bloom, "A Campaign against the Moqui Pueblos under Governor Phelix [*sic*] Martínez, 1716," *NMHR*, Vol. VI, No. 2 (April, 1931), 202–207.

76 *Ibid.*, 211–19.

77 *Ibid.*, 224.

78 Testimonio de la junta de guerra . . . y orden . . . para . . . la guerra ofensiva a los Yutas y Cumanchy . . . , Año de 1716[?] SANM, Documento 279. Also in Escalante, Noticias, BNM, Legajo 3. There is an account of an expedition against the Comanches in Amado Cháves, *The Defeat of the Comanches in 1717*. However, there are flagrant errors noted in this source. These include the author's conclusion that in 1717 "so severe was the punishment inflicted upon the Comanches that they never again went on the warpath against the Spaniards." This is absolutely not true when one examines the difficulties experienced in the province with them in the period before 1754 and those of the late 1750's, as well as the decades of 1770's and 1780's.

suggestion that Sierra Blanca and Jicarilla Apaches be employed also since they were known to be on friendly terms with the Spanish authorities.[79] The expedition met at Taos on October 22, making contact occasionally with bands of the enemy, killing a few, putting the rest to flight, and returning to the capital.[80]

Apparently another campaign in the following year, led by Juan de Padilla with 500 men (a large portion of whom must have been Pueblos), was much more successful. Entirely mounted and equipped with firearms, machetes, lances, and bows and arrows, this expedition marched through Pecos to Antón Chico and thence to the *llano estacado*. There, after everyone had painted his face to look like an Indian, the force surprised the Comanches while encamped, killed several, and took nearly 700 prisoners.[81]

After considerable uncertainty and much internal conflict over the governorship, including a fierce personal rivalry among three officials—Martínez, Páez Hurtado, and Antonio Valverde y Cosío—stability was finally established in the administration of Valverde from 1719 to 1721. Although other events occupied the Governor's attention, the most spectacular were his own campaign east of the mountains in the first year of his administration and that of Pedro de Villasur, which ended in disaster on the banks of the Platte River in present western Nebraska in 1720.

Although his campaign of 1719 was principally concerned with punishing the Utes for their raids on the northern pueblos, in the course of it the Governor learned of renewed Comanche activity, and investigated rumors of French incursions within the realm.

---

79 Testimonio de . . . la guerra ofensiva a los Yutas y Cumanchy . . . , Año de 1716[?], SANM, Documento 279.

80 Escalante, Noticias, BNM, Legajo 3.

81 Cháves, *The Defeat of the Comanches in 1717*, 6–7. An ironic observation may be made here when one considers that the Spaniards attempted to take away the arms and prohibit the ancient traditions, such as painting, among the Pueblos in 1714. Scarcely three years later it is apparent that the auxiliaries had firearms again and that everyone, including the Spaniards, resorted to painting himself in preparation for engagements with enemy tribes.

Periodically from 1719 to 1762, when Louisiana was transferred to her control, Spain was deeply concerned with rumored French encroachment along the northern frontier.

On August 13, 1719, Governor Valverde ordered a council of war to hear Pueblo, Spanish, and *coyote*[82] complaints about raids in the northern jurisdiction. Important Pueblos such as José Naranjo were interviewed and asked their opinions regarding the need for a campaign against the Utes and Comanches. Naranjo, a resident of Santa Cruz whom the viceroy had entitled *capitán mayor de la guerra,* discussed the Ute raids at Taos and Cochití and concluded that war was necessary. This opinion was shared by Miguel Tenorio, *alcalde mayor* and war captain of Taos, and by others.[83]

Over a month later, on September 15, Valverde took 60 troops from the presidio, obtained 40 settlers who volunteered for the reconnaissance (for whom he furnished most of the arms and horses), recruited 200 Pueblo allies, and set out for Taos.[84] There, at the rendezvous point, he added more volunteers, who swelled his command to over 600 individuals.

A review of the muster list completed at Taos reveals the composition and equipment of the expedition. The 60 soldiers of the presidio were counted and named with their horses, arms, and munitions. However, it was necessary to supply some of the 45 settlers with powder, balls, and leather jackets, which they lacked. The Pueblo auxiliaries comprised nearly 80 per cent of the expedition, numbering some 465 individuals who cared for 680 beasts (horses, cows, and probably sheep). Captain Luis García, under whose care

82 This term, meaning "mixed blood," was frequently used in the eighteenth century throughout the province. It is sometimes seen today and may be considered equivalent to the more commonly used terms of mestizo or "*ladino.*"

83 Autos y diligencias que . . . declara la guerra a los Yndios Yutas, Año de 1719, SANM, Documento 301. There is a translation of this source in Thomas (ed.), *After Coronado*, 99–110.

84 Antonio de Valverde to Marqués de Valero, Santa Fe, November 30, 1719, in Thomas (ed.), *After Coronado*, 141.

the Pueblos were placed, counted the animals, and great care was taken throughout the campaign to insure that the Indian horse herd did not become mixed with that belonging to the soldiers and settlers.[85]

This huge expedition departed from Taos on September 20, taking pinole, chocolate, tobacco, and presents for the Indians whom they expected to encounter. The marching order, according to custom, divided the main force into two parts. One was composed of soldiers and settlers while the other entirely consisted of Indian auxiliaries. Usually the two were separated by the herd of pack animals, and scouts flanked the whole line. A small group of Spaniards, led by the governor, comprised the vanguard and a similar group brought up the rear. At night two separate camps were made—one of the Spaniards and another for the auxiliary forces—and all were careful to see that the horse herds remained apart.[86]

Valverde proceeded to the vicinity of La Jicarilla (present Cimarron, New Mexico), where he accepted twelve additional allies from the Apache Indians there, who offered to accompany him.[87] The expedition then turned northward, probably crossing Ratón Pass, and in the vicinity of the Purgatoire River near present Trinidad, Colorado, Valverde accepted the offer of Chief Carlana of the Sierra Blanca Apaches to have sixty-nine Indians of that tribe accompany the expedition.[88] Apparently there was widespread

[85] Diario y derrotero que cuyo . . . Antonio Valverde . . . de . . . la campaña . . . contra las naciones Yutas y Cumanches, Año de 1719, in Thomas (ed.), *After Coronado*, 110–33. Hereinafter cited as Diario de la campaña contra las naciones Yutas y Cumanches. The muster may be found in Thomas on pages 28, 112, and 117. Bancroft, *History of Arizona and New Mexico*, 236, erroneously states that only thirty Indians were taken on this expedition. Hotz, *Indianische Ledermalereien*, 333–34, also relates the course of events for the Valverde expedition without significant alteration.

[86] Thomas (ed.), *After Coronado*, 28.

[87] Valverde to Valero, Santa Fé, November 30, 1719, in *ibid.*, 141. Here he found the Indians "very close to embracing our holy faith." Hotz, *Indianische Ledermalereien*, 334, states that over 100 Jicarillas accompanied Valverde.

[88] Diario de la campaña contra las naciones Yutas y Cumanches, in Thomas (ed.), *After Coronado*, 119.

99

fear of the Comanches among the Apaches at this time, for they desired to obtain every possible assistance, even from their former enemies, in combating the new menace on their frontiers.

Although the expedition failed to find and defeat the Comanches and Utes, it did reach the Arkansas River, proceeding downstream from a point east of present Pueblo, Colorado, to another perhaps near Las Animas. Valverde, knowing he was short of Cuartelejo, held a council of war, heard rumors of French intrusion from the east, and decided to return to Santa Fe, from whence he would dispatch a new expedition in the following year.[89]

From this venture of 1719, the Governor derived considerable information and reached the conclusion that a defensive settlement should be established on the eastern slope of the mountains at La Jicarilla, where the natives were friendly and "suitable for being commanded under arms as in all emergencies that have presented themselves they have shown their aptitude."[90] However, the Viceroy, not being familiar with frontier distances and terrain, ordered that the establishment be made at Cuartelejo.

Valverde contested the order, offering letters of explanation and his diary, and summoning a special *junta de guerra* on June 2, 1720, to obtain support from José Naranjo and others for his opposition to the Viceroy. Naranjo concluded that Cuartelejo was not a feasible site,[91] being situated some 130 leagues from Santa Fe. Valverde pointed out in his protest that to establish twenty-five men, as he had been ordered to do, at such a great distance from the capital and in the center of the "Apachería" was impossible since they could not be assisted by military forces in New Mexico. He added that he believed there had been an error made and that La Jicarilla had been the intended site.[92] However, neither location

89 Thomas (ed.), *After Coronado*, 29–31.

90 Valverde to Valero, Santa Fé, November 30, 1719, in *ibid.*, 145.

91 Junta de guerra, June 2, 1720, SANM, Documento 308. Twitchell, *The Spanish Archives of New Mexico*, errs in citing this date as 1719.

was subsequently selected and no such outpost was established. Valverde was relieved hereafter and a general inspection recommended that no post east of the mountains be founded.

Having resolved to block the French in their rumored penetration of New Mexico, the Viceroy ordered that a second expedition be conducted to find the enemy.[93] This was the ill-fated expedition commanded by Don Pedro de Villasur. Seventy Indian auxiliaries, with Naranjo as the chief scout, were selected to accompany forty-two soldiers, only three settlers, the priest Fray Juan Minguez, and the interpreter Juan de l'Archévèque. Tobacco was carried to reward the Indian guides and to please the unfaithful Indians whom they expected to meet.[94]

Although this expedition is important for many reasons, including the weakening of New Mexico's defensive posture and the investigation of Valverde, it is also significant for the study of the Pueblo auxiliaries in a disastrous defeat. On the banks of the Platte River in central Nebraska, perhaps near its junction with the Loup River, the Pueblo Indian sentinels were surprised by a dawn attack of *indios bárbaros*, probably from the Oto, Optata, Pawnee, and

92 Valverde to Valero, [El Paso], May 27, 1720, AGN, Historia 394, Documento 20. (There is also a copy in SANM, Documento 308.) Although no location is specified, the content of the document indicates that it was written from El Paso, not from Santa Fe. The reason for Valverde's temporary visit in the south is not stated.

93 Marqués de Valero to Valverde, México, September 26, 1720, SANM, Documento 310. There is a translation in Thomas (ed.), *After Coronado*, 234–39.

94 Valverde to Valero, Santa Fé, June 15, 1720, Historia 394, Documento 20, in Thomas (ed.), *After Coronado*, 162. The number of Indian allies who departed is not specified in Valverde to Valero, Santa Fé, October 8, 1720, in *ibid.*, 163. Note Thomas' conclusion, on page 36, that sixty Indian allies went. In view of the losses noted in the subsequent massacre it is possible that this is the correct number of auxiliaries accompanying the expedition. Of major importance in the study of the Villasur expedition and the subsequent massacre is the Indian skin painting, Segesser II, concerned entirely with the massacre itself, and published in Hotz, *Indianische Ledermalereien*. This painting, now possessed by the Segesser family at Lucerne, Switzerland, was perhaps ordered painted by Valverde while he was later preparing his defense at El Paso. Hotz, page 338, maintains that forty-five Spaniards and only sixty Pueblo Indians participated in this exploratory venture in search of the French. He adds that Carlana and Jicarilla Apaches co-operated as guides, receiving corn, knives, short swords, sombreros, and half a mule load of tobacco for their services.

Missouri nations.[95] Both the Spaniards and their Indian allies fled in great confusion as a result of this attack upon their encampment.[96] Apparently forty-five persons, including thirty-three officers and soldiers, José Naranjo, and eleven Indian allies were killed,[97] while a retired officer, a corporal, eleven soldiers, one settler, and forty-nine Indian allies escaped.[98] As a result of this disaster, it was reported that even the Indian allies in the province became so overbearing that it would take "little for them to declare themselves enemies" of the Spanish authorities. Fearing an uprising among the native auxiliaries, the informant warned that "there is no certain instant in which the kingdom of New Mexico may not be lost."[99]

During the decade of the 1720's, Indian campaigns continued, captured Pueblos were rescued, sometimes ransomed with horses,[100] and further requests from the Carlana and Sierra Blanca Apaches for a presidio were considered. Occasionally temporary measures were taken to relieve the pressures of the Comanches on the frontiers of the province.[101] Although the difficulties with the French arose from time to time after peace had been restored be-

95 Hotz, *Indianische Ledermalereien*, 346–47. There is considerable uncertainty over the actual site of the massacre, but Hotz presents ample evidence to support the choice of this point. However, for the view that the clash occurred near the junction of the North and South Platte rivers in western Nebraska, see Thomas (ed.), *After Coronado*, 287, and Bernard DeVoto, *The Course of Empire*, 183. All sources, however, agree that no Frenchmen were found by the Spaniards, and Hotz adds that those painted later on the skin itself were imagined. The painting itself (p.355) shows the Spanish soldiers and Pueblo auxiliaries in an elliptical formation near a fork of an unidentified river, and one of the auxiliaries is shown shielding Father Minguez. Villasur was apparently killed early in the assault.

96 Thomas (ed.), *After Coronado*, 38.

97 Martínez to Valero, México, 1720, in *ibid.*, 185–87. The list of individuals killed appears on pages 186–87, comprising thirty-four names, including Naranjo, and eleven allies. As usual there is some confusion of numbers after exchanges of correspondence occurred regarding the attack. Those killed included l'Archévèque, Villasur, and the friar.

98 Thomas (ed.), *After Coronado*, 276.

99 Martínez to Valero, Mexico, 1720, in *ibid.*, 185.

100 See Anon. Félix Martínez, Sentence and Judgment . . . , August 16, 1723, SANM, Documento 323 for one such rescue in 1723.

101 Thomas (ed.), *After Coronado*, 194–96.

tween the two countries in 1720, there were no major clashes. Indeed, the threat from the French was more imagined than real. Some New Mexicans apparently carried on an extensive illegal trade with them in 1724,[102] but this did not seriously jeopardize Spanish control over New Mexico. Campaigns against the Comanches continued,[103] as did others against the Apaches in the Ladrón and Sandía Mountains, where an expedition of 1724 employed 50 soldiers and 150 Indians of the Río Abajo jurisdiction.[104]

However, the most important event of the decade was undoubtedly the inspection of New Mexico during the summer of 1726, by Brigadier Pedro de Rivera. Appointed by the Viceroy to conduct an inspection of the entire northern frontier and to recommend necessary changes to improve the defensive status of the northern provinces, Rivera's visit to New Mexico was only part of a four-year tour. Although investigations had begun as early as 1722 under Don Antonio Cobían Busto, Rivera's was the only actual visit to New Mexico to examine the defenses of the province and to recommend improvements. The Spanish military officer, appointed officially as *visitador general*, reached New Mexico from El Paso about the twentieth of May, marching through Isleta and Albuquerque to Santo Domingo Pueblo, where he met Governor Juan Domingo de Bustamante on June 2. Rivera and the Governor reached Santa Fe together two days later, and Rivera remained in the capital until August 24.[105]

Rivera examined the responsibility for the Villasur massacre of 1720 and concluded that former Governor Valverde had been at

---

102 Juan Domingo de Bustamante, Interrogatorio, April 22–May 2, 1724, SANM, Documento 327. A translation may be found in Thomas (ed.), *After Coronado*, 245–46.

103 Junta de guerra . . . , Año de 1724, SANM, Documento 324.

104 Bustamente to Captain Antonio de Tafoya, Santa Fé, June 20, 1724, SANM, Documento 329.

105 Vito Alessio Robles (ed.), *Diario y derrotero de lo caminado, visto y observado en la visita que hizo a los presidios de Nueva España Septentrional el Brigadier Pedro de Rivera*, 48–52. This source is hereinafter cited as *Diario y derrotero de Pedro de Rivera*. There are summaries of the visit also in Hallenbeck, *Land of the Conquistadores* and Thomas (ed.), *After Coronado*.

103

fault for not leading the expedition himself. On the question of the proposed presidio at La Jicarilla, Rivera declared that there was no pressing need for such an establishment.[106] More significant for purposes of understanding this period, however, were his observations regarding the Pueblos and other friendly Indians.

Having predetermined his policy of retrenchment before his arrival in Santa Fe, Rivera concluded that if every proposal for new presidios was accepted, "the treasury of Midas would not suffice."[107] He therefore recommended that the Indians in the Jicarilla vicinity be invited to settle near Taos since there was too much unprotected land in New Mexico already. This caused the Jicarilla Apaches to split two years later. Some fled to Pecos Pueblo and other regions, while the remainder were removed to a point twelve miles north of Taos.[108] Thereafter the Spanish lost the benefit of an excellent Indian barrier northeast of their settlements to resist the incursions of the Comanches.[109]

Rivera decided to retain the Santa Fe presidio at its existing strength of eighty men, but he also commented unfavorably on the soldiers' dual role as commercial agents and military men. Turning to the Christian Indians or Pueblos, he found twenty-four towns of them, representing the following nations: Mansos, Piros, Tewas, Keres, Zuñis, Halonas, Jémez, Xeres[?], Picurís, Tanos, Pecos, Tiwas, Taos, and Sumas. In all, he concluded that there were probably 9,747 friendly Indians in the province.[110]

106 Alessio Robles, *Diario y derrotero de Pedro de Rivera*, and Rivera to Marqués de Casa Fuerte, Presidio del Paso del Río del Norte, September 26, 1727[*sic*], AGN, Historia 394, Documento 20, in Thomas (ed.), *After Coronado*, 212–14.

107 Rivera to Casa Fuerte, September 26, 1727[*sic*], in Thomas (ed.), *After Coronado*, 214.

108 Hallenbeck, *Land of the Conquistadores*, 217–18.

109 Thomas (ed.), *After Coronado*, 46.

110 Alessio Robles, *Diario y derrotero de Pedro de Rivera*, 54, 153–55. Although most of the Indian nations can be readily identified (i.e. the Alonas were undoubtedly Zuñis who resided at Halona Pueblo), nothing seems to explain the Xeres. Certainly Rivera could not have meant the Seris of Sinaloa and Sonora in this summary. The total number of natives is also surprisingly low for so many nations. Perhaps Rivera meant the number of families, not the number of individuals.

Commenting upon the Pueblos themselves, Rivera noted that they were well proportioned and of better appearance than any of the other nations. He noted further that the Pueblos always went about dressed, that they were hard workers, that their women wove woolen and cotton blankets, and, significantly, that they all traveled on horseback. The houses of the pueblos also received the attention of the Spanish officer, for he considered them to be vastly different from those he had seen in other provinces he had visited earlier. Particularly noted were the defensive achievements of the villages: the thick, strong walls, the fine construction, the terraced three- or four-storied buildings, the absence of doors on the ground floors, and the removable ladders to the entrances on the second floor.[111]

Lastly, Rivera commended the Pueblos for their concurrence and ready assistance in campaigns which the governor of the province conducted against the enemy nations. The inspector thought it highly unusual that the Pueblos would go out from their villages in the numbers requested, and without submitting a bill to the Royal Treasury for their time, their expenditures, or the horses and arms they needed. He concluded that the fidelity of the Pueblos was exemplary and, indeed, a great credit to them.[112]

Rivera's inspection eventually led to the noted *Reglamento de 1729*, a long list of rules and regulations designed to standardize and improve the defense of the northern frontier. The portions of that *reglamento* which applied specifically to New Mexico merit special attention, particularly those passages which applied to the treatment and use of Pueblo Indian auxiliaries.

New Mexico was assigned a presidial company of eighty men, including one lieutenant, one *alférez*, one sergeant, and seventy-

---

111 *Ibid.*, 54–55. The comment about Pueblos traveling on horseback is particularly unique since officials of the Spanish government did not regularly report to higher authorities on this practice, as Spanish law supposedly forbade Indians to ride horses.

112 *Ibid.*, 55.

seven soldiers. Her governors and commandants, as those of other provinces, were prohibited from using soldiers for their own interests, for guarding horse herds, for carrying messages, for negotiating business matters, or for service in locations away from the presidio.[113] They were forbidden to make war against friendly or neutral Indian nations, or even against hostile tribes until efforts to pacify them by persuasion had failed. They were further prohibited from employing one non-Christian nation against another unless it had specifically asked for Spanish help. On the other hand, the raising of Indian auxiliaries within the jurisdictions of the *alcaldes mayores* was encouraged.[114]

The governor of New Mexico was specifically instructed to visit all of the pueblos in May and October of each year and to maintain the Indians in their tranquil state. Further, he was to explain with great care to the *alcaldes mayores* selected for these districts that they were not to mistreat their subjects or give them cause to flee to the Moqui area as they had previously done in some instances. If such abuse occurred again, the governor was to replace these officials and assess on them a fine of 1,000 ducats to be paid to the treasury and the Indian community concerned.[115]

Whenever a pueblo of the province was threatened by the infidel tribes, the governor was to send a squadron from the presidio to dissuade the hostiles with a show of arms. Captains and other presidial officers were forbidden from requisitioning horses, mules, or equipment from the pueblos through which they passed without "just payment," under penalty of loss of office and a fine of 100 *maravedíes*. Soldiers were prohibited from creating disorders in the pueblos and *rancherías* of friendly Indians, or entering into any

---

113 Reglamento de 1729, in *ibid.*, 200–201. The translation of *alférez* as "ensign" would not be quite correct here. Such an official was usually the traditional standard-bearer, but as an officer in the presidio, he might be expected to exercise the functions of a modern second lieutenant.
114 *Ibid.*, 204–205, 216.
115 *Ibid.*, 222–23.

A view of Jémez Pueblo, New Mexico, as it looked about 1900.

Architecture of Jémez Pueblo, New Mexico, around 1900.

trade or obligation with them except at fair prices. When expeditions of war succeeded in taking prisoners of both sexes and all ages, captive families were not to be divided for any reason whatsoever lest the Indian warriors be induced to wreak vengeance. Finally, whenever natives sued for peace, commandants and governors were obliged to admit them to such an arrangement under a signed, written agreement.[116]

The *Reglamento de 1729* marked the end of one era and the beginning of another. For two and one-half decades prior to 1729, Spain's Indian policy in New Mexico was in a stage of transition characterized by vacillation and inconsistency. The controversy over arming and painting friendly Indians is most illustrative of this tendency. Yet, throughout this period there was one consistency—the continued allegiance of the Pueblo Indians. Not only had they refrained from rebellion of their own, but they had also materially aided in the defense of the province from the revolts and raids of other tribes.

When the Spaniards returned to New Mexico in the last decade of the seventeenth century, the fundamental problem was the conquest and control of the Pueblo Indians. Vargas had largely accomplished these tasks, and in his Sandía Mountain campaign of 1704, he had begun to co-ordinate Spanish and Pueblo military operations against the *indios bárbaros*. From that uncertain beginning, the use of Pueblo auxiliaries on military expeditions became standardized in the campaigns of 1715–17 against the Faraón Apaches, Moquis, and Comanches. Toward the end of the era, the task became one of defending the province against incursions of various Plains tribes, and this remained the paramount problem of the eighteenth century.[117]

The *Reglamento de 1729* noted the advantages to be derived from the continued use of Pueblo auxiliaries. It was an official

[116] *Ibid.*, 222–23, 229.
[117] Espinosa, *Crusaders of the Río Grande*, 369.

recognition of a basic policy adopted by Spanish authorities in New Mexico to meet the numerous threats presented by the hostile nations in the early eighteenth century. Thus, the *Reglamento*, although it attempted to establish a uniform Indian policy for the northern frontier, only confirmed what settlers in New Mexico had already devised. By 1729 the Pueblos had become an important component of the Spanish community along the Rio Grande. They had their own privileges, the respect of visiting officials such as Rivera, and the distinction of being the major dependable force of auxiliaries in New Mexico. Although it is apparent that the settlers did not accept them as equals, but kept them segregated on the campaigns, it is clear that many of the Pueblos gained official respect. An excellent example was José Naranjo, who supported the Spanish cause continually for one and one-half decades, until he lost his life as an auxiliary in the Villasur massacre of 1720. However, it must be remembered that the *Reglamento de 1729* was simply another in a long line of rules established to govern the Spanish colonies. It indicated the official intent, not the accepted practice, and enforcement of the provisions of this regulation, as of other legislation, varied according to circumstances, the integrity of the administrators, the behavior of the settlers, and the nature of the military campaigns.

By 1729 there was no longer any fear of Pueblo Indian uprisings. Unity among these natives had been established in support of Spanish policies in New Mexico. Control of these friendly Indians had been effectively demonstrated, particularly on the more regularized and organized campaigns. Pueblo assistance on these expeditions had provided the necessary strength with which to meet the many, widely scattered enemies. Indeed, as the period progressed, the number of auxiliaries seemed to increase until, at the end of the era, a larger proportion of the combined force was recruited. In addition, problems of organization were gradually worked out during this period. Likewise, the Pueblos furnished numerous other forms of assistance as scouts, interpreters, and informants. Their ready supply of foodstuffs and equipment, their effective fighting techniques, and their willingness to offer their villages as rendez-vous points for campaigns were other contributions of the Pueblos. Certainly, they provided an attractive example to other Indians such as the Jicarilla and Sierra Blanca Apaches. This formative period provided the basis in New Mexico for an intersocietal exchange which increased and endured until the end of Spanish authority in the province.

★ 4 ✦

Pacification and Integration, 1729–1754

With the *Reglamento de 1729* and the establishment of a nucleus for the Spanish-Pueblo alliance in New Mexico, the defensive posture of this northern region began to change. In the next twenty-five years new and serious threats appeared, jeopardizing Spanish control in the area even more than the frequent Apache incursions of the previous two and one-half decades. Yet, even in the face of the growing Comanche threat, the newly established unity was maintained and the bond grew in scope and strength.

Prior to 1754, ties between the various Pueblos on the one hand and the Spaniards on the other were considerably strengthened. Pueblo assistance was provided as before on numerous campaigns against Apaches, Utes, and Comanches, but new and greater uses were found for these loyal Indian auxiliaries. It is evident that Pueblos were expected to be equally responsible with European settlers for the defense of the province, and they seem to have been used extensively as military escorts for friars on mssionary ventures into the lands of the Hopi, Navaho, and Apache in the decade of the 1740's. By the time of Governor Tomás Vélez Cachupín (1749–54), they had become part of a well-integrated and formalized system of defense.

Perhaps the most important contribution of the Pueblos in this era, however, was their attraction of other Indians to alliances with the Spaniards. With their privileges, gifts, equipment, and military organization, these Indians provided an excellent example of what the *indios bárbaros* could attain if they would but agree to peace. Indeed, as the pacification of other tribes occurred, new alliances were possible with Indian groups other than the Pueblos.

Defense was still the key problem from 1729 to 1754. Apache raids persisted in the 1730's, although less frequently than before, and in the retaliatory campaigns the Spaniards established a new and aggravating practice. The Apaches whom they captured were now sold in slavery to friendly tribes of the realm. Governor Gervasio Cruzat y Góngora, recognizing the practice in 1732, issued an order to halt it. He levied a fine of seven pesos against the Spaniards for each captive sold, and a punishment of 200 lashes on the Indians for each Apache purchased. The alcaldes of all jurisdictions were instructed to be vigilant for violations of the order and to comply with its provisions completely.[1]

There is little doubt, however, that Governor Cruzat and his successor, Enrique de Olavide y Micheleña (1736–37), were as concerned with defense as with justice. Each placed New Mexico under alert, requiring both settlers and Pueblos to present themselves for military service on a moment's notice. The alcaldes were made responsible for mobilizing the inhabitants, provisioning

[1] Don Gervasio Cruzat y Góngora, Bando, Santa Fé, December 6, 1732, SAMN, Documento 378.

111

El Coronel Dn. Geruasio Cruzat, y Gongora, Gouernador
y Capitan General de este Reyno de la Nueua Mexico, y sus
Prouincias, Castellano de sus Fuerzas y Presidios por su Magd.

Por quanto combiene al Real seruisio de su Magd.
el q. todos los Españoles, é Indios. de este Reyno esten promtos, y Proueydos para lo q. se
pueda obrar en seruisio de su Magd., y deber
sa del Reyno, hordeno, y Mando q. todos los Ve-
sinos, y Naturales esten Promtos, y auiados para
Juntarse en la Plasa de Armas q. se les señalara
quando lo pidiera el caso. Y para q. llegue á
noticia de todos hordeno, y mando a los Alcaldes
Mayores hagan notoria esta horden en sus respec-
tiuas Jurisdiciónes, y en inteligensia de ella
salgan, quando se les mandare, equipados de
Armas, y cauallos y de mas pertos ofensiuas, y
defensiuas q. tubieren, quedando en las Villas,
y Pueblos la gente nesesaria para su resguardo, y
con toda las de mas vendran los mismos Alcaldes

Mayores condusiendola al parate q.e se les hor
denase prouejdos de bastimento para quinse
dias: Y esta horden pasara de Jurisdicion en Ja
risdicion sin la mas leue demora, y detension
hasta q.e debuelua á este superior Gouierno. Assi
lo mandé, y firmé con los testigos de mi asis
tensia á falta de Escriuano Publicô, y Real
q.e no lo ay en este Reyno =

D.n Gervasio Cruzat, y Gongora

Gaspar B.mo

Juan Antonio de Ynanue

them, and assembling them at whatever place might be designated for their service.[2]

Governor Cruzat's order of 1733 is of utmost importance in the development of Spanish-Pueblo relations. It demonstrates that Pueblos and Spanish settlers were equal in their military obligations. Both were subject to immediate call, whenever and wherever the governor might require, and both together with their respective *alcaldes mayores* were responsible for furnishing their own arms, horses, and provisions. They were expected to serve on campaigns of up to fifteen days duration, and only such men as were required for the defense of the *villas* and pueblos were to be left behind. So that all might be apprised of their duties, this order was to be broadcast in each major district of the province.[3]

A proposed campaign against the Utes in 1736 illustrates the Spanish plan for joint operations of presidial soldiers, settlers, and Pueblo Indians. Residents of Santa Cruz complained on April 14 that the Utes had raided the horse herds and cattle at Santa Clara Pueblo three days earlier.[4] In view of this complaint against the "Apaches Yutas,"[5] the governor called a *junta de guerra* which convened at Santa Fe on April 18. It was agreed there that warfare against the Utes was justified under the provisions of the "ninth law, fourth title, third book" of the *Recopilación de leyes de los reynos*

2 Don Gervasio Cruzat y Góngora, Bando [Santa Fé, June 23, 1733], SANM, Documento 384. The original, somewhat water damaged, has been photographed with the assistance of Dr. Myra E. Jenkins of the Spanish Archives of New Mexico and is included herein for detailed study and references; Enrique de Olavide y Micheleña, Bando, March 30, 1737, SANM, Documento 415.

3 Cruzat y Góngora, Bando [Santa Fé, June 23, 1733], SANM, Documento 384. Publication occurred at Santa Cruz on June 23 by Captain José Esteban García Noriega, *alcalde mayor*, and at Taos on June 26 by Diego Romero, *teniente alcalde mayor* of the "Pueblo and its jurisdiction." It is these promulgations which enable the document itself to be dated by internal evidence, since the actual date is not reflected in the record itself.

4 Cruzat y Góngora, April, 1736, SANM, Documento 409. The settlers were Joseph Gomes, Roque Jaramillo, Rosaleo Valdés, and Juan Manuel de Herrera. The complaint was forwarded by *alcalde mayor* Juan[?] Esteban García Noriega.

5 An interesting term since the Utes were in no way related to the Apaches. However, from the viewpoint of New Mexicans, all nomadic, raiding *indios bárbaros* were associated with Apaches. Thus we have the "Apaches Yutas" and the "Apaches Navajos."

de las indias.[6] This law required that warfare should not be conducted against Indians converted to the Catholic faith or who had rendered allegiance to the Spanish sovereigns unless they had become apostates or had negated their pledge, in which case they could be treated as "apostates and rebels, conforming to whatever excesses they merited."[7]

Governor Cruzat concurred in the justification and decision for the campaign and ordered that military operations should be conducted as quickly as possible. Three squadrons of soldiers from the presidio were to lead the expedition; settlers from Santa Fe and Santa Cruz and Indians from the Tewa pueblos were to assist the campaign force; and all would assemble and depart from Chama.[8] Under the over-all command of Lieutenant Governor Juan Páez Hurtado, this expedition of thirty-six presidial soldiers, fifty settlers, and seventy Pueblo Indians was to proceed northward in pursuit of the Utes.[9] Thus, the organization of this campaign reveals the relative strength of the elements employed, the preoccupation with proper justification for the warfare, and the time-lag in actually commencing punitive operations. Results, however, were meager and little contact with the enemy was made.

The practice of periodic official visits to the pueblos, begun by Vargas during the reconquest, was continued in this period by Cruzat. The purpose was to determine the justification of complaints from individual Indians and to make restitution for wrongs committed by soldiers and settlers. Most of the aggravations were minor, involving a horse, a cow, or a small monetary sum. In his

6 Cruzat y Góngora, April, 1736, SANM, Documento 409.

7 *Recopilación de leyes,* Tomo I, Libro III, Título IV, Ley *ix.* It is interesting to note that the law provided that even if the Indians began the warfare against "our vassals, settlements and peaceful lands," three or more efforts would be made to attract them to peace as desired by the sovereigns; war could be waged only if these measures did not suffice. If open and formal warfare were necessary, the Consejo Real de Indias was to be advised of the causes and motives.

8 Cruzat y Góngora, April, 1736, SANM, Documento 409.

9 Horden que deve observar el theniente General Dⁿ· Juan Páez Hurtado . . . , in Cruzat y Góngora, Santa Fé, April 24, 1736, SANM, Documento 409.

visits to Galisteo on July 27, 1733, and to Pecos five days later, the Governor was quick to grant restitution. Particularly notable is the fact that one Indian at the latter pueblo was reimbursed with a musket.[10] These restitutions illustrate the official desire to treat the Pueblos fairly and thus to preserve the amicable relations which existed between the two peoples. Such a policy not only enhanced the internal security of the realm but also tended to encourage out-lying tribes to seek peace with the Spaniards.

Whereas the previous decade had been one of sporadic activity against the Apaches, Utes, and Comanches, the period after 1739 was one of increasing alarm, requiring renewed efforts—both military and missionary. By then the Comanches had driven the Apaches from the region east and north of the Spanish settlements in New Mexico, and their trade with the French for firearms enabled them to conduct their own raids on the province itself. Devastating attacks by the Comanches depopulated the eastern frontier settlements of the province[11] and led to excesses on both sides. Spaniards and Indian auxiliaries who participated in expeditions against this increasing menace mistreated Comanche women and children, prompting the issuance of a remedial order in 1741. The Spanish inhabitants were to be fined 300 pesos for the first such offense and a similar amount plus six months exile for its repetition, while their Indian comrades were to receive 200 lashes and six months in prison.[12] Apparently the law was loosely enforced, because another decree was issued three years later, condemning the same practice as one against the "Catholic faith and the will of His Majesty"; the same punishments for offenses as before were set except that the number of lashes to be given Indian offenders was reduced to 100.[13]

[10] Visita . . . hecho por el Coronel Dn. Gervasio Cruzat y Góngora . . . , SANM, Documento 389.

[11] Alfred B. Thomas, *The Plains Indians and New Mexico, 1751–1778*, 16.

[12] Gaspar Domingo de Mendoza, Bando, Santa Fé, March 21, 1741, SANM, Documento 438.

Because campaigns against the "*bárbaros Cumanches*" were a constant requirement, authorities warned all alcaldes to be vigilant and quick to punish the culprits for their widespread robberies and depredations.[14] In spite of the unity among the Spaniards and Pueblos, it appears that Taos Pueblo was unco-operative. Having received notice from some loyal subjects,[15] the governor reported in 1746 that the Taos Indians traded and corresponded with the Comanches, pointing out that there was no pueblo, place, or dwelling which was safe from the robberies and murders of the Comanches, and that it was quite probable that some of the Taos natives were informing the enemy of military movements from the presidio.[16]

Governor Joaquín Codallos y Rabal ordered the *alcalde mayor* of San Gerónimo de Taos to collect on a festival day all the principal Indians, governors, caciques, and war captains, notifying them of his order to halt their dealings with the enemy and that the death penalty would be authorized for any Indian who traveled over a league from his pueblo without a license. Natives were not to offer any excuse, such as hunting or searching for lost animals, and they were absolutely forbidden to trade with the Comanches. Alcaldes were advised that the fine for violations of the order was 500 pesos and that they were not to grant licenses nor even give verbal permission for the Indians of Taos Pueblo to treat or communicate with the Comanches.[17]

Although the Comanches constituted the principal enemy in

13 Joachín Codallos y Rabal, Bando, Santa Fé, May 30, 1744, SANM, Documento 465.

14 Mendoza, Bando, Santa Fé, February 20, 1742, in Ordenes . . . sobre el cuidado y bigilencia en sus jurisdiciones, SANM, Documento 443.

15 Quite probably these informants could have been Pueblo Indians from Taos itself or from a nearby pueblo, such as Picurís, or even from the highly loyal San Juan Pueblo.

16 Codallos y Rabal, Santa Fé, February 4, 1746, included in Diferentes ordenes . . . , Años de 1744, 1745, 1746, 1747, y 1748, SANM, Documento 495. Hereinafter cited as Diferentes ordenes.

17 *Ibid.*

117

this eventful decade, occasional difficulties were experienced with the Faraón and Gila Apaches. Settlers of the Río Abajo district (embracing Albuquerque, Bernalillo, and neighboring pueblos) reported in 1744 that the Faraones had committed many livestock robberies in that area. Governor Codallos ordered Lieutenant Manuel Sanz de Garbuzu of the presidio to take 20 soldiers and proceed to Isleta Pueblo. There on December 10 they were joined by 30 settlers from La Cañada and Albuquerque and 100 Indians from the pueblos of Isleta, Laguna, Zía, Jémez, Santa Ana, San Felipe, Santo Domingo, and Cochití, drafted with their arms, horses, and provisions by their respective alcaldes. For their campaign into the Ladrón and Magdalena Mountains to the southwest, the Indian auxiliaries were to be employed not only as troops but also as spies, to reconnoiter the mountains and to determine the water holes used by the enemy. If Faraón *rancherías*, or those of other nations, were located, the commander of the expedition was enjoined to treat them gently and procure their friendship if possible.[18]

The Gila Apache campaign of 1747 was unique in the history of the northern frontier of New Spain during the first half of the eighteenth century. It was one of the few co-ordinated military efforts undertaken from different directions against a common enemy. The Viceroy of New Spain, Juan Francisco de Güemes y Horcasitas, better known as the first Conde de Revilla Gigedo, ordered the Governor of New Mexico to participate with soldiers, settlers, and Indians from El Paso and from the presidios of Terrenate and Fronteras, in Sonora, and Janos, in Nueva Vizcaya, in an extended general campaign against the Gila Apaches. The Governor was advised to prepare for a four-month campaign and to furnish thirty presidial soldiers, forty Spanish settlers, and sixty

---

[18] Codallos y Rabal, Ordenes, Santa Fé, December 2, 1744, and February 6, 1745, SANM, Documento 495.

Pueblo Indians. This force was to advance southward into the Gila Apache country until it made contact with detachments from the other presidios.[19]

Unfortunately, the New Mexico contingent was unable to participate in the general campaign as planned—a fact which may have contributed to its relative lack of success. Invasions of "Gentile Indians" and Utes in the vicinity of Abiquiú necessitated the dispatch of a military expedition to counter this threat in the north first.[20] Later "Lieutenant General" Bernardo de Bustamante with 30 soldiers, 15 settlers, and 110 well-equipped Indian auxiliaries finally assembled at Isleta on December 9 for the campaign which originally had been scheduled for September 30.[21] Since Governor Codallos could not provide 40 settlers as required by the viceroy's orders, he advised that he had augmented the number of Indians.[22] Thus, Pueblo Indian auxiliaries composed 71 per cent of the total force dispatched. Marching southward, Bustamante encountered only an independent Pueblo Indian army of 65 Lagunas and Acomas, whom he added to his own auxiliary force,[23] before snow and lack of supplies forced him to discontinue his tardy campaign.

Although the basic idea had been well-conceived and the planning for the general campaign had been extensive, the results were poor because of improper co-ordination, the diversionary attack on the northern frontier which necessitated an improvised defense in that direction, and the consequent insufficient force left to be employed. However, close analysis of the New Mexico portion of

---

19 Despacho del Superior Gobierno de este Nueva España . . . , SANM, Documento 479. The full title of the document and Twitchell, *The Spanish Archives of New Mexico*, II, 218, erroneously gives the number as seventy. The content of the document reveals in two separate places that the correct number was sixty.

20 Codallos y Rabal, Testimonio, Santa Fé, December 6, 1747, SANM, Documento 483.

21 Bernardo Antonio de Bustamante, Diario, Santa Fé, December 24, 1747, SANM, Documento 483.

22 Codallos y Rabal, Testimonio, Santa Fé, December 6, 1747, SANM, Documento 483.

23 Bustamante, Diario, Santa Fé, December 24, 1747, SANM, Documento 483.

this offensive reveals the importance of Pueblo auxiliaries in the composition of the total military forces, for nearly 80 per cent of the expedition (after the addition of the Acomas and Lagunas) was recruited from the pueblos.

Renewed missionary activity in the middle two decades of the eighteenth century also led to extensive use of the Pueblo Indians as escorts for the friars in their visits to remote, un-Christianized tribes. Missionaries made considerable use of the Pueblos as interpreters on their expeditions to the heathen nations and on individual visits to the pueblos themselves.

Some success was realized among the distant Moquis. There Father Carlos Delgado was successful in convincing 441 apostate Tiwas to return to the Río Grande, where they were settled temporarily at Jémez Pueblo. Later, in 1748, a grant was secured to provide them with a tract of land near the abandoned site of Sandía Pueblo. For Father Delgado's *entrada* of 1742, he was provided with an escort of eighty Pueblo Indians.[24] On a second such venture three years later, Governor Codallos ordered the governors and captains of Acoma, Laguna, and Zuñi pueblos to provide eighty Indians to serve the father as an escort to the Moqui villages.[25] Except for the return of the Tiwas, little success was realized in the attempt to transfer the Moquis, Navahos, and western Apaches to the east, to settle in pueblos, and expose them to Christianity.[26]

Two of the principal complaints often advanced by the civil against the religious authorities during the colonial period were that the missionaries failed to learn the Indian dialects and that they did not teach the Indians the Spanish language. The latter was not a valid criticism in New Mexico as can be observed in the many interpreters and informants found among the Pueblo Indians,

[24] Henry W. Kelly, "Franciscan Missions of New Mexico, 1740–1760," *NMHR*, Vol. XVI, No. 1 (January, 1941), 46–47.
[25] Codallos y Rabal, Zuñi[?], September 14, 1745, SANM, Documento 465b.
[26] Kelly, "Franciscan Missions of New Mexico, 1740–1760," *NMHR*, Vol. XVI, No. 1 (January, 1941), 50.

dating from the days of Bartolomé de Ojeda and the reconquest. Governor Codallos' *visita general* of 1745 further revealed his dependence upon these bilingual natives. This visit started with the northernmost pueblo, Taos, on August 16, and ended at Isleta and Albuquerque in the south on September 18–19. Throughout the thirty-five days required, Governor Codallos patiently heard complaints from individual Indians, made on-the-spot restitution where necessary, and examined the state of each pueblo.[27]

Although most of the complaints and requests made by the Indians dealt with minor items, and their nature is not here relevant, the use of Pueblo interpreters clearly reveals that in each village beneficial results of the Spanish-Pueblo alliance and the missionary efforts could be observed. At Taos the governor accepted "Estevan Nacion Taos" as his official interpreter because he was "*mui ladino*" in the Spanish language, and he paid him six pesos for his services.[28] Subsequent visits, ranging from Picurís in the north to Isleta in the south, also employed Pueblo Indians (all with Christian names) who were described as "*indios ladinos*" at each village.[29]

Military operations against the Comanches in New Mexico reached a climax during the first administration of Tomás Vélez Cachupín, from 1749 to 1754. This young, determined, and impetuous governor was one of the outstanding officials appointed to that office during the eighteenth century. He was remarkably successful in pacifying the Comanches and in establishing a temporary general peace on the frontier. However, he created another problem which marred his administration, by resurrecting the intense seventeenth-century conflict between the civil and religious authorities.

Since the beginning of the century the Utes and Comanches had

27 Codallos y Rabal, Visita general, Año de 1745, SANM, Documento 470.

28 *Ibid.* Undoubtedly the governor meant Esteban of the Taos nation. For an explanation of the "*muy ladino*" concept, see Chapter II, note 18 above.

29 Codallos y Rabal, Visita general, Año de 1745, SANM, Documento 470.

been faithfully allied with each other against all enemies, although the former were more frequently at peace with the Spanish settlements than were the latter. However, at some time before 1749, these two nations became deadly enemies. The reasons for this change in their relationship have not been specifically determined, but perhaps the difficulty can be traced to the temporary absence of the common enemy, the Apache. Since the Comanches had forced the Apaches southward by this time, the bond between them and the Utes may have been severed by quarrels over the trespassing of one upon territory claimed by the other.[30] Certainly, after mid-century, Comanches had begun to raid into the San Luis Valley of southern Colorado and northern New Mexico, perhaps encroaching upon territory formerly roamed by the Utes.

Whatever the cause of this separation, the Utes sought Spanish assistance against the Comanches, as did many small Apache bands. Governor Vélez Cachupín saw this changed relationship and, desiring to take advantage of it, employed the Utes and Apaches against the dreaded Comanches. He encouraged the Carlana, Paloma, and Cuartelejo Apaches in the northeast to continue their peaceful conduct and to move their *rancherías* nearer to Pecos Pueblo to escape the Comanches. In the southeast, he established friendly relations with the Faraones, who in turn ceased raiding Albuquerque and the southern settlements.[31] Thus, the governor was successful in creating a multi-nation "alliance" against the Comanches, which included Spaniards, Pueblos, Utes, and Apaches. Over thirty years later Governor Juan Bautista de Anza would create a similar combination against the Apache menace.

The loyal Pueblos were to serve as examples for the new allies. By 1752 an official census revealed that there were 6,453 of them

30 Thomas, *The Plains Indians and New Mexico, 1751–1778*, 29.

31 *Ibid.*, 30. Here we have a good illustration of the Spanish policy of having the *indios bárbaros* or *gentiles*, such as the Apache bands, settle near the Pueblo Indians. Thus, they might in turn be attracted to pueblo life, converted to Christianity, controlled effectively, and used as Indian auxiliaries for the Spaniards.

scattered in twenty-two pueblos with the largest numbers concentrated at Acoma, Zuñi, Taos, and Laguna. Of this total, 2,174 were classified as "men of arms" from fifteen to sixty years of age. Indeed, this was a remarkable figure for it meant that 33 per cent of *all* Pueblo Indians were considered capable of bearing arms in the defense of the province. They possessed 4,060 horses, 60,045 arrows, 414 lances, 57 swords, and 151 leather jackets for use on their campaigns. It was assumed also that all Pueblos were acquainted with the Castilian language since they had all grown up in the Catholic faith.[32]

In contrast to the 6,453 Pueblos, the Spanish population of the province numbered only 4,458 persons (3,402 of them in New Mexico proper and 1,046 in the district of El Paso). The total number of men-at-arms, although not included in the document listing these populations, must, therefore, have been less than that of the Pueblo Indians. New Mexican settlers, exclusive of those living in the El Paso area, possessed 1,370 horses, 388 muskets, 332 lances, 123 swords, 53 pistols, and 121 leather jackets.[33] Thus, the Pueblo Indians possessed three times as many horses as the Spaniards, undoubtedly many more men-at-arms, more lances, and a greater quantity of leather jackets for individual protection. Only in the number of swords and possibly firearms, although some Indians were known to possess them, did the Spaniards seem to be better equipped. A close examination of the municipal statistics reported in this survey reveals that the pueblos of Laguna, Acoma, and Zuñi (all western pueblos) each possessed more horses than

---

[32] Estado general y particular . . . del Nuevo México . . . en el año de 1752 . . . , AGN, Provincias Internas 102, Expediente 3, Foja 1. The absence of firearms is not unusual since this was an official report, and Spanish law supposedly forbade the distribution of firearms to Indians. However, the reader will note in the foregoing chapters that there is considerable evidence in support of the conclusion that the Pueblos did possess them.

[33] Estado general y particular . . . de . . . las 16 poblaciones españoles . . . del Nuevo México . . . el año 1752 . . . , AGN, Provincias Internas 102, Expediente 2, Foja 2.

any Spanish settlement, and that Laguna alone had almost as many as all of the Spanish settlements together.

Added to the greater mobility, better protective equipment, superior numbers, and general advantage of weapons were the fighting characteristics of the Pueblos themselves. One missionary, on his visit of 1754 to the villages of Pecos, Galisteo, and Santa Clara, among others, reported that these Indians were vigorous fighters. At Pecos he remarked that the mission was located in a beautiful valley, which was invaded repeatedly by the enemy, but that the Pueblos were so brave and warlike that they always defeated the Comanches. Likewise, he reported that the Christian Indians never claimed reimbursement for their services and that they went out voluntarily on campaigns.[34]

Later at the missions of Nuestra Madre de Santa Clara and Santa Cruz de Galisteo, he noted the staunchness of the Pueblos. At Santa Clara he stressed the proximity of the barbarian Utes but pointed out that even the women defended the pueblo by throwing stones from their slings upon the attackers. At Galisteo the missionary observed that:

> Although a victim of the barbarian hammer (*el bárbaro martillo*), its Indians are so courageous that on the occasion of an attack when I was there on a visit, boys of fifteen scaled the walls, the gates being shut, so as to be able to give the enemy a warm welcome with arrows and slings.[35]

Recognizing the Comanches as the principal Indian menace to the settlements and pueblos, Governor Vélez Cachupín personally observed that the most serious threat existed on the Pecos-Galisteo frontier, southeast of Santa Fe. After the enemy had raided Galisteo

[34] Father Manuel de San Juan Nepomuceno y Trigo to Very Reverend Father Procurador General Fray José Miguel de los Ríos, Istacalco, July 23, 1754, in Hackett, *Historical Documents*, III, 465.
[35] *Ibid.*, III, 466–67.

in the late summer of 1751, he conducted a general campaign through that village to the Great Plains.

For this expedition, commencing on September 4, Vélez Cachupín used fifty-four soldiers from the presidio of Santa Fe, thirty citizens, and eighty Pueblo Indians.[36] He employed the aborigines as scouts or spies, dispatching many of them as much as three leagues ahead of the main body to determine the whereabouts of Comanche camping places. Ten of these Pueblo scouts reported that they had seen two Comanches proceeding on foot to some springs on top of a nearby mesa, nearly a week after the expedition began its march eastward. Vélez Cachupín immediately dispatched twenty soldiers and an equal number of Indian auxiliaries to follow the Comanches "at a gallop" and to try to capture them. At the water hole this combined force succeeded in trapping the enemy in a canebrake until the main element of the expeditionary force arrived. The Governor ordered all, including the Pueblos, to dismount and penetrate the thicket, sword in hand, to attack the Comanches. After an overnight halt following the initial onslaught, the destruction of the enemy was completed the following morning. Women and children were allowed to surrender, but over 100 Comanches were killed in the engagement. In the aftermath, the Comanche "arms, guns, lances, swords, shields, and bows and arrows [were] collected and divided among the Pueblo Indians as well as their saddles and trappings of their horses."[37] As a result of

36 Tomás Vélez Cachupín to Conde de Revilla Gigedo, Testimonio de los auttos fechos . . . de la nación Cumanche, AGI, 103–5–19, in Thomas, *The Plains Indians and New Mexico, 1751–1778*, 69. Both this source and the accompanying report of the senior auditor agree that the number of auxiliaries was eighty. See Marqués de Altamira to Tomás Vélez Cachupín, México, April 2, 1752, Copia, SANM, Documento 518, for corroboration of this number. However, the governor's report contains a minor error in the title when he states that only eight Indians were taken. In view of the numbers subsequently specified in this report, this small quantity could not have been possible.

37 Vélez Cachupín, Testimonio de los auttos fechos . . . de la nación Cumanche, AGI, 103–5–19, in Thomas, *The Plains Indians and New Mexico, 1751–1778*, 69–73, Twitchell is in error when he observes that this expedition went to the Arkansas River. This campaign may have reached the vicinity of the Canadian River in eastern New Mexico or

this crushing blow and Vélez Cachupín's subsequent leniency toward the captives, the Comanches sued for peace with the Spaniards. This the governor granted, and the Comanches maintained their new relationship faithfully for the remainder of his term of office.

By 1752 Governor Vélez Cachupín was employing Apaches as well as Pueblos as auxiliaries, especially Carlanas, Palomas, and Cuartelejos, who had proved trustworthy since their resettlement near Pecos the previous winter. Vélez Cachupín found them particularly qualified as spies because of their agility, astuteness, and extensive knowledge of the terrain.[38] This marks a departure from the policy in New Mexico of relying solely on Pueblos as Indian auxiliaries.

Of unusual significance in Spanish-Indian relations in New Mexico during the eighteenth century is the detailed system of military preparedness and defense devised by the Governor during the early 1750's. His well-organized, integrated plan may be examined and studied in detail in the instructions of 1754 which he left for his successor, Francisco Antonio Marín del Valle.[39] This policy statement may be divided arbitrarily into three separate assessments and recommendations: (1) on the domestic Pueblo nations; (2) on the other Indians, such as the Utes, Apaches, and Comanches; and (3) on military preparations and techniques.

Disgusted with the haphazard co-operation of the local Spanish citizenry, Vélez Cachupín pointed out that they wanted a soldier

west Texas. It is particularly important because it reveals that Pueblo auxiliaries were both equipped with firearms and mounted. This decisive defeat of the Comanches may be compared to a similar one dealt them in 1779 by Juan Bautista de Anza. Both led eventually to general peace settlements between the Comanches and the Spaniards.

[38] Vélez Cachupín to Conde de Revilla Gigedo, Informe, Santa Fé, September 29, 1752, in Thomas, *The Plains Indians and New Mexico, 1751–1778*, 124.

[39] Copia de Ynstrucción que dejo Dⁿ. Tomás Vélez Cachupín . . . a su sucesor Dⁿ. Francisco Marín del Valle, August 12, 1754, AGN, Provincias Internas 102, Expediente 2, Fojas 270 ff. Although the document has been consulted in this study, an accurate translation exists in Thomas, *The Plains Indians and New Mexico, 1751–1778*, 129–43. Hereinafter the document is cited as Vélez Cachupín, Instrucción.

to defend every horse and cow, whereas each settler should defend his own hacienda.[40]

In contrast to the Governor's attitude toward the Spaniards, he recommended the Pueblos highly. They were satisfied with the laws passed for their protection and assistance and supported the government to the best of their ability. Vélez Cachupín suggested that the policy of treating them benevolently be continued so that they might enjoy all possible comforts and so that "the example of their well being and freedom from want would be an attraction for the conversion of the heathen Indians."[41] He pointed out that humane consideration, affection, and protection should be given them because during the five years of his administration they had not given him the slightest cause for suspicion of infidelity, but were always prompt to serve whenever war broke out.[42]

Vélez Cachupín also cautioned his successor to treat the Utes with the greatest friendship possible, displaying generosity, sincerity, and a humane attitude. He recommended that all graciousness, the best of friendship and affection, and good faith be adopted as the policy for the Ute captain, Tomás, because if he were alienated it would be difficult to pacify him again. If the Utes should commit further robberies of horses, Marín del Valle was advised not to threaten the entire tribe with retaliation, but simply to inform the Ute captains of the deed and allow them to remedy the situation.[43]

Likewise, Vélez Cachupín proudly pointed out that the Comanches had been at peace since their punishment by force of arms in the late summer of 1751. He recommended that this situation be continued since the Comanches, if alienated, possessed the strength to ruin New Mexico. With their allies from the plains and their

[40] Vélez Cachupín, *Instrucción*.
[41] *Ibid.* Thomas' translation for this passage, in *Plains Indians and New Mexico, 1751–1778*, page 137, conveys the same meaning.
[42] Vélez Cachupín, *Instrucción*.
[43] *Ibid.* This is an early recognition of the advantages to be derived from the recognition of native leadership.

firearms, the enemy could not be resisted continuously by the forces available within the province.[44]

To prevent depredations, robberies, and incursions of the *indios bárbaros* from all directions, Governor Vélez Cachupín had devised a military system which integrated Pueblos and Spaniards of all jurisdictions in New Mexico. He also established an extensive vigilance which must have been one of the first "early warning" systems devised on the North American Continent.

To the north and east he sent Pueblo Indian auxiliaries from Taos, Pecos, Picurís, and Galisteo as scouts to reconnoiter the passes and routes usually followed by the Comanches to enter the Río Grande Valley. Especially vulnerable were the gaps in the mountains near Mora, where he assigned Picurís and Taos Indians to examine and patrol the mountain slopes as far north as the Canadian River. The most prompt and reliable intelligence reports on Comanche movements, he noted, were those obtained from the natives of Pecos and Galisteo. Vélez Cachupín recommended that these Pueblos be maintained ever on the alert, since the strategic passes they patrolled might otherwise allow the enemy to penetrate and overpower the Spanish defenses.[45]

In the south the governor had maintained a continuous summer patrol of forty Indians from the six Keres pueblos and, when practicable, two squadrons of soldiers from the presidio. These contingents guarded against the entrance into the Río Grande settlements of Faraón and Natagé Apaches to raid Albuquerque, Santo Domingo, and San Felipe.[46] They were stationed at "Coara"[47] and Tajique[48] in the "ancient missions in the cordillera of the Sandía

44 *Ibid.*

45 *Ibid.* Vélez Cachupín refers here to the negligence of some scouts near Galisteo in 1751, which caused the disastrous raid and the subsequent campaign against the Comanches as discussed earlier.

46 *Ibid.*

47 This is the abandoned seventeenth-century mission of Quarai, located east of the Manzano Mountains (an extension southward of the Sandías) and southeast of Albuquerque. It is now a New Mexico state monument.

Mountains."[49] Such outlying patrols were to inspect all the terrain in their vicinity and to reconnoiter the entrances used by the Apaches, particularly the *bocas* of Abó,[50] to gain access to the Río Abajo region. As a result of these preventive measures, the Governor reported that these jurisdictions in the south were free from robberies, although the Gila Apaches could still reach Albuquerque from the southwest by way of the Río Puerco and the Ladrón Mountains.[51]

This elaborate, co-ordinated scouting system was provided to make initial contact with the enemy. The Pueblos assigned to these patrols were instructed that should they meet enemy Indians in numbers too great to be overcome, the loyal auxiliaries were to advise their pueblos promptly so that forces could be gathered to drive out and pursue the attackers. Behind this outer Pueblo defensive screen, Vélez Cachupín kept 200 men armed and equipped at Santa Fe, able to march within one day, and he provided instruction in cavalry movements for 150 settlers there.[52]

Pueblo Indian auxiliaries contributed greatly to the defense and military operations of New Mexico during the period beginning with the *Reglamento de 1729* and ending with Governor Vélez Cachupín's completion of his first term of office. These faithful Indians were a bulwark of defense, for they possessed traditional deep-seated hatreds for the nomadic *indios bárbaros*, especially the Apaches, Utes, and Comanches. They were vigorous fighters, and

48 Located on the eastern slope of the Manzano Mountains about fifteen miles north of Quarai. All of these pueblos and missions had been established in this saline region during the early seventeenth century and had been abandoned because of their exposed position to the Apaches before the Pueblo revolt of 1680.

49 Vélez Cachupín, Instrucción. Thomas' summary in *The Plains Indians and New Mexico, 1751–1778*, page 33 contains some minor errors such as the statement that the squads were stationed in the "Albuquerque jurisdiction," and placing them in the cited missions along the "Sandía Mountains," which do not extend that far southward.

50 Just west of the present site of the abandoned seventeenth-century mission of Abó, now a New Mexico state monument.

51 Vélez Cachupín, Instrucción.

52 *Ibid.*

129

their courage in the defense of their pueblos was unquestioned. These characteristics, given official recognition in this era, helped to negate the popular image of the Pueblo Indians as docile tribesmen unfit for war.

Certainly the Spanish-Pueblo alliance grew during this period of consolidation, pacification of hostiles, and integration of Indians into one defensive plan. Protected and privileged, the Pueblos served as a magnet in the pacification of other, non-Christianized tribes, gradually convincing them that peace with the Spaniards would be beneficial to them. The first fruits of the changing alliance situation and the "attractive power" of the Pueblos may be seen in the uses made by Vélez Cachupín in the 1750's of the Utes, Carlana Apaches, and Cuartelejos to supplement his auxiliary forces.

Indeed, the Pueblo Indians not only served promptly and well on campaigns as reliable and well-equipped soldiers, but also as indispensable escorts, interpreters, and scouts. They were the "eyes and ears" of the detailed vigilance system initiated by Governor Vélez Cachupín and were relied upon by him as the first line of defense for the province. By the end of his administration he was successful in establishing a temporary peace on the New Mexican frontier—a peace which seemed loosely to unite Spaniards, Pueblos, Utes, Comanches, and even some Apaches in his integrated defensive plan. Had his policies been followed, it is most likely that New Mexico might have enjoyed a long era of stability in the latter half of the century. Instead, nearly continuous Indian warfare ultimately jeopardized Spain's hold on the province.

★ 5 ✦
Defensive Crisis, 1754–1776

Fifty years had passed since the first Apache campaign had been conducted in the Sandía Mountains by Diego de Vargas. That expedition had failed to accomplish its objective of chastising the marauders, just as many others over the course of the next half-century did not achieve their goal. Several methods were employed to combat the threats presented by the Utes, Comanches, and Apaches, but the technique most consistently used in this continuous warfare was the employment of Pueblo Indian auxiliaries. They served on every campaign in the first half of the eighteenth century, if it can be assumed that the documentation available for this period is anywhere nearly complete and accurate.

Although this was not an era of lasting achievement in many respects, there were positive gains in the formation of Indian policy. Political quarrels, controversies between secular officials and the Franciscans, struggles within the Church, difficulty in converting the Moquis, and clandestine apostasy among the Pueblos were only a few of the major problems of this period. According to the reports of the friars, the Indians were always treated harshly by the Spanish authorities.[1] Yet, one cannot conclude, as Ralph E. Twitchell does, that "little was accomplished by the Spaniards" and that the era may be characterized as "unprogressive."[2]

By mid-century, after much experimentation with various methods of warfare, a basically sound policy had been devised for controlling the *indios bárbaros* and making use of the Christian Indians to combat their traditional enemies. It had largely been consolidated from previous experience throughout the century, but Governor Vélez Cachupín had developed the first integrated policy during his first term of office, from 1749 to 1754. Primarily this program involved the use of presidiaries, citizen militia, and Pueblo Indians in punitive expeditions against nomadic tribes, as before. However, the native auxiliary force now had been augmented by Utes, Comanches, and some Apaches, all attracted to the Spanish cause by the apparent benefits accruing to the Pueblo troops. This basic policy of uniting the several amenable Indian nations against the implacable Apaches was ultimately to be extended to all the northern provinces. Had it been pursued diligently and with consistency after Vélez Cachupín's administrations, in all probability there would have been no defensive crisis in Spanish New Mexico from 1754 to 1776.

That the basic policy adopted by Vélez Cachupín was successful cannot be denied. In 1754, when he left office the province enjoyed a relatively peaceful state. Pueblos, Utes, and some Apaches aided in the pacification of the dreaded Comanches, who, in turn, had established an alliance with the Spaniards. Only the Apaches, now hopelessly outnumbered, remained as the enemy. The prospect of general peace and stability for the province seemed bright as Vélez

---

[1] Twitchell, *Leading Facts*, I, 443. For some examples of missionary reports chastising the governors, see the accounts of Fray Juan de Lezaún and Fray Pedro Serrano in Hackett, *Historical Documents*, III, 470–76 and 485–86.

[2] *Leading Facts*, I, 443.

Cachupín turned over the *gobernación* to his successor, Francisco Marín del Valle. In the next eight years, when three different governors ruled New Mexico at various times, warfare returned to the isolated province. It is not clear why Comanche raids upon the Spanish settlements and Pueblo communities resumed, causing the depopulation of the northern missions in this period. Missionaries reported that the governors were responsible for these retaliatory raids. Apparently the overbearing attitude of these Spanish officials, their denial of peaceable Comanche trade at Taos, and a surprise attack made upon the Comanches encamped near that pueblo by Governor Manuel del Portillo y Urrisola on December 22, 1761, had destroyed the earlier tranquility.[3]

From the turmoil of this era, peace was once again restored in the second term of Vélez Cachupín (1762–67). This governor's first concern upon resuming office was to solve the problems which had alienated the Comanches. In fact, he so reassured his former allies of his continued desire to maintain friendly relations with them that the powerful Plains tribe seems to have kept the peace during the five years of his second administration. Visitors on the northern frontier in this period, such as the Marqués de Rubí, noted this fact upon inspecting New Mexico.[4]

However, this stable situation was not destined to continue during the long administration of Governor Pedro Fermín de Mendinueta (1767–78). For some unknown reason, this official decided on a policy of all-out warfare against the Comanches, necessitating the use of Pueblo Indian auxiliaries and the undertaking of extensive defensive measures, most of which were not successful.[5] This resulted in probably the most tumultuous period in New Mexico's history. The frequency and extent of nomadic raids upon the province increased markedly from year to year. There were few,

3 Thomas, *The Plains Indians and New Mexico, 1751–1778*, 34.
4 *Ibid.*, 35.
5 *Ibid.*, 39.

if any, respites from the pressures and threats of Indian attack, although Mendinueta conducted more campaigns perhaps than any other governor save Diego de Vargas during the reconquest period. By 1776, the effect of these widespread and devastating attacks was a challenge to continued Spanish occupation of New Mexico. In that year the province had become an isolated frontier region, almost totally encircled with warlike tribes. Spanish settlers and their loyal Pueblo Indian allies were confronted with marauding Navahos to the northwest, Utes to the north and northwest, Comanches to the north and east, and various Apache bands to the east, south, and southwest.[6]

Spanish defenses and military forces within the province were inadequate to combat these threats. Against the depredations of the *indios bárbaros*, Spain had only eighty presidial soldiers, some unreliable militia elements, and the Pueblo Indians. Although the governors were responsible for the control of the Pueblos, including their mobilization, the native allies were under the direct administration of district officials, the *alcaldes mayores*. By the third quarter of the eighteenth century, New Mexico was divided into eight *alcaldías*, each administered by an *alcalde mayor* who was responsible to the governor for the conduct of Indian affairs in his district. His duties included settling problems among his charges, notarizing legal documents, investigating requests for land grants, placing grantees in possession of their land, collecting legal fees and tributes, and sometimes leading forces against hostile tribes. Usually *alcaldes mayores* were appointed from among the most influential Spaniards of a given district. They frequently abused their Indians, confiscated native supplies for their own benefit, reducing them to forced labor, mistreating their women, and appropriating their lands.[7] These individuals, who resided in the various pueblo dis-

6 Thomas (trans. and ed.), *Teodoro de Croix*, 7.
7 Myra E. Jenkins, "The Baltasar Baca 'Grant': History of an Encroachment," *El Palacio*, Vol. LXVIII, No. 1 (Spring, 1961), 53.

tricts, were responsible for complying with the governor's requests for certain numbers of auxiliaries to accompany each of the proposed expeditions.

By the middle of the eighteenth century, Pueblo Indians had organized their own military units. For a time these were commanded by a native *capitán mayor de la guerra*[8] who was subordinate when on campaign to the commander of the expedition. Generally, the governor or his designated representative, often an officer from the presidio of Santa Fe, commanded campaign forces. Father Manuel de San Juan Nepomuceno y Trigo observed in 1754 that the "mission Indians" were brave and warlike, particularly those from Pecos whom he admired for their "voluntary" and continued resistance to the barbaric tribes. He also considered the natives of Isleta Pueblo "brave warriors" and noted that those of Jémez sacrificed their corn crops to the settlers and soldiers who passed through their village.[9]

In the early 1770's, there were only 250 persons in the province who reportedly possessed firearms, and these were outdated *escopetas*, or flintlock muskets, common to the northern frontier of New Spain in the seventeenth and eighteenth centuries.[10] Pueblo auxiliaries, although they possessed some firearms of this type, relied chiefly upon the bow and arrow and the lance. Apparently some of

[8] Alfonso Rael de Aguilar, Protector General, Certificate, Santa Fé, January 10, 1706, in Hackett, *Historical Documents*, III, 366. This position had been created as early as 1706, was renewed in 1747, but seems not to have been authorized after 1767.
[9] Father Manuel Nepomuceno y Trigo to Fray José de los Ríos, July 23, 1754, in Hackett, *Historical Documents*, III, 462–65.
[10] Frank D. Reeve, "Navaho-Spanish Diplomacy, 1770–1790," *NMHR*, Vol. XXXV, No. 3 (July, 1960), 211. An excellent sketch of the type of *escopetas* used by the Spanish and their auxiliaries may be found in Carl P. Russell, *Guns on the Early Frontiers: A History of Firearms from Colonial Times through the Years of the Western Fur Trade*, 32. In his chapter "Arming the American Indian," the author noted that the *escopeta* persisted in New Mexico from the Pueblo revolt to the middle of the nineteenth century. He obviously was not aware of the new firearms received there during the administration of Juan Bautista de Anza. Also, he erroneously states that the Spaniards were "very conscientious" in withholding guns and ammunition from the Indians of the Southwest, although he admits that there were "some leaks" in this policy. Evidence in this book would refute Russell's contention that the Spaniards failed to arm the natives.

these weapons, especially the firearms held by the settlers and Pueblos, were traded to the Plains Indians at the fairs held in Taos. Governor Marín del Valle, early in his term of office, ordered all persons to stop selling such items to the Comanches; he further prohibited Spaniards, mulattoes, *coyotes*, and Pueblo Indians from visiting any *ranchería* of the Apaches, Comanches, or Utes. Violators of this decree were to be punished with fifty lashes.[11] Undoubtedly this stringent policy, being such a radical departure from that pursued by his predecessor, Vélez Cachupín, was a factor in the resumption of warfare between the Comanches and the Spanish-Pueblo forces in the decade of the 1750's.

Extensive campaigns in the period prior to the arrival of Vélez Cachupín for his second term of office created many problems for the Pueblos themselves. In addition to all the work normally done by the Indians in their own villages and elsewhere for the Spaniards, the natives were frequently employed as auxiliaries on individual campaigns. Their greatest sacrifice, however, was of their livestock. The many horses, cattle, and sheep raised by the Pueblos were either consumed by the campaign forces or stolen by the enemy. According to one sympathetic report, there was no compensation whatsoever for these losses.[12] The Pueblos furnished corn as well as livestock to the expeditionary armies. Whenever the alcalde required, Christian Indians from the pueblos, sometimes amounting to half the population of a given village, were dispatched to a central point to shell corn for the soldiers' rations.[13]

Bishop Pedro Tamarón y Romeral, visiting New Mexico in 1760, was alarmed by the ineffective defense of the province

[11] Francisco Antonio Marín del Valle, Bando, Santa Fé, November 26, 1754, SANM, Documento 530.

[12] An Account of the Lamentable Happenings in New Mexico and of Losses Experienced Daily in Affairs Spiritual and Temporal written by Father Fray Juan Sanz Lezaún in the Year 1760, in Hackett, *Historical Documents*, III, 472.

[13] Report of the Reverend Father Provincial Fray Pedro de Serrano to the Most Excellent Señor Viceroy Marqués de Cruillas in Regard to the Custodia of New Mexico, Year of 1761, in Hackett, *Historical Documents*, III, 485.

against the hostile Indians. He believed that the danger presented by these tribes threatened the very life of the frontier provinces and suggested that greater use of infantry forces, such as a unit of 3,000 men recruited from the presidios and settlers of the northern provinces, be made. Although such a force would attract less enemy attention than a mounted expedition and would free troops from the duty of guarding the horse herds,[14] such a recommendation was highly impractical for conducting warfare against such a highly mobile enemy as the hostile tribes of New Mexico. Most of the suggestions offered by visitors in the period from 1760 through 1776 were impractical.

The only realistic frontier Indian policy in this critical period was that of Vélez Cachupín. Once he had taken office again in 1762, he re-established the peaceful situation he had achieved during his first term. As before, he made peace with the Comanches, sent Pueblos to scout the distant frontiers of the province, especially to the east and south, and increased his auxiliary forces by enlisting former enemy tribes. In addition, he reinstituted the practice of trading with the Plains Indians at Taos. Instead of maintaining one central arsenal of weapons at Santa Fe, he dispersed his equipment, sending some to the individual pueblos, where *alcaldes mayores* were made responsible for its maintenance and use. At Pecos Pueblo the governor reported that he had one small campaign cannon, 3 pounds of powder, and 250 musket balls. At Galisteo, the equipment was about the same, but Picurís and Taos had greater quantities of powder and more musket balls. Each of the locations included in this report had one small campaign cannon, but all of the equipment distributed to the designated villages was administered by the district *alcaldes mayores.*[15] Although there were no Pueblo Indians settled in the capital itself, the

[14] Eleanor B. Adams (ed.), *Bishop Tamarón's Visitation of New Mexico, 1760.*
[15] Tomás Vélez Cachupín, Informe, February, 1762, AGN, Provincias Internas 102, Expediente 2, Foja 172.

people residing there being all castes and Spaniards (*gente de razón*),[16] Vélez Cachupín noted that a *genízaro* Indian named Diego de Sena possessed one musket.[17]

The judicious Indian policy pursued by this official was particularly important to Spain during the period following the conclusion of the Seven Years' War. With the acquisition of Louisiana from France, the threat of French traders dealing arms to the Plains Indians had subsided, but in the next half-century English traders became an even more serious menace. At the same time Spain was plagued by her involvements in foreign wars, which drained off troops and funds sorely needed to defend and administer her enlarged North American territory.

To deal with the continuing problem of her vast northern frontier, Spain tried a variety of remedies. She established new presidios, relocated others, subjected them to official inspection, examined detailed reports, ordered expensive campaigns against the hostiles, and entertained recommendations from all quarters. Yet, the results were always the same. In the quarter-century ending in 1772, 4,000 persons and over 12,000,000 pesos were lost to the marauding tribes in the region north of Chihuahua.[18] Even the great *visitador-general* José de Gálvez (1765–71) was frustrated in his efforts to pacify the frontier.[19]

The best way to stabilize the northern frontier of New Spain was to establish a relative peace such as Vélez Cachupín had done on two occasions in New Mexico. However, such a situation was not destined to continue there, especially under a new governor with different policies. Mendinueta, upon assuming office in 1767,

16 Father Manuel Nepomuceno y Trigo to Fray José de los Ríos, July 23, 1754, in Hackett, *Historical Documents*, III, 465.

17 Vélez Cachupín, Informe, February, 1762, AGN, Provincias Internas 102, Expediente 2.

18 Alfred B. Thomas, *Forgotten Frontiers: A Study of the Spanish Indian Policy of Don Juan Bautista de Anza, Governor of New Mexico, 1777–1787*, 5.

19 Herbert I. Priestley, *José de Gálvez: Visitor-General of New Spain (1765–1771)*, 268.

View of Zuñi Pueblo about 1900, showing mission church, terraced architecture, and typical ladders for access to upper stories.

Walpi, First Mesa, Hopi or Moqui Reservation, Arizona, as it looked around 1900.

initiated a decade of open warfare against the *indios bárbaros*, concentrating especially upon the Comanches to the north and east of the settled areas of the province. His emphasis upon martial activity necessitated all sorts of defensive measures, many of which included the use of Pueblo Indians as auxiliaries in the over-all defense of New Mexico.

For the first time, the Comanches had penetrated the Sangre de Cristo Mountains north of Taos Pueblo, perhaps using La Veta Pass in present southern Colorado. Once the mountain barrier had been crossed, the raiders from the plains near the Arkansas River met with no obstacles. They extended their depredations into the San Luis Valley and toward Taos, Santa Fe, and new Spanish settlements in the Río Arriba district. The recently established community of Ojo Caliente, north of San Juan Pueblo and on the west bank of the Río Grande, which was composed largely of *genízaros*, was in the direct path of the Comanches who approached New Mexico from that direction. Formerly the Utes had resided in this area, but they had now been pushed westward into the San Juan Mountains along the modern Colorado-New Mexico boundary.

To meet this new threat, Mendinueta established by the end of May, 1768, a new temporary post on the Cerro de San Antonio, north of Ojo Caliente.[20] For a garrison force, the Spanish official detailed fifty men from the presidio and nearby Indian villages (probably from Taos and Picurís) to watch the ford on the Río Grande generally used by the Comanches to reach the west bank of the river and thus facilitate their raids southward. Alfred B. Thomas believes that this was the earliest military post to have been established within the present boundaries of Colorado,[21] but it

20 Thomas, *The Plains Indians and New Mexico, 1751–1778*, 39. This is probably the modern San Antonio Peak, some sixteen miles west of the Río Grande and north of Tres Piedras, New Mexico. There are no outstanding hills in southern Colorado which could rival this as a landmark in the San Luis Valley. Anza's map of 1779, however, appears to place the peak too close to the Río Grande.

21 *Ibid.* Thomas' error is apparently based upon his use of Anza's latitude readings, which are erroneous. The thirty-seventh parallel marks the southern boundary of

was obviously located in northern New Mexico, overlooking the Río Grande.

As Comanche activity increased in eastern and northern New Mexico, it also gradually pushed the Apaches further southward, forcing them to forage deep into the northern provinces of New Spain, where they frequently devastated Coahuila, Nueva Vizcaya, and even Sonora. The Viceroy of New Spain reported in 1772 that 140 inhabitants had been killed, 7,000 horses and mules had been stolen, and that whole herds of cattle and sheep had been destroyed in the northern provinces during the previous year.[22] These widespread activities often ranged westward across New Mexico, especially in the southern part of the province between El Paso and the Jornada del Muerto, severing this region from continuous communciation with the more populous areas to the south. When such occurred, and as the raids reached Zuñi, Tubac, and Sonora by November, 1772, New Mexico became virtually an island colony.[23]

Recommendations for resolving the Indian problem were received from all sources, including the *visitador-general*, José de Gálvez, and the Marqués de Rubí, who inspected the frontier presidios between 1766 and 1768. The latter's suggestions were reflected in the *Reglamento de 1772*, which abolished some frontier presidios and moved others so as to establish a new line of fifteen presidios from Texas to Sonora. New Mexico, although it retained

---

Colorado today. However, on Anza's map this line lies just north of Santa Fe. If Thomas' conclusion is correct about the Cerro de San Antonio, then Ojo Caliente and the "Valley and Pueblo of Taos" on this same map also lie in Colorado. Obviously this is an error which could have been avoided had the author carefully examined the river systems and other geographic features depicted by Anza. Triangulation, using at least three other known points, would have revealed the error. Robert W. Frazer, "Governor Mendinueta's Post on the Cerro de San Antonio," (University Studies No. 49) University of Wichita *Bulletin*, Vol. XXXVI, No. 4 (November, 1961) also concludes that the present San Antonio Peak in northern New Mexico and Mendinueta's Cerro de San Antonio are one and the same. The location is therefore clearly in New Mexico, not Colorado.

[22] Antonio María de Bucareli to Julián de Arriaga, Ministro General de Indias, No. 193, México, January 27, 1772, in Thomas, *Forgotten Frontiers*, 6.

[23] Thomas, *Forgotten Frontiers*, 8.

its presidio, was not within this perimeter of defense but remained an exposed northern salient well beyond it. Since the presidio of Santa Fe obviously contained an insufficient force to protect the province, a more permanent solution to the problem of defense had to be sought. Of necessity, the province had to resort to the extensive use of a citizen militia and Indian auxiliaries just to hold the areas already settled. In the critical period before 1776, Spanish authorities had no Indians but the Pueblos upon whom they could rely for consistent and quantitative support in the defense of New Mexico.

The assistance of these natives was favorably noted by Hugo O'Conor, who was dispatched to the northern frontier in 1775–76 to implement the provisions of the *Reglamento de 1772*. O'Conor found conditions in the northern provinces vastly changed from the peaceful ones encountered by Rubí, from 1766 to 1768, upon which the *Reglamento* was based. Therefore, he suggested extensive changes be made on the basis of his own observations. He recommended that ten frontier detachments be formed, two of which were to be in New Mexico. The two groups in that northern province were to be composed of *vecinos* and friendly Indians. They were to defend the frontier primarily against the Comanche menace, but against other frontier tribes as well. O'Conor reported that "the friendly Indians" were the Pueblos, namely those from Jémez, Zía, Santa Ana, Sandía, Isleta, Laguna, Acoma, and others he admittedly didn't know. He was confident, however, that they were a peaceful people, devoted to agricultural pursuits and the raising of livestock.[24]

The detachments that O'Conor proposed for New Mexico were to have a total of 565 men. He suggested that a body of 100 troops be added to the recruitment of citizen militia from each of the

[24] Enrique González Flores and Francisco R. Almada (eds.), *Informe de Hugo O'Conor sobre el estado de las Provincias Internas del Norte, 1771–1776*, 106–107.

141

provinces, thus establishing a total of 2,228 men for a general campaign on the northern frontier. The levies for New Mexico were to be about two-thirds Pueblo Indian:

Communities	Spaniards	Indians
Jémez	0	40
Zía	0	50
Santa Ana	0	80
Vicinity of Bernalillo	15	0
Sandía	0	25
Town of Albuquerque	80	0
Atrisco and Pajarito	25	0
Isleta	0	40
Vicinity of Valencia and Tomé	30	0
Vicinity of Belén and Pueblo of *genízaros*	40	40
Laguna and Acoma	0	100
Totals	190	375[25]

Governor Mendinueta closely observed the problems of defense in New Mexico and made recommendations to improve conditions there. Unique among his proposals was the suggestion that the Spaniards, who were widely dispersed along the Río Grande, be collected into centrally located, easily defended, fortified towns resembling those of the Pueblo Indians. He cited the lack of unity among the Spanish settlers and recommended that they emulate the Pueblos in defending themselves against the Comanches, Apaches, Utes, and Navahos.[26] Here was a reversal of the normal Spanish pattern of settlement and Indian policy. Usually it was the Spaniards who settled in villages and tried to reduce the Indians to easily

[25] Hugo O'Conor, Plan, Carrizal, March 24, 1775, AGN, Provincias Internas 87, Expediente 5. Thomas, *Forgotten Frontiers*, 10, states that the total for New Mexico was 595, but supplies no basis for this figure.

[26] Pedro Fermín de Mendinueta to Viceroy Antonio María de Bucareli Santa Fé, March 26, 1772, photostat from BNM, Legajo 10, Part 1. Another copy of this manuscript has been published in Alfred B. Thomas, "Governor Mendinueta's Proposals for the Defense of New Mexico, 1772–1778" *NMHR*, Vol. VI, No. 1 (January, 1931), 27–30.

controlled towns.[27] In this case, however, the natives had the better system and therefore exerted an influence upon the Europeans.

Mendinueta tried to augment his small presidial force of eighty troops with settlers and *"indios cristianos."*[28] He admonished the settlers for their reluctance to respond to his orders and pointed out that *all* should obey his instructions. No matter what time or under what conditions the orders for a campaign arrived, each settler was to appear with his horse, lance, pike, or whatever type of arms he possessed, since every inhabitant of the province had an obligation to perform eighteen days of public service annually.[29]

The cacique of each pueblo was instructed to maintain constantly in readiness a force of fifteen or twenty Indians. He was to supply them with the necessary horses and provisions for campaigns so that they could depart immediately when directed by the Governor. Once the summons had been received, the cacique would collect his force and personally conduct it in pursuit of the enemy. By this practice it was hoped that the hostiles could be prevented from escaping unpunished for their raids upon the settled communities.[30]

For general campaigns, Governor Mendinueta faced the problem of maintaining a sufficient number of horses. Since the hostile tribes had no fixed encampments and could ride wherever they pleased, the pursuing force had to be equally mobile and durable. Therefore, each man in the campaign force required at least three or four horses.[31] There was also a shortage of firearms for these expeditions, and when the auxiliaries returned, the Governor was hard-pressed to compensate them for their service. Finally, he

27 *Recopilación de leyes*, Tomo II, Libro VI, Título III, ley *i*.

28 Mendinueta to Bucareli, Santa Fé, March 26, 1772, BNM, Legajo 10.

29 Mendinueta, Bando, Santa Fé, November 16, 1771, SANM, Documento 663.

30 The Form of Government Used at the Missions of San Diego de los Jémez and San Agustín de Isleta by Father Fray Joaquín de Jesús Ruíz, Their Former Minister, [1773?], in Hackett, *Historical Documents*, III, 506.

31 Mendinueta to Bucareli, Santa Fé, March 26, 1772, BNM, Legajo 10.

could never draw on all the pueblos at once. It was impossible to use allies from Zuñi, Acoma, and Laguna in the campaigns against the Comanches, as these three western pueblos were too far from the Comanche frontier and were also usually occupied in defending themselves against the Apaches.[32]

Mendinueta used numerous Indian auxiliaries, largely recruited from the pueblos, in annual campaigns against the Utes, Navahos, Apaches, and Comanches, but, although the pursuing forces sometimes marched hundreds of miles, they seldom yielded notable results. Pueblo auxiliaries served a dual purpose on campaigns, as the backbone of military strength and as informants.

In 1768, a Taos Indian, who had earlier been a Comanche captive, advised the Spanish Governor of the whereabouts of the Comanches and of their trade to the east for weapons. Apparently they were obtaining firearms from the Jumanos, who lived in the Red River area between present Oklahoma and Texas. These Indians, also known as the Taovayas and later as the Wichitas, had obtained the arms from the advancing English traders. As a result of this information, Mendinueta personally led an expedition of 546 men, including presidiaries, militia, and Indian allies, northeastward to the vicinity of the Arkansas River. The native auxiliary force, although primarily composed of Pueblos, included some Utes and Apaches (probably from the Jicarilla, Sierra Blanca, and Cuartelejo bands who had occupied the region near Pecos Pueblo during the administration of Vélez Cachupín).[33] This campaign, however, was without apparent success.

Expeditions in 1774 were made from Albuquerque, the Keres pueblos, Laguna, and Acoma against the newly aroused Navahos. These campaign forces consisted largely of Pueblo Indian auxiliaries, supplemented by militiamen and presidiaries from Santa Fe.[34]

[32] *Ibid.*
[33] Thomas, *The Plains Indians and New Mexico, 1751–1778*, 40.

144

Before the forces departed upon each of the forays into hostile territory, mass was said for all the participants, and a brief sermon was usually given on the concept of "just wars" against the resisting natives. Occasionally, control of the Indian auxiliaries while on campaign was either lost or relaxed. In one such instance, reported by Father Francisco Atanasio Domínguez, Christian Indians removed the scalps of the hostiles before they were dead and danced with them in token of victory and revenge.[35]

Sometimes Pueblo Indians were called upon to resist the attacks of the Comanches and to conduct their own punitive campaigns without assistance from the Spanish authorities and the presidial forces. This was especially true when the enemy unexpectedly raided their villages to obtain food, horses, cattle, sheep, and captives. Then the natives of the offended pueblo had to provide their own immediate defense. An example of this type of warfare occurred at Santa Clara Pueblo in 1774, where nine Indians of that community defended themselves when attacked outside of the village. The raiding Comanches were unable to inflict any injuries on the Pueblos and were put to flight by the defenders. The Comanches were also unable to run off any of the horses, because the Santa Clarans dismounted and hobbled their horses together before the skirmish began.[36]

As the frequency and extent of the devastating raids by the *indios bárbaros* increased yearly from 1774 to 1776, the problem of defending New Mexico grew in importance. On one occasion the Comanches even raided Sandía Pueblo, which was in the heart of the settled region on the Río Grande. Apparently they were successful in running off that village's horse herd, for the Pueblos pursued

34 Frank D. Reeve, "Navaho-Spanish Diplomacy, 1770–1790," *NMHR*, Vol. XXXV, No. 3 (July, 1960), 207.
35 Domínguez, *The Missions of New Mexico, 1776*, (trans. by Eleanor B. Adams and Fray Angelico Chávez), 257, 271.
36 Mendinueta to Bucareli, Santa Fé, September 30, 1774, in Thomas, *The Plains Indians and New Mexico, 1751–1778*, 170.

them on foot. Feigning retreat, the Comanches suddenly turned on their pursuers and killed thirty-three of them in one engagement.[37]

Even the Viceroy of New Spain, Antonio María de Bucareli y Ursua, recognized the necessity for providing a better defense of New Mexico in this period. In 1775 he gave the Governor permission to arm the settlers and offered to send the province additional firearms at cost.[38] Mendinueta, however, reported that the province already had 600 muskets and 150 pairs of pistols. He believed that additional firearms could not aid in the defense of New Mexico, particularly since the inhabitants did not possess the necessary money to purchase them even at original prices. The real difficulty, according to the Governor, was a shortage of horses since the hostile Indians had been successful in stealing many from the herds of the Pueblos and Spaniards in the past few years.[39] In October of the same year, the Viceroy authorized the purchase of 1,500 horses for New Mexico to replenish the lost herds and to aid in the preservation of the province.[40]

By 1776, defense of the protruding salient of the northern frontier had reached a critical point. The hostile invasions of New Mexico were among the most serious on the entire extent of this vast region.[41] If anything, the situation had grown worse throughout the decade of the 1770's. No Spanish settlement or Indian village was safe from these depredations. To meet these attacks, Spanish Indian policy had evolved gradually to include two basic practices. The first of these, consisting of peace treaties with the Indians, was preventive. This had met with little success, except during Vélez Cachupín's terms of office, because of the independence of one band from another and the consequent inability of establishing a general peace with all the hostiles. The second was punitive and

37 Thomas, *The Plains Indians and New Mexico, 1751–1778*, 45.
38 Bucareli to Mendinueta, México, February 18, 1775, in *ibid.*, 178.
39 Mendinueta to Bucareli, Santa Fé, August 19, 1775, in *ibid.*, 184–85.
40 Bucareli, Decree, México, October 24, 1775, in *ibid.*, 189.
41 Thomas (trans. and ed.), *Teodoro de Croix*, 24.

required many campaigns into Indian country to recapture animals, rescue prisoners, and especially to chastise the enemy so as to discourage further raids.[42] The success of both practices was extremely limited by the insufficiency of presidial and regular forces, the inadequate training and discipline of militia and Indian allies, the ineptitude of leaders recruited from the local populace, the difficulty of operations and supply over such an extensive terrain, the dispersal of the settlements, the shortage and obsolescence of weapons, and the lack of co-ordination of the several campaigns on the entire northern frontier.

The continued Spanish occupation of New Mexico was more seriously jeopardized by 1776 than it had been at any time in the eighteenth century. Not since the expulsion of the Spaniards by the Pueblos in the rebellion of 1680 had the colonies of the province been in such a serious state. Now, more than ever before, the Spanish authorities were dependent upon the Pueblo Indians for information concerning the whereabouts of the many marauding bands of *indios bárbaros*. Likewise, they relied more upon them for military recruits, for campaign provisions, and for horses. But other policies had also to be devised to offer better protection for the New Mexican settlements. In the formation of these new plans, the Spaniards had one loyal element which was absent during the reconquest of the area by Vargas some eighty-four years earlier. This was a unified, organized, highly experienced auxiliary force which could attract still other native allies to the Spanish colors, and thus aid in pacifying the province.

[42] *Ibid.*, 10–11.

★ 6 ✛
The Crisis Resolved, 1776–1794

Drastic frontier reorganization began on August 22, 1776, with the instructions issued by Charles III to Teodoro de Croix. This Caballero of the Teutonic Order and brigadier in the army was appointed governor and commandant-general of the Interior Provinces of New Spain, which included Texas, Coahuila, Nueva Vizcaya, Sonora, Sinaloa, New Mexico, and the Californias. Such an extensive region thus became virtually a separate governmental unit, independent, with some minor exceptions, from the Viceroyalty of New Spain.[1]

There is some uncertainty as to why the king chose this particular moment to create the commandancy-general. Alfred B. Thomas' conclusion that the threatened collapse of the entire northern frontier demanded attention,[2] although open to question since the amount of information on frontier conditions available to the

[1] Bernard E. Bobb. *The Viceregency of Antonio María Bucareli in New Spain, 1771–1779*, 143–44. There is an excellent chapter in this work on the general aspects of the reorganization of the Provincias Internas and the early efforts of Croix to overcome the Indian problem in the North.

[2] *Teodoro de Croix*, 16.

148

Council of the Indies was limited,[3] is not entirely without application to the region. New Mexico is most illustrative of this fact, for its condition in 1776 was among the worst in the vast Spanish empire. Indeed, the province probably was involved in more warfare over a continuous period of time for the decade preceding the reorganization of the Provincias Internas than any other region in the New World.

Yet, from this uncertain and unstable situation in 1776, New Mexico's problems were gradually reduced in the course of the next eighteen years. By 1794 the province had once more become stabilized, as it had been in 1754 under Governor Vélez Cachupín. What caused this relatively sudden change in Spanish-Indian relations after nearly a century of open warfare with the *indios bárbaros* surrounding the province? The answer may be found in the adoption of a more aggressive, consistent, and better administered Indian policy for New Mexico and all of the northern region. Basically this involved the continuance of military campaigns, but these were now co-ordinated with similar efforts throughout the entire northern area. Also, Spain employed balance of power tactics in dealing with the northern provinces, defeating strategic hostile tribes and then effecting alliances with an increasing number of these former enemies.[4] In addition, there was much greater co-ordination of effort between the various isolated districts, and the personnel involved in both the formation and carrying out of frontier policy were more familiar with the local problems and the Indian tribes with whom they dealt.

Neither the concept of the commandancy-general in the Provincias Internas nor the particular Indian policy in this era was entirely new. Recommendations for a separate authority to administer the vast northern reaches of New Spain had been made for over twenty

3 See Bobb, *Viceregency of Bucareli*, 144–45, for a detailed discussion of this subject.
4 Joseph E. Park, "Spanish Indian Policy in Northern Mexico, 1765–1810," *Arizona and the West*, Vol. IV, No. 4 (Winter, 1962), 344.

years preceding Charles III's instructions of 1776. Likewise, the specific practices and techniques adopted for dealing with the hostile tribes had been advanced on many occasions. Some of the suggestions for particular practices, as well as the actual execution of many of the earlier recommendations, were evident in the first few decades of the eighteenth century, even if often applied sporadically.

It is also important to note that difficulties with many raiding Indians on the northern frontier, including those menacing New Mexico, were not immediately resolved by the appointment of Croix. The new commandant-general deliberately studied the situation, first from reports and records in Mexico City and later from actual observations on the frontier itself. He examined the reports from each province, as well as prior recommendations, before he undertook any specific action to improve the situation. In addition, it must be pointed out that the policies developed after 1776 could not be universally employed on every frontier. Certain adjustments had to be made for the special conditions encountered within each province, but the general objectives and the broad outlines of policy remained essentially the same. Delays were, of course, frequently encountered. These were caused by a variety of factors, beginning with Croix's exhaustive survey of conditions, which consumed nearly two years. In the period following his arrival on the frontier, other factors arose to divert primary attention from Indian problems. The necessity of employing royal troops to wage the war against Great Britain, and to defend against invasion after 1779, further delayed the enforcement of the basic Indian policy. Local conditions also contributed to the lack of uniformity in the pacification of the hostile Indians. Some areas were relatively well armed, were provided with better presidial forces, and had greater experience in combating the attacks of the wild Indians. In certain regions the marauders were neither numerous nor well equipped for long-term opposition to the Spaniards.

Consequently, Apaches and Comanches continued to plunder Indian and Spanish settlements on the northern frontier while the inhabitants lived in constant dread of their attacks. From June through August, 1777, these two enemy nations killed 61 persons, captured 18, and killed more than 1,200 head of livestock.[5] In the following year the Comanches alone either killed or captured 127 persons solely in New Mexico.[6] Once his study of frontier depredations and defenses was completed, Croix called for a general council of war to meet in Chihuahua to establish a basic Indian policy for the northern frontier. This body adopted fifteen specific objectives within its general program, including these five major points:

1. An alliance of Spaniards with the Indians of the North against the Apaches.

2. The conclusion that Apaches were unreliable and would not keep either promises or peace treaties.

3. The belief that the Comanches were in every way superior to Apaches, and, therefore, their assistance must be obtained in subduing the common enemy, the Apaches.

4. An observation that the average frontier presidio, consisting of only fifty-six men, could not attend to all its duties, such as guarding horse herds, escorting supplies, carrying mail, and performing other minor duties, and still defend the area assigned to it.

5. A conclusion that settlers had to be recruited to supplement the presidios, but the simultaneous recognition that they had to pay the costs themselves, and that their absence on campaigns deprived their families of support, while exposing their possessions to raids by other hostile Indians.[7]

Croix considered the defense of New Mexico particularly impor-

[5] Mendinueta to Croix, Santa Fé, September 9, 1777, in Alfred B. Thomas, "Antonio de Bonilla and Spanish Plans for the Defense of New Mexico," *New Spain and the Anglo-American West* (ed. by George P. Hammond), I, 184.

[6] Teodoro de Croix, General Report, 1781, in Thomas (trans. and ed.), *Teodoro de Croix*, 111.

[7] Thomas, *The Plains Indians and New Mexico, 1751–1778*, 53–55.

tant to the security of New Spain's northern provinces. He directed much of his attention toward overcoming the extensive problems faced by this frontier salient. He made a continuing effort to coordinate activities in that province with those of other regions to the south, concentrating upon reducing the Comanche threat first, then establishing an alliance with them, and finally gradually subduing the resisting Apache bands one by one. Thus, the policies determined by the Chihuahua Council could be applied particularly well in New Mexico. With only one presidio, the province was forced to rely for defense upon its settlers and its only large native auxiliary force, the Pueblo Indians. Since the citizen militia was a comparatively unreliable element for military service, the great weight of the task fell upon the loyal allies.

Military authorities, such as Lieutenant Colonel Antonio Bonilla, had previously noted the presence of an abundant supply of man power in New Mexico to defend the province, but their estimates were based upon total numbers of both settlers and Indians. These officials simultaneously emphasized that lack of arms and horses rendered the citizenry of that region useless. Bonilla observed that Spanish authorities in the province were unable to obtain assistance from Zuñi, Acoma, and Laguna, since they were too far away from the principal area of the war against the Comanches and had to defend themselves from Apache threats in their own districts. He concluded that hardly 250 Spaniards and an equal number of Indians were equipped with horses and proper arms for the defense of the province.[8]

Bonilla pointed out that all the inhabitants of New Mexico had an obligation to serve in the general defense of the province, but that at present they were a "congregation of dissident, discordant, scattered people without subordination, without horses, arms,

---

[8] Lieutenant Colonel Antonio Bonilla, Puntas historicas sobre Nuevo México, Año de 1776, AGN, Historia 25, Expediente 7, Paragraphs 16–17. Bonilla's observations and recommendations may also be examined in Thomas' essay cited in note 5, this chapter.

knowledge of their handling, and were governed by their [own] caprice."[9] He proposed that formal militias be created with experienced individuals in command and that remuneration be provided since the cost of each man on campaign could exceed 150 pesos. This revenue could be obtained, he suggested, from a levy upon local trade.[10]

Pueblo Indians were one of the most well-organized, experienced elements used in the defense of New Mexico during this period. In 1782 the province still contained eight *alcaldías*, centered at Santa Fe, Santa Cruz de la Cañada, Taos, Keres, San Carlos de Alameda or Sandía, Albuquerque, Laguna and Zuñi.[11] Each pueblo within these jurisdictions was ruled in local matters by an alcalde, or sometimes by a war captain, and various subordinates who were elected yearly and were under the direct supervision of the district *alcalde mayor*, who was appointed by the governor.[12] During the last half of the eighteenth century, after a slight drop during the first decade of the period, Pueblo population gradually increased, but the Spanish settlers of the province began to increase at a much more rapid pace. A comparison of the population elements for New Mexico in this era follows:

	1750	*1760*	*1793*	*1799*
Spaniards	3,779	7,666	16,156	18,826
Indians	12,142	9,104	9,275	9,732
Totals	15,921	16,770	25,431	28,558[13]

9 Bonilla, Puntas historicas, AGN, Historia 25, Expediente 7, Paragraph 44.

10 *Ibid.*, Paragraph 47; Thomas, "Antonio de Bonilla and Spanish Plans for the defense of New Mexico," *New Spain and the Anglo-American West* (ed. by George P. Hammond), I, 186. Bonilla also noted that the population of New Mexico in 1776 consisted of 5,781 Spaniards, and 12,999 Indians, for a total of 18,780 persons. The estimates of the Indian population are considerably higher than those made by other observers in the period before 1800.

11 Morfi, Descripción geográfica, Año de 1782, AGN, Historia 25, Expediente 6. This is a copy of the original.

12 Bancroft, *History of Arizona and New Mexico*, 271, citing 1793 letter of the second Viceroy Revilla Gigedo.

13 *Ibid.*, 279. These estimates of population, like all other statistics in New Mexico

Father Juan Agustín de Morfi noted many changes in the locations of Pueblo people in his report of 1782. Galisteo, for example, had already begun to feel the effects of the continued Comanche pressures in the preceding decade and a half before peace was established with that tribe. Only fifty-two Indians remained there; three times that number had fled to Tesuque, north of Santa Fe. The decline at Pecos was even more marked. Morfi reported that the depopulation at both of these places was largely due to the frontier position of the villages, the enemy having destroyed other sites such as those of San Marcos, San Cristóbal, and San Lázaro. The situation in the north was much the same. Many of the formerly occupied settlements were now abandoned because of Comanche raids. Even the Taos jurisdiction, although still held by friendly Indians, had experienced a decline in population, and the mission founded for the Jicarilla Apaches in 1733, some five leagues north of Taos, was abandoned. Despite frequent hostilities and the numerous campaigns made from the southern and western *alcaldías*, including Zuñi, Laguna, and Alameda, Morfi noted that these pueblos were still "well populated."[14]

In 1778 another military officer, Lieutenant Colonel Juan Bautista de Anza, was appointed governor of New Mexico. Charged with the execution of the policy determined at Chihuahua in that same year, Anza reviewed presidiaries, militia, and auxiliaries in

---

during this century, must be examined critically. Except for the numbers of Indians, these figures agree closely with those of Bonilla in 1776. However, the only two categories of people reflected are Spaniards and Indians. The former must have included the castes and mixblood population, whereas the latter showed only the pureblood Indians residing in the villages. Some pueblos did decline in population, but the figures evidently conceal the fact that many mestizos undoubtedly still resided in the native communities. Tesuque is an excellent illustration. There were no Spaniards shown at that pueblo as of 1760, whereas there were 232 Indians; by 1793 this same pueblo had 293 "Spaniards" and only 138 Indians. Many of the so-called Spaniards must have been mestizos, still very much a part of the Indian community. The same observation can be made for Santa Clara, San Juan, and San Ildefonso—all of which declined as the population of nearby Santa Cruz increased. Thus, population figures for this period can be very misleading for there were more "Indians" available for duty as auxiliaries than the actual figures for the pueblos reveal.

14 Morfi, Descripción geográfica, AGN, Historia 25, Expediente 6.

Ruins of Quarai, north of Mountainair, New Mexico, as they now appear.

Present-day view of the ruins at Gran Quivira (Tabirá), southwest of Mountainair, New Mexico.

the El Paso district before reaching Santa Fe in the latter part of the year. Soon after his arrival in the capital the new Governor established two definite policies to meet the problem of provincial defense. First, he campaigned against and negotiated with the frontier tribes to ward off their attacks and to secure their friendship. Second, he attempted to reorganize Spanish settlements by collecting the scattered, unprotected families into towns similar to the Indian pueblos, which provided a better defense against Apache, Comanche, and Ute raids.[15]

The Governor's military campaigns were extensive and gradually resulted in reducing the number of enemy tribes. Comanches received most of his attention in the early years of his administration. During Anza's term their raids became increasingly less frequent because of tribal losses and the defeats inflicted upon them. By the end of 1778 they conducted only a few minor attacks in the vicinity of Abiquiú, Ojo Caliente, and the valley of the Río Chama.[16]

Anza even decided to carry the war into the home country of the hostile tribes. For these ventures he adopted many of the policies and practices of his predecessors. He employed a large number of Pueblo Indian auxiliaries at first and later augmented them with other tribes whom he had either conquered or conciliated. In August and September, 1779, Anza personally led a force of 600 men[17] on a punitive expedition from San Juan de los Caballeros, north of Santa Cruz, to find and defeat the Comanches in the north under the chieftainship of Cuerno Verde. Anza's large military unit included an auxiliary force of 259 Indians, who served as scouts

---

15 Thomas, *Forgotten Frontiers*, 374.

16 Croix to Juan Bautista de Anza, January 8, 1779, SANM, Documento 714.

17 This figure has been established by analysis of the document entitled Expedición de Anza y Muerte de Cuerno Verde, August and September, 1779, Santa Fé, November 1, 1779, AGN, Historia 25, Fojas 267–88. This report was prepared by Anza for the commandant-general. The table included by Anza shows a total force of 645 men, but there are two errors in addition. Thomas, *Forgotten Frontiers*, 67, says that the number was 573, but no basis for such a total can be found.

and as an integral portion of the expeditionary element.[18] The new Governor outfitted settlers and Indians alike, allotting each a good horse, although the "best" persons were said to have two mounts. Their equipment, however, was limited and their munitions were in short supply, as reflected by the fact that there were only three charges of powder for each musket.[19] Nevertheless, the expedition achieved two resounding victories over the Comanches, one culminating in the death of Cuerno Verde in an engagement between present Pueblo and Walsenburg, Colorado.

Having broken the Comanche resistance, Anza turned his attention to other trouble spots. He always took Pueblo auxiliaries with him on his visits as well as his campaigns. Thus, on September 10, 1780, he led 126 men, including 88 Pueblo Indians (40 Tewas, 40 Keres, and 8 converted Moquis) to the Moqui villages of present northeastern Arizona.[20] In his campaign of November, 1780, against the Apache threat from the south, he took 151 men, including 34 Indians.[21] His later Apache campaigns of 1785 involved forces of, first, 120 horsemen, 30 foot soldiers, and 92 Pueblos, and, second, a combined operation of Pueblos, Spaniards, and Navahos against the Gila Apaches.[22]

In these expeditions Anza assured his faithful allies of all spoils taken in battle except horses. There was, however, to be no pillaging until the engagement with the enemy was completed so that none of the foe might escape. Looting would be permitted by all members of the expedition once an encounter was concluded.[23]

18 Expedición de Anza y Muerte de Cuerno Verde, August and September, 1779, AGN, Historia 25, Foja 270.

19 Thomas, *Forgotten Frontiers*, 67.

20 *Ibid.*, 228. Note that the author errs on page 27 when he concludes that there were only forty-eight Indians.

21 *Ibid.*, 193. Again there is a discrepancy between this figure and the one of thirty-six used on page 37 by Thomas.

22 *Ibid.*, 47.

23 *Ibid.*, 253.

In addition, rewards were offered for the head of each hostile which the auxiliaries might kill and for each captive taken alive.[24]

In his reorganization of the settlements, Anza required that each Spanish town have a minimum of twenty families settled in a pueblo-like village with plazas and construction similar to the native towns. These buildings were to be complete with gunports and bastions. He attempted to relocate some of the settlers and concentrate them in a few selected locations, but this met with violent opposition and appeals to the commandant-general.[25] In pursuing such a policy, Anza only repeated a practice previously employed by Vargas and recognized as beneficial by both Mendinueta and Bonilla in the previous decade. Although popular opposition largely nullified the relocation of New Mexico's Spanish citizenry, Anza did succeed in improving the general defensive position of the province.

By 1786 conditions had changed in New Mexico. Spain's participation as an ally of France in the North American War for Independence had ended, peace had finally been restored with the Comanches, the size of the presidial force at Santa Fe had been increased from 80 to 119, and the population of the province had grown to 20,810.[26] It was now possible to concentrate on defense against the Apaches, for Anza had succeeded in adding new allies—Comanches, Utes, Navahos, and Jicarilla Apaches—to his already closely established alliance with the Pueblos. Now there were six nations allied against one highly scattered and disunified enemy.

New weapons, especially *carabinas*, had reached the northern

24 Croix to Anza, Arizpe, October 23, 1780, SANM, Documento 809. The bounty for captives taken was 100 pesos each.

25 Thomas, *Forgotten Frontiers*, 379.

26 Croix, General Report, 1781, in Thomas (trans. and ed.), *Teodoro de Croix*, 105–106. Although these figures are for 1781, they present a fair estimate of the size of the presidio and population five years later.

frontier by the end of Anza's term of office. Although not carbines in the nineteenth-century or modern sense, these were refinements upon the old *escopeta* of earlier times. Governor Anza in April, 1786, received 200 of these new firearms, which had been sent for the aid of the inhabitants of the province. He distributed them throughout the area under his administration. This dispersal of weapons is of unusual importance since it clearly proves that the Spanish policy of prohibiting Indians from carrying such weapons was not the standard practice in New Mexico by this time. Anza's report of the following year reveals that he provided one of the *carabinas* for an interpreter, Francisco García, and one each to the alcaldes of Laguna and Zuñi. Eight of them were sent to the alcalde of Laguna Pueblo for distribution among his people on the occasion of campaigns against hostiles. One was presented to Tomás, an Indian from Santa Ana Pueblo, and another to Juan Luján, an Indian of the Santa Cruz de la Cañada jurisdiction.[27]

Yet, this distribution of firearms to officials and Pueblo Indians is not the only significant aspect of Anza's report, for it reveals that he also presented Comanches and Utes with *carabinas*. One was given to the Comanche Josef (alias "El Sarco"), another to the "captain" of the same tribe, Pasaginanchi, a third to the Ute captain Muguisachi, and a fourth to another Ute captain named Pinto. Eleven other *carabinas* were divided among various "settlers, Pueblo Indians, and allied Utes and Comanches."[28] Anza's summary reveals the wide dispersal of these weapons:

In control of the Indians cited	25
At Laguna	8
Gifts for the wild Indians	10

[27] Juan Bautista de Anza, Relación de las carabinas ... del Nuebo México ... Santa Fé, October 28, 1787, AGN, Provincias Internas 65, Expediente 6, Foja 9. This is a copy of the original. Although the document does not so state specifically, these *carabinas* presumably went to *alcaldes mayores* for their control, not to individual Pueblo Indian alcaldes.

[28] *Ibid.*

Lost	11
Storage in armories	146
Total	$\overline{200}$[29]

Viceroy Bernardo de Gálvez, who had been exposed to frontier conditions and policy-making while serving as governor of Louisiana during the war of the English colonies against their mother country, promulgated extensive instructions on August 26, 1786, for a new and uniform Indian policy on the northern frontier. These called for "swift and vigorous warfare with the Indians who declared it, peace with those who solicited it, and an effort to win allies among the warlike nations by spreading the use of Spanish foods, drinks, weapons, and customs among them."[30] Gálvez urged widespread use of the Indian auxiliary in New Mexico, Sonora, and Nueva Vizcaya and observed that troops must operate in those areas with the aid supplied them by both Spanish settlers and the Indians of the pueblos.[31]

Pueblo Indians were to be employed in conjunction with other native allies for a unified campaign against the Gila Apaches in the region of present southwestern New Mexico and southeastern Arizona. According to the instructions of the new commandant-general, Jacobo Ugarte y Loyola, Navahos also were to join the Spanish troops, Pueblos, and settlers of the province for this expedition. Governor Anza was directed to purchase supplies for all the allies and to send gifts, such as scarlet cloth and medals, to the Navahos. Additional horses and mules were sent to New Mexico specifically for the Indian auxiliaries, and their use by the soldiers of the regular military forces was expressly forbidden.[32]

---

29 *Ibid.*

30 Bernardo de Gálvez, *Instructions for Governing the Interior Provinces of New Spain, 1786* (trans. and ed. by Donald E. Worcester), 23. Unique recommendations to furnish firearms and livestock to the hostile Indians are included in these instructions with the objective of making the Indians dependent upon the Spaniards.

31 *Ibid.*, 69, 72.

32 Thomas, *Forgotten Frontiers*, 48, 54, 269.

For the Gileño campaigns, Pueblos generally comprised a large part of the total Spanish force. The expedition of 1786, involving a total of 235 men, included 60 Pueblo Indians, 22 Comanches, and 26 Navahos.[33] In the following year a highly-organized general expedition under Commandant-Inspector Joseph Antonio Rengel, encompassing resources from various provinces, included 99 Pueblos among the 340 men from New Mexico. The expeditionary force from that province met at Laguna Pueblo, one of the three customary rendezvous points for western campaigns, and was organized in the following marching order:

1st Division

Troop of Santa Fe (mounted)	22
Pueblo of Acoma (foot)	24
Comanches (mounted)	30
Settlers from Sandía (mounted)	4
Jicarilla Apaches (mounted)	5
Total	85

2nd Division

Troop of Nueva Vizcaya (mounted)	21
Settlers from Albuquerque (mounted)	22
Settlers from Santo Domingo (mounted)	20
Pueblo of Laguna (one mounted, others on foot)	6
Pueblo of Acoma (foot)	12
Settlers from Sandía (mounted)	4
Total	85

3rd Division

Troop of Nueva Vizcaya (mounted)	23
Settlers from La Cañada (mounted)	14
Settlers from Santa Fe (mounted)	21
Settlers from Santo Domingo (mounted)	3
Pueblo of Zuñi (foot)	25
Total	86

[33] Letter of the Commandant-General [Jacobo Ugarte y Loyola], July 1786, AGN, Provincias Internas 65, Expediente 2, Paragraph 46.

4th Division

Troop of Santa Fe (mounted)	13
Settlers from La Cañada (mounted)	25
Settlers from Santo Domingo (mounted)	13
Pueblo of Laguna (foot)	28
Pueblo of Zuñi (foot)	5
Total	84[34]

From this organizational plan it may be noted that each division was now a separate army in itself, complete with experienced regular troops and leaders from the presidios, settlers from Spanish jurisdictions, and Pueblo, Jicarilla, and Comanche auxiliaries. Pueblo Indians, principally from the western villages of Zuñi, Acoma, and Laguna, still comprised the major portion of the native allies, but strangely they participated in this expeditionary force on foot in spite of the horses provided for their use. Perhaps these animals dispatched earlier from the south did not reach them. The Comanche auxiliaries, on the other hand, had 120 horses, which completely surprised the Apache enemy.[35]

Monetary payments were rendered to the friendly tribes for their assistance on this expedition,[36] and 6,000 pesos were sent, along with horses and *carabinas*, for further campaigns of this type.[37] The agility and physical stamina of the Pueblos was noted in 1788 by the new Governor Fernando de la Concha, who admired the obedience of these natives to his campaign summons.[38] As for the enemy, La Concha was advised by Commandant-General Ugarte to save the lives of his Apache prisoners so that they could be converted to the Spanish way of life. This procedure, Ugarte observed,

34 Diario de la campaña ... de Don Joseph Antonio Rengel, October 21, 1787, AGN, Provincias Internas 128, Expediente 2.

35 *Ibid.*

36 Fernando de la Concha, Bando, Santa Fé, [1788?], SANM, Documento 1025.

37 Estado que ... esta provincia ... , Santa Fé, June 20, 1788, AGN, Provincias Internas 65, Expediente 7, Foja 28.

38 Fernando de la Concha, Informe ... , Año de 1788, AGN, Provincias Internas 254.

would continue to reduce the number of enemies in this region.[39] It might be added that it would also continue to increase the number of potential auxiliaries supporting the Spanish cause.

By the time La Concha became governor, there were 2,647 persons in Santa Fe, Santa Cruz, Keres, Alameda, and Albuquerque employed in military pursuits. In addition, there were 2,354 Indian auxiliaries who were organized as follows:

Jurisdiction	*Pueblos*	*Cap- tains*	*Lieu- tenants*	*Pri- vates*	*Number*
Santa Fe	Tesuque	1	1	50	52
La Cañada	Abiquiú	1	1	54	56
	San Juan	1	1	47	49
	Santa Clara	1	1	62	64
	San Ildefonso	1	1	85	87
	Pojoaque	1	1	26	28
	Nambé	1	1	40	42
	Picurís	1	1	55	57
Keres	San Felipe	1	1	105	107
	Santo Domingo	1	1	140	142
	Cochití	1	1	160	162
	Santa Ana	1	1	115	117
	Zía	1	1	120	122
	Jémez	1	1	118	120
Alameda	Sandía	1	1	94	96
Albuquerque	Isleta	1	1	90	92
Taos	Taos	1	1	118	120
Laguna	Laguna	1	1	204	206
	Acoma	1	1	240	242
Zuñi	Zuñi	1	1	294	296
Pecos	Pecos	1	1	95	97
9 Jurisdictions	21 Pueblos	21	21	2,312	2,354[40]

[39] Jacobo Ugarte y Loyola to Fernando de la Concha, January 23, 1788, SANM, Documento 998.

[40] Estado que . . . esta provincia . . . , Santa Fé, June 20, 1788, AGN, Provincias Internas 65, Expediente 7, Foja 28. Note the decline in relative strength from the older auxiliaries such as those at Pecos, Tesuque, and Picurís.

New practices and concepts particularly pertinent to the use of Indian auxiliaries were evident after 1788. Pueblos often are mentioned only incidentally on military campaigns, and sometimes it appears that they did not participate at all.[41] Increasing use of Comanches, Navahos, Utes, and converted Apaches may be noted. However, numerous Pueblo Indians were included on special campaigns such as Governor La Concha's expedition of August through early October, 1788. Like the earlier forays against the Gila Apaches, this effort was made not only to defeat the enemy but also to drive him southward. The long-range objective was to crush these hostile bands between Spanish and Indian auxiliary forces from New Mexico in the North and similar forces operating from Sonora and Nueva Vizcaya in the South. With the final defeat of the Gileños, New Mexico would no longer be isolated from the province of Sonora.

The campaign itself is worth a detailed study because it reveals the organization, employment, and fighting characteristics of the native auxiliaries. When the Governor departed from Santa Fe on August 22, 1788, only sixty-four presidiaries, eight Comanches, and eight Jicarilla Apaches accompanied him. At each of his camping places—Santo Domingo, Alameda, and Isleta—he added friendly Pueblo Indians and settlers to his force. From Isleta he dispatched a scouting expedition of twenty soldiers and an equal number of settlers (probably including some Pueblo Indians from that southern village, since Spaniards did not normally reside in quantity at Indian pueblos). This party was instructed to reconnoiter the Ladrón and Magdalena Mountains southwest of Isleta and then rejoin La Concha at Laguna Pueblo, the *plaza de armas*, for the general campaign. The Governor then proceeded to that Keresan

41 The absence of Pueblo auxiliaries may be observed in many documents of the era following 1788. An example is [La Concha] Instrucciones al alférez Pablo Sandoval, Santa Fé, July 14, 1790, SANM, Documento 1087. See also La Concha to Pedro de Nava, November 1, 1791, SANM, Documento 1164(3) and La Concha to Viceroy Revilla Gigedo, May 6, 1793, SANM, Documento 1234.

village where, at the end of August, he recruited more allies, including Navahos, obtained cattle, horses, and sheep for the sustenance of the expedition, and finally organized his command into four basic elements. Although he held a final review of his forces and equipment on August 28, he failed to provide any muster rolls or other details which would clearly indicate the strength and organization of his expeditionary force.[42]

Despite the fact that the scouting unit returned from its reconnaissance without finding the enemy, La Concha departed from Laguna after mass had been said, leaving behind two soldiers and four settlers who were reported to be ill. He proceeded to Acoma Pueblo, where he also became ill, and sent the troop on its way southward under the command of Lieutenant Manuel Delgado. By September 2, however, La Concha rejoined the force, and three days later he sent forty-eight men ahead as spies or scouts under the leadership of the Navaho (?) chieftain El Pinto. Upon encountering a band of Apaches in the Gila Mountains on September 10, La Concha observed that he could not restrain his Indian allies. They surged ahead directly at the enemy, killing eighteen of them and taking four prisoners. A few days later the governor reported that some Taos Indians,[43] who had separated from the main army to follow the fleeing Apaches, returned with a saddled horse, two Apache horses, and a *coyote* girl whom they said the Apaches had held as a captive. The Taos war captain presented these prizes to the governor.[44]

The expedition returned through Fray Cristóbal on the Río Grande, where La Concha dismissed the Navahos and Pueblo Indians of Jémez, Zía, and Santa Ana before returning to the

[42] Fernando de la Concha, Diario, Santa Fé, November 19, 1788, AGN, Provincias Internas 193. This is a copy of the original.

[43] The governor does not mention Taos Indians as part of the auxiliary force upon departing from Santa Fe. Unless this was an error of omission, the only logical place where they could have joined the expedition was at Laguna.

[44] La Concha, Diario, November 19, 1788, AGN, Provincias Internas 193.

capital on October 6. The Governor reported favorably on his impressions of the loyalty and suffering experienced during the campaign by the officers, troops, settlers, Pueblo Indians, and other allies who had served as auxiliaries in his army. Because of a lack of supplies and the poor state of the horse herd, La Concha had curtailed the campaign.[45] Although the results were not particularly outstanding, the record of the expedition is important for the information it provides on the uses made of the native auxiliaries. The foray did succeed in driving the Gila Apaches southward and at least temporarily away from the New Mexican settlements.

During the six years of La Concha's administration as governor, progress in overcoming the menace of the numerous *indios bárbaros* is apparent. No longer was there any threat to New Mexico from the northeast, east, north, or northwest. Comanches, Utes, Navahos, and Jicarilla Apaches remained allied to the Spaniards throughout the period. Only in the southwest, where there were occasional troubles with the Gileños, was there any notable hostility. Indeed, New Mexico had reached a state of relative peace when compared to the turmoil of the proceding decades. The quantity of cattle and mules within the province increased markedly, and horses were in plentiful supply by 1791.[46] By the last decade of the eighteenth century, probably the greatest difficulty was in maintaining unity among the auxiliaries since there were long-standing hatreds of one nation for another. The antipathy between the Utes and the Comanches, by then nearly a half-century old, is an outstanding example of this difficulty, but no serious problems seem to have arisen in this area. Every effort must have been made to insure that these rivalries did not flare up anew, thus jeopardizing the tranquility of the province.

Retaliatory campaigns continued against various Apache bands.

[45] *Ibid.*
[46] La Concha to the Commandant-General of the Provincias Internas del Oriente Pedro de Nava, Santa Fé, November 1, 1791, SANM, Documento 1164(3).

Raiding Natagé Apaches in the vicinity of Tomé and Belén, south of Albuquerque, were pursued by fourteen Indians from Isleta Pueblo, all mounted bareback, during June, 1791,[47] and Gila Apaches were followed in a more extensive western campaign in 1793. In this latter expedition, forty Indians from Acoma and Laguna, led by the *alcalde mayor* of the district, caught up with the fleeing hostiles after a chase of some twenty-five miles, but they were ambushed by a band of twenty-two Apaches which attacked from behind, killing three Pueblos and putting the rest to flight.[48] To punish the victorious Gileños, the Governor personally led a large military expedition composed of most of the regular troops from the presidio, militia forces, and Indian auxiliaries (who served additionally as scouts) from the pueblos of Taos, Laguna, and Jémez.[49] Heavy snow and inability to locate any major groups of the enemy rendered the campaign generally unsuccessful.

In his lengthy instructions prepared for his successor, Fernando de Chacón, Governor La Concha provides an excellent and fairly complete analysis of the Indian situation in New Mexico in 1794. A Spanish alliance and friendship had been maintained with the intrepid Comanches, the Utes, the Jicarilla Apaches, and the Navahos since their close relations with the Gila Apaches had been severed in 1786, but La Concha saw the need for continued warfare against the one remaining enemy, the rebellious Apache bands variously known as Faraones, Mimbreños, Gileños, and Natagees. He further noted the need for obtaining interpreters and furnishing them with provisions. Outlining some of the Indian hatreds and friendships, he cautioned the incoming governor to be aware of them at all times. La Concha recommended the continuance of the

47 La Concha to Revilla Gigedo, Santa Fé, July 1, 1791, SANM, Documento 1129.
48 La Concha to Pedro de Nava, Santa Fé, April 30, 1793, SANM, Documento 1231.
49 *Ibid*. Although the governor states that the last-named natives were "Tiguas," it is probable that he meant Jémez Pueblos. He refers to that pueblo as an ally in this campaign during the course of his letter of November 19, 1793, to Pedro de Nava, SANM, Documento 1266.

important practice of giving the heathen tribes presents of clothing, hats, mirrors, knives, cigars, oranges, and indigo whenever they visited Santa Fe in peace.[50]

Defense of the province received much of the outgoing Governor's attention. In this analysis, La Concha reviewed Anza's organization of militia companies under *alcaldes mayores* and lieutenants. He recommended that both settlers and Indians be considered for campaign duty, always designating the former by name and title and the latter only by number. Evidently, like many of his predecessors, he had become disillusioned with the role played by the settlers, for he warned Chacón not to give them anything other than arms and munitions even though they would often ask for horses and provisions.[51]

Contrary to his impressions of the settlers, La Concha had nothing but the highest praise for the exemplary service of the Pueblo Indians. He noted that they would never ask for anything except the munitions to which they were entitled, that they were truthful and obedient, and that they did not steal. He further pointed out that the six Keres pueblos should not be counted in the total native force available for service since they maintained their own detachment to resist the invasion of the Apaches. From the remaining total of the Christian Indians, however, the new Governor was advised that he should count on each individual for fifteen days of military service every two years, whereas the settlers were required to give only fifteen days every six years.[52]

By the end of La Concha's administration in 1794, there was a notable change in the conditions within the province of New Mexico. For the first time in over a century the region enjoyed an extended, relatively peaceful state. The population began to in-

50 La Concha, Instrucción . . . , Chihuahua, June 28, 1794, AGN, Historia 41, Expediente 10, Fojas 1–26, Paragraphs 3–10.

51 *Ibid.*, Paragraphs 13–15.

52 *Ibid.*, Paragraphs 15, 23.

167

crease at a more rapid rate, and the livestock industry began to prosper. Crops could be raised without fear that they would be stolen by hostile Indians or confiscated by campaigning troops. Certainly, all of New Mexico's problems with marauding Indians had not been completely overcome by this time. They would not be solved to such a degree for nearly another century. But it is apparent that the resolution of the major difficulties with the *indios bárbaros* not only had preserved the province for Spain but had insured that it would prosper in many respects.

What had caused this major improvement in the security of the province? Why was New Mexico never again to experience the decline and uncertainty to which it had been exposed in 1776? One of the major reasons for this reversal was the adoption of a sensible, consistently enforced Indian policy. This program was based not on innovation, but on a consolidation of the techniques and practices learned by over a century of experience.

The near pacification of New Mexico's enemy tribes between 1776 and 1794 was basically achieved by the enforcement of the general Indian policy for the Provincias Internas. This policy was formulated by Commandant-General Croix and his Council at Chihuahua in 1778, and elaborated by Viceroy Gálvez in his celebrated *Instrucción* to Commandant-General Ugarte in 1786. Basically, this policy called for effecting an alliance with the powerful Comanches, intensifying their war on the Apaches, turning the Apache bands against each other, and waging a co-ordinated war of Spaniards and Indian allies against the remaining hostile Apaches, which would annihilate them, force their complete surrender, or, at least, reduce their capability to raid the settlements.

In New Mexico the main tenets of this policy were successfully carried out by Governor Anza. After twice defeating the Comanches in battle, he succeeded by 1786 in winning them to an alliance with the Spaniards, a reconciliation with the Ute allies, and a revitalized war on the eastern Apache tribes. By the same year, Anza had detached the Navahos from their alliance with the Gila Apaches in the west, added them to the growing number of friendly nations, and turned them against their former friends.[53]

One basic aspect of this locally developed general policy was the continuous use of Pueblo Indian auxiliaries. These loyal allies provided the strength and sustenance for the defense of Spanish New Mexico. In addition, they attracted the former enemies of the Spaniards, thus increasingly augmenting the balance of forces in favor of the Europeans and simultaneously rendering their own immediate role in the pacification of the region less arduous. In Anza's successful strategy the Pueblo auxiliaries were employed against the hostile Apaches less directly than indirectly, as diplomatic and military allies in inducing the Utes, Comanches, and Navahos to join the Spanish cause. In fact, for operations against the recalcitrant Apaches, the Spaniards relied less on the Pueblo auxiliaries than in the past and more on the newly won Indian allies.

[53] For a discussion of the basic policies of Croix and Anza, see Thomas, *Forgotten Frontiers*, 47–56, 66–83.

★ 7 ✦
Spanish Employment of Pueblo Auxiliaries

S<small>PAIN SPENT A CENTURY</small> after the beginning of the reconquest of New Mexico in the establishment of the security of the province from the widespread depredations of the *indios bárbaros*. The period from 1692 to 1794 was one of trial and error in the formation of her Indian policy for the Northern Frontier. Policies and practices were not developed rapidly; experience played a great part in the growth of a standardized policy for dealing with the aborigines who surrounded New Mexico. The use of Pueblo Indian auxiliaries was one of the earliest techniques developed and most consistently employed throughout the era.

Repeated raids by hostile bands necessitated extensive campaigning by Spanish forces to protect the settlements and to punish the marauders. The more significant of these punitive forays chronologically, indicate, as best as the records reveal, the use, recruitment, organization, leadership, and fighting qualities of Pueblo auxiliaries. It might now be appropriate to synthesize these aspects by reconstructing a hypothetical campaign in which the Pueblo warriors were enlisted. It must be realized, of course, that not all of the characteristics and practices to be discussed were developed at any given time or, indeed, within a short period of years. Evolving from an initial system, established to meet an immediate need during the reconquest, they developed with modifications throughout the course of the ensuing century.

What necessitated such a foray against hostiles and how did it commence? Generally, the campaign was either punitive or preventative in purpose, to discourage the continuous depredations of nomadic bands on the settled parts of the province. The root of the Spanish problem lay in the cultural and economic differences between the Spaniards and Pueblos on the one hand and the nomadic Indians on the other. The latter depended upon what the former produced or possessed, and obtained by plundering what it was unable to get by trading. From the Pueblos the "barbarians" took food, livestock, and captives; from the Spaniards, horses and firearms.

Friendly Pueblo informants, widely distributed over the province, reported these raids or the approach of the marauders. Sometimes they came directly to Santa Fe, and at other times they submitted their information through the local alcaldes. On occasion they even wrote directly to the governor. Once the complaint or report had been received in the capital, that Spanish official decided whether or not to call a *junta de guerra* to consider the report and to recommend what should be done to punish the offenders. Occasionally, prominent Pueblo leaders, such as the caciques and war captains, were invited to participate in these councils. Yet, the practice of consulting a junta was not followed religiously throughout the century. It was time-consuming and frequently did little more than endorse the governor's recommendations that the raid justified waging war on the offenders.

Once the decision to conduct a campaign had been reached

171

either by the governor or the *junta de guerra*, the former instructed the *alcaldes mayores* as to the quota of men to be provided from each Indian jurisdiction, the number of weapons and horses required, the time and place of assembly, and the anticipated duration of the campaign. Generally, the governor led the presidial and militia forces from Santa Fe and collected other civilian militia and Pueblo auxiliaries along his route to the designated rendezvous point. The *alcaldes mayores*, acting through the individual pueblo governors, caciques, and war captains, recruited the Christian Indians and assembled the horses and arms which were regularly maintained within each jurisdiction to meet the governor's requirements. When the necessary warriors and equipment had been obtained at each village, they joined forces and marched together to the mobilization center, each pueblo led by its own alcalde, cacique, governor, or more frequently by its war captains. In the first half of the eighteenth century, the entire body of auxiliaries from a particular jurisdiction was under the over-all command of an Indian *capitán mayor de la guerra*.

At the designated assembly point the Spanish presidiaries and militia joined the Pueblo auxiliaries. Here a final muster was held as the governor reviewed his forces preparatory to the departure upon the campaign. The *plaza de armas*, or rendezvous point, was usually an Indian pueblo, particularly one near the enemy's last reported position. Thus, if the Comanches had created the immediate threat, the assembly point was usually at Pecos or Taos. If the punitive campaign was against the Utes, the assembly was at Taos, Abiquiú, or San Juan. Western campaigns against the Navahos or the Moquis departed from Jémez, Laguna, or Zuñi. Expeditions against the Apaches, however, were launched from a variety of locations, depending upon the particular band involved and their position at the time. Sandía Pueblo and the Bernalillo district served as assembly points for the campaign against the Faraones in

1704, but later in the century, after Comanche pressures had forced most of the resisting Apaches southward, Isleta became the leading rendezvous for the majority of the campaigns against the southern Apaches, although Laguna and Acoma were used occasionally for expeditions against the Gileños in the southwest.

The campaign itself usually involved a well-organized force. Until the latter half of the eighteenth century the expedition was divided into two basic elements: the Spanish soldier-settler unit as one body, and the Indian auxiliaries as the other. The combined force was usually preceded by a group, often quite large, of Pueblo scouts from the auxiliary element which maintained a position three leagues or so in front of the main column, frequently reconnoitering the advanced area as virtually independent bodies under the leadership of their own war captains.

The basic expeditionary force remained at all times under the over-all control and command of the provincial governor or his designated representative—either the lieutenant governor, an officer from the presidio, or the *maestre del campo*. During the early part of the century the horse herds, livestock, and warriors of the auxiliary force were not allowed to mingle with the stock of, or with the regular soldiers and militia. Separate camps were pitched at night for each of the major elements within the campaign force. In the latter half of the century, especially in the last two decades, this segregation seems to have been abolished. Perhaps the presence of other native allies necessitated such a change, since the placement of Comanches near Utes or the Pueblos without the presence of Spanish troops would undoubtedly have caused friction. At any rate, the expeditions of Anza and La Concha included auxiliaries integrated within a basic four-divisional organization. Each division included presidial troops, civilian militia, and native allies—Pueblos, newly pacified Comanches, Utes, Jicarillas, Navahos, and even *genízaros*. There were no longer any *capitanes mayores* in this

173

period. Divisional officers were always Spaniards appointed by the governor, usually from among the officers of the presidial company, but occasionally from the prominent citizenry. Still, native war captains led their own forces within these basic divisions.

Pueblo auxiliaires performed a variety of services throughout these campaigns. Primarily, they constituted the principal quantitative element in the total force, usually over half the total number of men. On occasion, the proportion increased, especially as the century advanced, until it reached a maximum of 75 to 85 per cent of the expeditionary force. In addition to this major function, Pueblo allies also served as scouts, spies, messengers, and interpreters. Although no mention is made of it in the records, these natives must have performed also as guards for the horse herds and the droves of cattle and sheep which usually accompanied the expeditions.

Pueblo auxiliaries seem to have performed very well in all of the capacities in which they were employed. Their knowledge of both the terrain and the enemy made them invaluable as scouts. Their acquaintance with the languages of the hostile tribes obviously made them significant in parleys, conferences, and treaties. Most of all, however, they performed and fought well in actual engagements with the enemy. The Spaniards apparently never withheld them from battle nor relegated them to a subsidiary or rear-guard type of action. Instead, the opposite seems to have been the case, since Spanish commanders, upon encountering the enemy, had difficulty restraining the enthusiasm of the auxiliaries. Only when the expeditionary force was surprised, as at the Platte River in 1720, did the Pueblos, like all other elements of the force, behave improperly. Then, when the enemy warriors threatened to annihilate the entire expedition, the auxiliaries virtually disintegrated, retreating in utter confusion. In circumstances in which the Spanish authorities were in complete control, there was no reluctance to use the auxiliaries in any phase of combat. Both military

174

and civil officials, and even the missionaries, frequently noted the loyalty, willingness to serve, and the over-all value of Pueblo assistance on these campaigns.

Why did the Pueblo participate so willingly and so extensively on these campaigns? The answer appears to be twofold. First, these expeditions provided the Pueblo with an opportunity to carry the warfare to his traditional enemy, to chastise him for his raids, and to prevent his further depredations. Second, they supplied the Pueblo with an opportunity to share in the spoils of battle. After the enemy had been defeated, the Spanish commander usually divided their possessions among the troops, and the Indian allies shared along with the soldiers and settlers, frequently receiving captive warriors, weapons of all types, horses, other livestock, and supplies of food. Not only did they recover their own animals but also some of their own people who had been captured by the marauding enemy. Profitable as these rewards for participation on Spanish campaigns may seem, there were still other incentives in the form of privileges, titles, and special recognition to the exceptionally valorous warriors and their leaders. Moreover, by the latter half of the century, the Spanish authorities made auxiliary service even more attractive by regularly distributing annual presents to the loyal allies.

When a campaign had been concluded and the spoils divided, the Pueblo auxiliaries were dismissed and returned expeditiously to their villages. This demobilization seems to have occurred either at the original *plaza de armas* or at the first pueblo encountered on the return route. The Spanish element, soldiers and militia, continued to Santa Fe or to their respective jurisdictions under the over-all commander of the expedition, whereas Pueblos were detached to return to their villages under their own native leaders. The arrival of the governor or his designated representative in the capital marked the conclusion of the campaign.

175

Pueblo Indian auxiliaries performed a major role in the Spanish reconquest and pacification of New Mexico in the late seventeenth and most of the eighteenth century. As the constant allies of the Spaniards, these loyal mercenaries contributed to the defense of the province in many ways. They served repeatedly on campaigns against the hostile tribes which surrounded the province. Also, they accompanied missionaries and Spanish officials on expeditions to aboriginal groups not yet converted to the Iberian way of life. They served as interpreters and informants, demonstrating both their knowledge of Castilian and their fidelity to the Europeans. In addition, they contributed to the sustenance of campaign forces, providing food, horses, and other livestock as needed. Their economic assistance was as valuable, perhaps as their military aid in the establishment of tranquility within the province.

Yet, one must remember that Pueblos were not the only auxiliaries used by Spain in the expansion of her authority in the Americas. The practice of relying upon Indian auxiliaries was widely employed throughout the Spanish colonial period in almost all of her kingdoms. Nor was this the only technique used in dealing with the natives encountered in the New World. The use of missionaries, the establishment of presidios, the extension of Spanish governmental institutions to Indian communities, the retention of native political structures under the control of designated Spaniards, and the employment of certain tribes, like the Tlaxcalans and Otomies, to colonize remote problem areas—all were practices resorted to by Spanish authorities in the control and assimilation of various aboriginal elements. The use of Pueblo Indians, although an important aspect of the reliance upon auxiliaries, is only an illustration of one commonly adopted technique in one restricted area of the Spanish Empire.

Was the system of employing Pueblo auxiliaries for New Mexico's defense a good one? Naturally, the answer to such a question must involve many factors, including an understanding of problems encountered and other means available to solve these difficulties *at that time*. Above all, it is necessary to weigh the strengths and weaknesses of the practice.

The greatest benefit Spain derived from her close affiliation with the Pueblos was the establishment of unity in a province formerly torn by internal dissension and native hatred for the conquerors. This early disunity, so prominent in the seventeenth century, ultimately resulted in the expulsion of the Spaniards from New Mexico for nearly a dozen years. Beginning with the reconquest, Pueblos gradually were attracted to the cause of the Iberians, thus forming a nucleus for future development and expansion. Without the unification of the Pueblos and their subsequent association with the Spaniards, Spain could not have controlled New Mexico with the limited resources she maintained in that area. Except for rare occasions in the early part of the period when conspiracies were reported, Spain in the eighteenth century never again had to worry about her Pueblo allies rebelling against her imposed authority.

To achieve this unity, Spanish authorities rewarded Pueblo Indians with titles, recognition, privileges, gifts, and the spoils of battle. Of singular importance in this regard is the Spanish permission for Pueblos to carry firearms and ride horses almost continuously throughout the century after the reconquest. Although there is no documentary evidence to indicate that these privileges were officially sanctioned by authorities in Spain, they were so widely recognized by governors, missionaries, military officers, and visiting officials that it became an accepted fact for Pueblos to be armed and equipped like the presidiaries and settlers of New Mexico. Therefore, the generally accepted statement that Spain prohibited natives within her empire from riding horses and carrying firearms is, indeed, not true for New Mexico.

177

Pueblo auxiliaries served as the most consistently reliable element in the pacification of hostile tribes and the defense of New Mexico during the eighteenth century. The presidial force at Santa Fe, numbering only eighty troops during the major portion of this era, was too small to control the province adequately by itself. Militia forces were unreliable, poorly equipped, and often untrained and undisciplined. From Vargas to La Concha, authorities complained of the reluctance of the settlers to serve in the defense of the province. At the same time they praised the loyalty, self-denial, and military preparedness of the Pueblos in fulfilling their obligations to defend the kingdom. Of unusual importance is the fact that both civil and religious authorities seemed to agree that the natives contributed greatly to the defense of the province.

Hostile tribes gradually joined the Spanish-Pueblo side. Attracted by the privileges granted to the Pueblos, the nomadic elements realized that they, too, could share in the benefits accruing to their traditional enemies. In addition, alliance with the Spaniards did not mean that these nomads must discontinue their warlike practices. Instead, it provided an opportunity to continue fighting, but on the side of the Iberians and Pueblos against a dwindling number of rebellious tribes. Toward the end of the century it is evident that Spain actually subsidized her allies, providing them arms, horses, and even cash payments for assistance rendered.

Another great strength of the Spanish system of employing Pueblo auxiliaries was the acceleration of cultural interchange between the two groups of people. The association of Spaniards with Pueblos on campaigns, visits, and inspections facilitated the assimilation of the Pueblos and the growth of a homogeneous population, basically devoted to agricultural development, throughout the province. Evidence of this trend is provided by the more rapid increase of the general population in the last three decades of the century, whereas Pueblo Indian numbers increased only slightly. Since immigration into the province was never very great, the only logical explanation for this increase lies in the expansion of the mestizo element. With the establishment and growth of such a society, New Mexico became a region where mixbloods dominated and the economic pursuits of both Spanish settlements and Indian pueblos closely resembled each other.

Nevertheless, despite these many strengths in the use of Pueblo auxiliaries, there were drawbacks to such a system. The greatest weakness may be observed in the relative lack of success experienced by individual campaign forces. Only in a comparatively few instances were these expeditions successful enough in chastising the enemy to compensate for their extensive preparations. The system of employing native auxiliaries in conjunction with presidiaries and settlers necessitated long delays in the execution of particular campaigns. It took time for all the elements to be advised, recruited, equipped, and assembled prior to their departure in pursuit of the marauding enemy. These delays of weeks, sometimes months, allowed the enemy to scatter, thus weakening the effect of the planned expedition to chastise them. Also, in the time so consumed, other hostile tribes struck elsewhere on New Mexico's frontiers, requiring diversionary efforts by Spanish-Pueblo forces and further delaying the expedition against the original enemy.

Pueblo participation on Spanish military campaigns probably intensified the hatreds of hostile tribes for the Spaniards. Traditional native antipathies of one tribe for another only increased when it was realized that Spanish authorities were using Pueblos against the enemy as a means for the enemy's reduction. Thus, the struggle may have been prolonged, rather than shortened, since Pueblos were allowed the spoils of battle after the nomadic tribes had been defeated, and rewards were offered for captives, heads,

179

and ears. No doubt this practice led the enemy to choose resistance since the consequences of defeat were so severe.

Certainly, there were other weaknesses in the system of using Pueblo auxiliaries. Absence on campaigns injured the harvests and domestic pursuits of the sedentary natives. Likewise, it reduced the number of Indians left to defend the pueblos, thus exposing them to attacks by other tribes or even by the same enemy, should he be successful in eluding the original campaign force. All this military activity established a focus upon the pueblos since they were the rendezvous and provisioning points designated by the Spaniards. As a result, there was a continual drain on their agricultural resources and their stock-raising industry.

Like all mercenaries on campaigns, the Pueblos were often difficult to control. Their enthusiasm occasionally knew no bounds once the enemy was in view. In addition, once the Spaniards lost the advantageous element of surprise, it is obvious that the Pueblos were of no great value, fleeing in disorganized, full-scale retreat. It must be noted finally that the employment of Pueblo auxiliaries may have had an effect upon the social and political structures of their own villages. Naturally, duty as an auxiliary increased the prestige of individual native military leaders, enhancing their position relative to the traditional Pueblo chieftains. Thus, the positions of war captain and *capitán mayor de la guerra* became much more influential than those of the native governor, the cacique, or the Indian alcalde. It appears that the military and civil positions were sometimes combined as a result. On occasion, the overbearing attitude developed by auxiliaries seems to have been demonstrated within individual pueblos, further unbalancing the former social structure.

Even though there were identifiable weaknesses in the system of employing Pueblo auxiliaries, the technique was a highly realistic and practical one for the defense of New Mexico. Without the

assistance of these allies, the province could not have been recon-
quered in the last decade of the seventeenth century. At that time
only a portion of the Pueblo Indians served as the sole auxiliaries
of the Spaniards. In the early decades of the following century
these natives were first unified in support of the Spanish cause.
Then they were organized effectively, after much experimentation and vacillation. Finally, near mid-century, Governor Vélez
Cachupín integrated them into an over-all defensive concept for
the province. Later they were combined with the nomadic tribes
they had attracted, so that all could then serve as auxiliaries. By
1794 the Pueblos were only one of the many native allies employed by Spain in the defense of New Mexico, and their role in
relation to the newer auxiliaries was in decline.

Throughout the period of 1692–1794, Pueblo Indians constantly contributed to the stabilization and pacification of the
Spanish Empire in America. Their extensive support of the Spaniards in the remote province of New Mexico, especially through
their service as Indian auxiliaries, helped to reconquer, control,
and defend the province. Gradually they aided in pacifying this
northernmost interior province, not only directly through their
military aid but indirectly by attracting the resisting tribes to the
Spanish-Pueblo alliance. This constructive contribution of the
Pueblos has largely been ignored by historians and the general
public. Instead, interest has been devoted to the destructive acts
of the Pueblos in overcoming the Spaniards during the great
rebellion of 1680. The loyalty, courage, constancy, and organizational ability of the Pueblo auxiliaries in the century following the
reconquest are more notable aspects of their character, however,
than their destructive tendencies in the expulsion of the Spaniards.
Indeed, their aid was invaluable to the Spanish soldiers and settlers
of the eighteenth century, and was a positive contribution to the
defense and pacification of New Mexico.

Epilogue

SPANISH EMPLOYMENT of Pueblo auxiliaries did not end in 1794. It continued until the end of the colonial period, although authorities relied principally upon Comanches, Utes, Navahos, and some Apache bands to combat local threats as they arose. Often in the period from 1794 to 1821, difficulties were experienced with the Navahos themselves. When this occurred, Pueblos were once again recruited to join other friendly Indian allies in campaigns against the rebellious bands. Thus, even though one of the allied tribes would desert the Spanish cause temporarily, the remainder was always sufficient to chastise the dissident elements.

As a last resort, Spain could always fall back on the faithful Pueblos for military and economic assistance in subduing the *indios bárbaros*. Usually these native allies accompanied other auxiliaries, as in the last decades of the eighteenth century, but occasionally they alone participated with their Spanish allies, both presidiaries and militia, in retaliatory expeditions. In addition, they often conducted their own forays against the enemy. Essen-

182

tially, all these practices had originated in the preceding century.

Over the course of the last three decades of Spanish occupation in New Mexico there were long periods of relative peace and tranquility. After 1804, however, sporadic efforts were necessary to suppress rebellious bands of Navahos, but Spanish control over the far-flung reaches of the province was not seriously jeopardized either by these recalcitrants in the west and northwest, or by the Gileño, Faraón, Mescalero, and Natagé Apaches in the south. To combat these latter threats, Spanish officials continued to rely upon a nucleus of regular troops from the presidio of Santa Fe, the civilian militia from the settlements of the Río Grande, and an overwhelming majority of native auxiliaries, often including the Pueblos as allies in this task. Muster rolls of the New Mexico militia, although they do not depict that the auxiliaries were officially a part of that body, reveal that there were 199 Indians at the four villages of Sandía, Cochití, San Felipe, and Santo Domingo who were mounted and armed, and over 300 who were armed but not mounted. However, the total number of firearms for these same communities seems to have remained low, being only seventy-six as of 1806.[1]

For their performance as loyal allies, Pueblos and other natives received rewards or gifts of commercial articles and clothing. The interim governor of New Mexico was advised in 1810 to use all possible means to acquire and maintain their friendship, but particularly he was to offer gifts and trade goods which the aborigines especially appreciated.[2] It is evident that Indian auxiliaries also received food when on campaigns (although it may have been their own in the first place) because cattle were slaughtered to provide meat for them.[3] The policy of giving presents, which was

1 Revista de Nuevo México, San Carlos de Alameda, July 19, 1806, SANM, Documento 1995.
2 Nemesio Salcedo, Commandant-General, to Interim Governor Joseph Manrrique, Chihuahua, May 14, 1810, SANM, Documento 2321.
3 Sergeant José Alaxi, Cuenta de gastos, March 7, 1810, SANM, Documento 2296.

reported to have been initiated by Anza but which had been in existence under Vélez Cachupín nearly thirty years earlier, was continued for all tribes. These gifts included coats and blue capes with red lapels for the chiefs, three-cornered hats, medals, food, and wine.[4]

Not all of the expeditions undertaken by the Spaniards and their Indian auxiliaries were successful, but some must have achieved their objectives, for it was noted in 1810 that San Juan Pueblo had on display the heads of three Apaches taken on a foray of that year.[5]

By 1812 it was necessary to maintain 1,500 men under arms within the province. These consisted of the "veteran company" at the presidio of Santa Fe, militia, and auxiliaries. The "veteran company" was composed of 121 troops, of which 30 always guarded the horse herd, 15 were on guard duty in the capital, 7 were at Sevilleta to watch the Apache frontier, and the scattered remainder was supported at the expense of the settlers. To augment these inadequate forces, militiamen were organized into three companies, each commanded by a captain. They were recruited from the citizenry since each person (including Indians) was obligated to serve a tour of duty without pay. Each had to furnish his own horses, muskets, pistols, bows and arrows, and provisions for a forty-five day tour which was sometimes extended in length to two or three months.[6]

During the first two decades of the nineteenth century a new threat to the Spanish occupation of New Mexico appeared. The continued presence of foreigners and the increased activity of the

4 Pedro Bautista Pino, *Exposición sucinta y sencilla de la provincia del Nuevo México,* found in AGI, Guadalajara 561. This printed document is included within the cited tomo itself. See also the translation of it in H. Bailey Carroll and J. Villasana Haggard (trans.), *Three New Mexico Chronicles: The Exposición of Don Pedro Bautista Pino; The Ojeada of Lic. Antonio Barreiro, 1832; and the Additions by Don José Agustín de Escudero, 1849.*

5 Manrrique to Salcedo, Santa Fé, July 16, 1810, SANM, Documento 2339.

6 Pino, *Exposición sucinta . . . del Nuevo México,* 14–20.

norteamericanos from the United States necessitated the dispatch of many combined expeditions to determine their whereabouts. One such reconnaissance in 1817, for example, consisted of twenty-nine mounted Indians and twenty-three natives on foot, armed with thirty-three firearms, thirty-nine lances, and an unstated number of bows and arrows.[7]

By 1819, Pueblo Indian auxiliaries had been organized into both cavalry and infantry companies as depicted at Cochití.[8] To combat Navaho hostiles over the next three years, native allies from Jémez and Zuñi were employed in conjunction with settlers from various areas in the Río Abajo district.[9] Jémez contributed greatly to these Navaho campaigns. Alcalde Ignacio María Sánchez Vergara maintained constant direct communication with the governor, advising him of expeditionary activities and complying with the orders he received from the capital. Interpreter Antonio García of Jémez aided the Spanish forces on various military operations, and auxiliaries from Zía and Santa Ana made their rendezvous with Jémez Indians at that pueblo before their departure on a campaign to the west.[10] The expeditionary force of 1821 against the Navahos also assembled at Jémez Pueblo. It included 225 men in all, armed with 136 muskets, 150 lances, 3,625 arrows, 141 horses, and 126 mules.[11]

The use of Pueblo Indians as auxiliaries did not end with the Spanish withdrawal from North America in 1821 and the creation of an independent Mexico. Although troubles with the

7 Alfred B. Thomas (ed.), *Documents Bearing on the Northern Frontier of New Mexico, 1818–1819* (Santa Fe, 1929). This is a reprint of the author's article in the *NMHR*.

8 Compañía de caballería y infantería, Alcaldía de Cochití, November 5, 1819, SANM, Documento 2857.

9 See the Respuestas de Socorro, Sevilleta, Belén, Tomé, Jémez, Taos, etc., September 18–November 16, 1818, SANM, Documento 2747. See also Respuestas de las alcaldías de Belén, Albuquerque, Alameda, Cochití, Jémez, etc., May 5–22, 1819, SANM, Documento 2812.

10 Ignacio María Sánchez Vergara to Governor Pedro María Allande, Jémez, June 29, 1818, SANM, Documento 2728.

11 Estado general . . . pueblo de Jémez . . . , SANM, Documento 2994.

hostile Indians in New Mexico were not as serious as those of the previous century, when the province had been under Spanish administration, Pueblo Indians were occasionally employed by the Mexican government to combat rebellious Navaho and Apache bands over the next twenty-five years. Principal reliance, however, seems to have been placed upon Comanche allies.[12] Yet, retaliatory expeditions against these nomadic elements frequently included both Pueblo Indians and Mexican citizens.[13] In addition, the pueblos of Santo Domingo and San Juan furnished military aid to the governor of the province in his efforts to suppress internal disturbances, such as the anti-centralist insurrection of 1837.[14]

For three decades after the occupation of New Mexico by United States forces, Pueblo Indians continued to serve as auxiliaries. They aided Colonel A. W. Doniphan and Major William Gilpin in the pacification of the Navahos in late 1846,[15] and in 1849 they joined in another expedition, led by Colonel John M. Washington, against the same people.[16] By that time the United States had decided to furnish the Pueblo Indians with arms and ammunition to defend themselves against Navaho raids, but they were now prohibited from attacking their less-civilized enemies independently.[17]

That Pueblo Indian auxiliaries were still considered useful by United States authorities as late as 1868 is evident from the recommendations made in that year by John Ward, a special Indian agent in New Mexico, to the Indian Peace Commission. To resolve

---

[12] Bancroft, *History of Arizona and New Mexico*, 315.

[13] Spicer, *Cycles of Conquest*, 169.

[14] Bancroft, *History of Arizona and New Mexico*, 317.

[15] *Ibid.*, 421–22.

[16] *Ibid.*, 440. Full details on the use of Pueblo auxiliaries in this expedition may be found in Lieutenant James H. Simpson, *Navaho Expedition: Journal of a Military Reconnaissance from Santa Fe, New Mexico to the Navaho Country, Made in 1849* (ed. and annotated by Frank McNitt).

[17] Spicer, *Cycles of Conquest*, 170.

the "Navajo question" and to control the raids of these hostiles eastward, Ward suggested that fifteen Pueblo Indians or an equal number of peacefully disposed Navahos be employed as auxiliaries at each post in a proposed line from the San Juan River to Fort Bayard or Fort Cummings, thus establishing a defensive barrier west of the Río Grande and keeping the Navahos on their assigned reservation. These auxiliaries would serve principally as guides, scouts, trail-followers, and messengers. Each was to be properly armed and furnished two good horses. Ward further recommended that the United States government pay, feed, and clothe these allies and select one of their best warriors as their commander. The auxiliaries, he felt, should be housed in separate quarters, be treated kindly so as to gain their confidence, and be employed for a six- to twelve-month period. He concluded that:

> . . . every post in the Indian country, particularly in this territory, ought to have such an auxiliary force, for there can be no doubt that once they enter the service of their own accord, by proper management they can be made very useful.[18]

As the frequency and extent of Indian depredations in New Mexico were reduced in the twenty years following the Civil War, the need for Pueblo Indian auxiliaries diminished accordingly. Navahos, despite the frequent raids to secure food, horses, and other livestock in the early 1870's, were essentially pacified by the middle of that decade. Apache difficulties no longer threatened the Río Grande Valley, and their hostile bands were gradually eliminated, resettled on reservations, or pushed southward and westward into the Gila River area of present southwestern New Mexico and southeastern Arizona. By 1886, the last Apache resistance from

18 John Ward, Special Indian Agent, to Hon. S. F. Tappan, Indian Peace Commissioner, Santa Fé, August 4, 1868, Letters Received by the Office of Indian Affairs, 1824–81 MSS, New Mexico Superintendency, National Archives, Microcopy 234, Roll No. 555.

the Chiricahua, Mimbres, and Mogollones bands had been over-whelmed. After two hundred years of employment by three sep-arate governments, there was no longer any need for the Pueblo Indian auxiliary in the defense and pacification of New Mexico.

Sources Consulted

MANUSCRIPT MATERIALS

I. Primary

The great majority of the primary manuscript material used in this study has been examined at the New Mexico Archives, Santa Fe, and at the University of New Mexico Library, Albuquerque. Major attention has been devoted to the Spanish Archives of New Mexico (SANM). The original manuscripts of this collection are maintained in Santa Fe, and photostatic copies exist in the Coronado Room of the University of New Mexico Library. A second major archive consulted was the Archivo General de la Nación (AGN) in Mexico City, although it was not necessary to visit Mexico City since photostatic copies of pertinent documents exist at the University of New Mexico. Also, similar copies of documents from the Archivo General de Indias (AGI), Seville, Spain, and the Biblioteca Nacional de México (BNM), Mexico City, were examined in the Coronado Room in Albuquerque. Two of the manuscripts from the AGI were provided by Professor Max

L. Moorhead, of the University of Oklahoma, from his own research. Manuscripts are arranged below by archive, beginning with the Spanish ones, then the Mexican, and finally the New Mexican archives. One document from the microcopy of the National Archives, Washington, D. C., maintained at the University of Oklahoma Library, Norman, is included in this category. Within each archive, manuscripts are arranged, first, in alphabetical order, and, second, in chronological order under each alphabetized entry.

A. *Archivo General de Indias, Seville, Spain*

Cuervo y Valdés, Francisco, to His Majesty [Philip V], Santa Fé, July 13, 1706. Guadalajara 116, Number 260.

————, to His Majesty, Santa Fé, n. d. Guadalajara 116, Number 261.

Medina, Roque de. Extracto de la revista de inspección a la compañía de indios Pimas de San Rafael de Buenavista en los días 22 y 23 de Noviembre de 1785, San Rafael de Buenavista, November 26, 1785. Guadalajara 521 (104–5–23).

————. Extracto de la revista de inspección executada por mi dn. Roque de Medina, Teniente Coronel de cavallería y Auyadante Inspector de Presidios, en virtud del orden del sr. dn. Josef Antonio Rengel, Caballero del orden de Santiago, Coronel de Infantería de los reales Exércitos de S. M., Comandante Inspector de las tropas regladas y de milicias, que sirven en estas Provincias Internas de Nueva España, y Comandante General interino de ellas a la Compañía de Opatas de San Miguel de Bavispe en los días [*sic*] 16 de Enero de 1786, San Miguel de Bavispe, January 21, 1786. Guadalajara 521 (104–5–23).

Ugarte y Loyola, Jacobo, to Marqués de Sonora, Chihuahua, June 1, 1786. Guadalajara 521 (104–6–23).

190

B. *Archivo General de la Nación, Mexico City. Photostatic copies
in the Coronado Room, University of New Mexico
Library, Albuquerque*

Aguilar, Alfonso Rael de, Protector General, Certificate, Santa
Fé, January 10, 1706. Provincias Internas 36, Expediente 5.

———. Protector general de los indios naturales y de sus pueblos, Santa Fé, January 6, 1707. Provincias Internas 36, Expediente 1.

Anza, Juan Bautista de. Relación de las carabinas destinados
para auxilios de los vecindarios de esta Provincia del Nuebo
México recibidas en 7 de Abril de 1786, Villa de Santa Fé, October 28, 1787. Provincias Internas 65, Expediente 6, Foja 9.

Bonilla, Lieutenant Colonel Antonio. Puntas historicas sobre
Nuevo México, Año de 1776. Historia 25, Expediente 7.

Copia de Ynstrucción que dejo D[n.] Tomás Vélez Cachupín,
Gobernador del Nuevo México, a su sucesor D[n.] Francisco
Marín del Valle, August 12, 1754, Provincias Internas 102,
Expediente 2, Fojas 270 ff.

Cuervo y Valdés, Francisco, to Viceroy Duque de Alburquerque,
Santa Fé, May 18, 1705. Provincias Internas 36, Expediente 5.

———, to Viceroy Duque de Alburquerque, Santa Fé, September 23, 1706. Provincias Internas 36, Number 4, Fojas
149–50.

Diario de la campaña que sale de la villa de Santa Fé del Nuevo
México a las ordenes del Comand [t.e] Ynsp[or.] Don Jph. Antonio
Rengel, October 21, 1787. Provincias Internas 128, Expedi-
ente 2.

Diario y derrotero que hizo el Sargento Mayor Juan de Ulibarri
de la jornada que executo de orden del Señor Gobernador y
Capitán General de este Reino Don Francisco Cuerbo y Valdés,
Año de 1706. Provincias Internas 36, Expediente 4.

Diligencias hechas por el sargento mayor Juan de Ulibarri a pedimiento de parte sobre lo que en ellas se expresa, Año de 1708. Provincias Internas 36, Expediente 2.

Estado general y particular del numero de familias y personas que contienen los veinte y dos pueblos de indios reducidos del Reyno del Nuevo México, como constó de la revista, y visita general que hizo en el año de 1752 su Gobernador Don Thomás Vélez Cachupín. Provincias Internas 102, Expediente 3, Foja 1.

Estado general y particular del numero de familias y personas que contienen las 16 poblaciones españoles, y gente de razón establecidas, y pobladas en el Reyno del Nuevo México desde su consta como constó de la revista, y visita general que hizo en él, el año de 1752 su Governador Don Thomás Vélez Cachupín: y asimismo consta en él las establecidas en el Real Presidio del Passo del Norte que consta de una compañia de 50 soldados de á cavallo. Provincias Internas 102, Expediente 2, Foja 2.

Estado que manifiesta el numero de vecinos e indios que tiene esta provincia capaces de tomar armas, Santa Fé, June 20, 1788. Provincias Internas 65, Expediente 7, Foja 28.

Expedición de Anza y Muerte de Cuerno Verde, August and September, 1779, Santa Fé, November 1, 1779. Historia 25, Fojas 267–88.

Flores Mogollón, Juan Ignacio, Santa Fé, January 1713[?]. Provincias Internas 36, Expediente 3.

Galve, Conde de, to Diego de Vargas, May 28, 1692. Historia 38, Expediente 1.

Informe del Padre Fray Alonso de Posadas sobres [*sic*] las tierras del Nuevo México. Historia 3.

La Concha, Fernando de. Diario de la campaña que executó desde la Prov ª· del Nuevo México contra los Apaches Gileños, el Governador de aquella Provincia Dⁿ· Fernando de la Concha, empezado en 22 de Agosto y concluido en 6 de Octubre de 1788. November 19, 1788, Provincias Internas 193.

———. Informe general del gobernador del Nuevo México sre. el estado de aquella provincia, Año de 1788. Provincias Internas 254.

———. Instrucción formada por el Coronel Don Fernando de la Concha, Gobernador que ha sido de la Provincia del Nuevo México para que su sucesor el Teniente Coronel Don Fernando Chacón adapte de ella lo que le paresca combeniente a bien tranquilidad y fomento de la misma Provincia, Chihuahua, June 28, 1794. Historia 41, Expediente 10, Fojas 1–26.

La Peñuela, Marqués de, to Juan de Ulibarri, Santa Fé, September 6, 1709. Provincias Internas 36, Expediente 3.

———. Orden, Santa Fé, December 8, 1709. Provincias Internas 36, Expediente 3. (Another copy exists in SANM, Document 157.)

———, to Virrey, Santa Fé, January 26, 1710. Provincias Internas 36, Expediente 3.

Letter of the Commandant-General [Jacobo Ugarte y Loyola], July, 1786. Provincias Internas 65, Expediente 2.

Morfi, Fray Juan Agustín de. Descripción geográfica del Nuevo México, Año de 1782. Historia 25, Expediente 6.

O'Conor, Hugo. Plan, Carrizal, March 24, 1775. Provincias Internas 87, Expediente 5.

Páez Hurtado, Juan, to the Governor and Captain General [Marqués de la Peñuela], Santa Fé, October, 1707, in Diligencias hechas por el sargento mayor Juan de Ulibarri . . . , Año de 1708. Provincias Internas 36, Expediente 2.

Reconquista del Reyno del Nuevo México. Historia 39, Expediente 3.

Testimonio de los autos de guerra de la reconquista del reyno y Provincias de la Nueva México. Historia 38, Expedientes 1–3.

Valverde, Antonio de, to Marqués de Valero, [El Paso], May 27, 1720. Historia 394. (Copy in the SANM, Documento 308.)

Vargas, Diego de. Diario. Historia 38.

————. Diario después de veinte de Septiembre, Año de 1694. Historia 39, Expediente 3.

Vélez Cachupín, Tomás. Informe, February, 1762. Provincias Internas 102, Expediente 2, Foja 172.

C. *Biblioteca Nacional de México, Mexico City. Photostatic copies in the Coronado Room, University of New Mexico Library, Albuquerque*

Escalante, Fray Silvestre de. Noticias de lo acaecido en la custodia de la conversión de San Pablo en el Nuevo México sacadas de los papeles que se guarden en el archivo de la villa de Santa Fé empiezan desde el año de 1679. Legajo 3, Documento 2.

Flores Mogollón, Juan Ignacio. Auto, Santa Fé, July 5, 1714. Legajo 6, Documento 16. (Copy in the SANM, Documento 207.)

Interrogatorio de 1711–1712 y respuestas de indios, Año de 1711. Legajo 6, Documento 4.

Mendinueta, Pedro Fermín de, to Viceroy Antonio María de Bucareli, Santa Fé, March 26, 1772. Legajo 10, Part 1.

D. *Spanish Archives of New Mexico, Santa Fé, New Mexico. Photostatic copies also available in Coronado Room, University of New Mexico Library, Albuquerque*

Alaxi, Sergeant José, Cuenta de gastos, March 7, 1810. Documento 2296.

Alburquerque, Duque de. Mandamiento, México, July 30, 1706. Documento 124.

————, to Marqués de la Peñuela, México, July 8, 1708. Documento 143.

————, to the Governor and Captain General Peñuela, México, December 4, 1708. Documento 152.

————, to Marqués de la Peñuela, November, 1710. Documento 161.

Altamira, Marqués de, to Tomás Vélez Cachupín, México, April 2, 1752. Copia, Documento 518.

Anon. Félix Martínez. Sentence and Judgment against Him in the Matter of a Complaint of the Indians of the Pueblo of Pecos, Ordering Martínez to Make Payment in Restitution, August 16, 1723. Documento 323.

Autos de guerra de la primera campaña que Marqués de la Nava Brazinas sale a hacer la guerra a los Apaches Faraones desde la sierra de Sandía, Año de 1704. Documento 99.

Autos y junta de guerra sobre un robo que hicieron los indios Apaches del Navajo en el pueblo del San Ildefonso y orden para que el capitán Cristóbal de la Serna salga a castigarlos con cincuenta soldados, veinte vecinos, y ciento y cincuenta indios de los pueblos de este reyno, Santa Fé, October 30, 1713. Documento 199.

Autos y junta de guerra sobre si se le debe hacer la guerra a los indios gentiles de la nación Faraona, Año de 1714. Documento 206.

Autos y diligencias que se han hecho: en que se les declara la guerra a los Yndios Yutas, Año de 1719. Documento 301.

Bustamante, Bernardo Antonio de. Diario, Santa Fé, December 24, 1747. Documento 483.

Bustamante, Juan Domingo de. Interrogatorio, April 22–May 2, 1724. Documento 327.

————, to Captain Antonio de Tafoya, Santa Fé, June 20, 1724. Documento 329.

Codallos y Rabal, Joachín. Bando, Santa Fé, May 30, 1744. Documento 465.

———. Zuñi[?], September 14, 1745. Documento 465b.

———. Visita general, Año de 1745. Documento 470.

———. Santa Fé, February 4, 1746, in Diferentes ordenes politicas y militares de bandos, y otras providencias de este Governación que se contienen en este quaderno, para los efectos que en ellos se expressan, y dentro se perciben, Años de 1744, 1745, 1746, 1747, y 1748. Documento 495.

———. Testimonio, Santa Fé, December 6, 1747. Documento 483.

Compañía de caballería y infantería, Alcaldía de Cochití, November 5, 1819. Documento 2857.

Croix, Teodoro de, to Juan Bautista de Anza, January 8, 1779. Documento 714.

———, to Juan Bautista de Anza, Arizpe, October 23, 1780. Documento 809.

Cruzat y Góngora, Don Gervasio. Bando, Santa Fé, December 6, 1732. Documento 378.

———. Bando [Santa Fé, June 23, 1733]. Documento 384.

———. April, 1736. Documento 409.

Cuervo y Valdés, Francisco. Autos en campaña contra los Apaches, Santa Fé, April, 1705. Documento 110.

Despacho del Superior Gobierno de esta Nueva España, en orden a que de este R^{l.} Presidio se destaquen treinta soldados, quarenta vecinos, y setenta Yndios ausiliares con un oficial para que se junten con el campo que ba al comando del cap^{n.} D^{n.} Alonso Victores Rubín de Celis para la campaña que está mandado hacer por el exc^{mo.} Señor Virrey contra los Yndios Gentiles enemigos Nación Gilas Apaches, y sus confederados. Documento 479.

Diferentes ordenes politicas y militares de bandos, y otras providencias de este Governacion que se contienen en este quaderno, para los efectos que en ellos se expressan, y dentro se perciben, Años de 1744, 1745, 1746, 1747, y 1748. Documento 495.

Estado general que manifiesta el numero de los hombres en este pueblo de Jémez para operar en la expedisión al Navajo bajo el comandante de capitán Juan Antonio Cabeza de Vaca. Documento 2994.

Flores Mogollón, Juan Ignacio. Bando, Santa Fé, December 16, 1712. Documento 185.

Horden que deve observar el theniente General D$^{n.}$ Juan Páez Hurtado en la expedisión que se ha de executar en los requerimientos que se han de hacer a los Apaches Yutas sobre los daños que han cometido y cometen en la Jurisdisión de la Villa Nueva de S$^{ta.}$ Cruz, in Cruzat y Góngora, Santa Fé, April 24, 1736. Documento 409.

Investigación del levantamiento de indios. Documento 84.

Junta de guerra, June 2, 1720. Documento 308.

Junta de guerra que se formo en este Real Palacio de orden del Señor Capitán General Don Juan Domingo de Bustamante sobre si convenia a hacerles guerra a la nazión Cumancha, Año de 1724. Documento 324.

La Concha, Fernando de. Bando, Santa Fé, [1788?]. Documento 1025.

[La Concha, Fernando de], Instrucciones al alférez Pablo Sandoval, Santa Fé, July 14, 1790. Documento 1087.

———, to Viceroy Conde de Revilla Gigedo, Santa Fé, July 1, 1791. Documento 1129.

———, to the Commandant General of the Provincias Internas del Oriente Pedro de Nava, Santa Fé, November 1, 1791. Documento 1164(3).

———, to Pedro de Nava, Santa Fé, April 30, 1793. Documento 1231.

197

———, to Viceroy Conde de Revilla Gigedo, May 6, 1793. Documento 1234.

———, to Pedro de Nava, November 19, 1793. Documento 1266.

La Peñuela, Marqués de, to Roque de Madrid, Orden, Santa Fé, February 21, 1709. Documento 154.

———, to Roque de Madrid, Santa Fé, December 8, 1709. Documento 157. (Another copy exists in AGN, Provincias Internas 36, Expediente 3.)

Manrrique, Joseph, to Nemesio Salcedo, Santa Fé, July 16, 1810. Documento 2339.

Marín del Valle, Francisco Antonio. Bando, Santa Fé, November 26, 1754. Documento 530.

Martínez, Félix, Gobernador Interino. Diario de los acontecimientos y las operaciones. Documento 250.

Mendinueta, Pedro Fermín de. Bando, Santa Fé, November 16, 1771. Documento 663.

Mendoza, Gaspar Domingo de. Bando, Santa Fé, March 21, 1741. Documento 438.

———. Bando, Santa Fé, February 20, 1742, in Ordenes a los alcaldes mayores se este reyno sobre el cuidado y bigilencia en sus jurisdicciones. Documento 443.

Olavide y Micheleña, Enrique de. Bando, March 30, 1737. Documento 415.

Ordenes a los alcaldes mayores de este reyno sobre el cuidado y bigilencia en sus jurisdicciones. Documento 443.

Páez Hurtado, Juan. Relación de una conspiración de los indios pueblos, December, 1704. Documento 104.

Respuestas de Socorro, Sevilleta, Belén, Tomé, Jémez, Taos, etc., September 18–November 16, 1818. Documento 2747.

Respuestas de las alcaldías de Belén, Albuquerque, Alameda, Cochití, Jémez, etc., May 5–22, 1819. Documento 2812.

Revista de Nuevo México, San Carlos de Alameda, July 19, 1806. Documento 1995.

Salcedo, Nemesio, Commandant General, to Interim Governor Joseph Manrrique, Chihuahua, May 14, 1810. Documento 2321.

Sánchez Vergara, Ignacio María, to Governor Pedro María Allande, Jémez, June 29, 1818. Documento 2728.

Testimonio de los autos y junta de guerra que se mando formar por el Señor Don Juan Ignacio Flores Mogollón sobre si seria conveniente el quitar a los naturales de este reino el envije y uso de su anteguedad y los parezeres y resolvio dicho Señor Governador remitir con correo a S. M., Año de 1714. Documento 207. (See BNM, Legajo 6, Documento 16.)

Testimonio de las juntas de guerra que se formaron para hazerla campaña a la sierra de los ladrones, Año de 1715. Documento 224.

Testimonio de la junta de guerra que mando formar el señor gobernador y capitán general Don Félix Martínez y orden que se le dio al capitán Cristóbal de Serna para que se hiziece la guerra ofensiva a los Yutas y Cumanchy fronterisos deste reyno, Año de 1716[?]. Documento 279.

Ugarte y Loyola, Jacobo, to Fernando de la Concha, January 23, 1788. Documento 998.

Ulibarri, Juan de, to Governor Pedro Rodríguez Cubero, Zuñi Pueblo, March 8, 1702. Documento 85.

Valero, Marqués de, to Antonio de Valverde, México, September 26, 1720. Documento 310.

Vargas, Diego de. Diario de operaciones. Documento 53.

———. Bando, Santa Fé, May 31, 1695. Documento 57.

———. Diario, Año de 1696. Documento 60a.

———. Diario, Año de 1696. Documento 60c.

Visita de los Pueblos de S$^{ta.}$ María de Galisteo y de Nuestra Señora de los Angeles de Pecos—hecho por el Coronel D$^{n.}$ Gervasio Cruzat y Góngora, Governador y Capitán General de este Reyno de la Nueva [*sic*] Mexico. Documento 389.

E. *National Archives, Washington, D. C.*

Ward, John, Special Indian Agent, to Hon. S. F. Tappan, Indian Peace Commissioner, Santa Fé, August 4, 1868. Letters Received by the Office of Indian Affairs, 1824–81, New Mexico Superintendency, Microcopy 234, Roll No. 555.

II. Secondary

Peripheral information in the study of Pueblo Indian auxiliaries has been supplied by consulting dissertations and research papers. Although their major emphasis is upon other topics, they provide useful material on Indian policy, presidial activity, and the use of Tlaxcalans in the colonization of the northern frontier.

A. *Major Studies*

John, Elizabeth Ann Harper. "Spanish Relations with the *Indios Bárbaros* on the Northern Frontier of New Spain in the Eighteenth Century." Unpublished Ph.D. dissertation, University of Oklahoma, 1957.

Warner, Ted J. "The Career of Don Félix Martínez de Torrelaguna, Soldier, Presidio Captain, and Governor of New Mexico, 1693–1726." Unpublished Ph.D. dissertation, University of New Mexico, 1963.

B. *Minor Studies*

Adams, David. "Tlaxcalan Colonization in Northern New Spain, 1550–1777." Unpublished Seminar paper, University of Texas, 1963.

PRINTED MATERIALS

I. Primary

A. *Collected Documents*

There are in this category a few major works which include information on the use of Pueblo auxiliaries as well as those of other allies. Of great importance in any study of Spanish Indian policy is the theory developed by Spain and illustrated by the monumental codification in the *Recopilación de leyes*, originally published in 1681. On the actual day-to-day practices and experiences in dealing with the Indians, the works of Hackett and Thomas are invaluable. The former's three-volume collection of *Historical Documents* provides primary material, particularly from the missionaries in New Mexico. Their reports are important because of their criticism of civil authorities on the administration of the natives and because they supply first-hand accounts on the role of auxiliaries from observations at the pueblos themselves. Thomas, although sometimes subject to error, provides extensive documentation on frontier conditions and practices in his *After Coronado, Forgotten Frontiers, Teodoro de Croix,* and *Plains Indians and New Mexico,* all of which cover the period from 1696 to 1727, and 1751 to 1787. Other collections listed below provide background information on the Pueblo revolt of 1680 and the policies of Spain in the Mississippi Valley. All entries are arranged alphabetically.

Carroll, H. Bailey, and Haggard, J. Villasana (trans.). *Three New Mexico Chronicles: The Exposición of Don Pedro Bautista Pino; the Ojeada of Lic. Antonio Barreiro, 1832; and the Additions by Don José Agustín de Escudero, 1849 (Quivira Society Publications,* XI). Albuquerque, The Quivira Society, 1942.

Hackett, Charles W. (ed.). *Historical Documents Relating to New*

Mexico, Nueva Vizcaya, and Approaches Thereto, to 1773. 3 vols. Washington, D. C., Carnegie Institution, 1923–37.

———— (ed.). *Revolt of the Pueblo Indians of New Mexico and Otermín's Attempted Reconquest, 1680–1682* (*Coronado Cuarto Centennial Publications,* VIII, IX, ed. by George P. Hammond). 2 vols. Albuquerque, University of New Mexico Press, 1942.

Kinnaird, Lawrence (ed.). *Spain in the Mississippi Valley, 1765–1794: Translations of Materials in the Spanish Archives in the Bancroft Library* (*Annual Report of the American Historical Association for the Year 1945,* II–IV). 3 vols. Washington, D. C., Government Printing Office, 1946.

Recopilación de leyes de los reynos de las indias. 3 vols. Madrid, Impresora de dicho real y suprema consejo, 1943. (Originally published in 1681.)

Thomas, Alfred B. (ed.). *After Coronado: Spanish Exploration Northeast of New Mexico, 1696–1727.* Norman, University of Oklahoma Press, 1935.

————. *Forgotten Frontiers: A Study of the Spanish Indian Policy of Don Juan Bautista de Anza, Governor of New Mexico, 1777–1787.* Norman, University of Oklahoma Press, 1932.

———— (trans. and ed.). *Teodoro de Croix and the Northern Frontier of New Spain, 1776–1783.* Norman, University of Oklahoma Press, 1941.

————. *The Plains Indians and New Mexico, 1751–1778* (*Coronado Cuarto Centennial Publications,* XI, ed. by George P. Hammond). Albuquerque, University of New Mexico Press, 1940.

B. *Individual Documents*

Visitors to New Mexico in the eighteenth century, whether civil or religious officials, often provided astute observations on conditions and practices there. Although their recommendations were based upon their personal experiences at one particular time, occasionally they caused great changes of policy in the province and throughout the northern frontier. Of special importance in this regard are Vito Alessio Robles, *Diario y derrotero de Pedro de Rivera*, and Enrique González Flores and Francisco R. Almada, *Informe de Hugo O'Conor*. Particularly valuable in the determination of Indian policy for the 1780's is Bernardo de Gálvez, *Instructions for Governing the Interior Provinces of New Spain*, edited by Donald E. Worcester. Observations of two important ecclesiastical officials are in Eleanor B. Adams (ed.), *Bishop Tamarón's Visitation of New Mexico* and Fray Francisco Domínguez, *The Missions of New Mexico*, translated by Eleanor B. Adams and Fray Angelico Chávez. Irving Leonard's translation of *The Mercurio Volante of Don Carlos de Sigüenza y Góngora* is a useful supplement to the documentary study of Diego de Vargas' first *entrada* in 1692. Irwin R. Blacker and Harry M. Rosen have translated and edited the five dispatches of Hernán Cortés, providing the most recent version of those letters to the king which include comments on auxiliaries used in the famous conquest of Mexico. Documents are arranged below in alphabetical order.

Adams, Eleanor B. (ed.). *Bishop Tamarón's Visitation of New Mexico, 1760* (*Publications in History*, Historical Society of New Mexico, XV). Albuquerque, Historical Society of New Mexico, 1954.

Alessio Robles, Vito (ed.). *Diario y derrotero de lo caminado, visto, y observado en la visita que hizo a los presidios de Nueva España Septentrional el Brigadier Pedro de Rivera* (*Archivo Histórico Militar Mexicano*, No. 2). Mexico, Taller Autografico, 1946.

Blacker, Irwin R., and Rosen, Harry M. (eds.). *Conquest: Dis-*

patches of Cortés from the New World. New York, Grosset and Dunlap, 1962.

Domínguez, Fray Francisco Atanasio. *The Missions of New Mexico, 1776.* Trans. by Eleanor B. Adams and Fray Angelico Chávez. Albuquerque, University of New Mexico Press, 1956.

Gálvez, Bernardo de. *Instructions for Governing the Interior Provinces of New Spain, 1786.* Trans. and ed. by Donald E. Worcester (*Quivira Society Publications in History*, XII). Berkeley, The Quivira Society, 1951.

González Flores, Enrique, and Almada, Francisco R. (eds.). *Informe de Hugo O'Conor sobre el estado de las Provincias Internas del Norte, 1771–1776.* México, Editorial Cultura, 1952.

Hodge, Frederick W., Hammond, George P., and Rey, Agapito (eds. and trans.). *Fray Alonso de Benavides Revised Memorial of 1634 (Coronado Cuarto Centennial Publications*, IV). Albuquerque, University of New Mexico Press, 1945.

Hotz, Gottfried. *Indianische Ledermalereien.* Berlin, Dietrich Reimer, 1960.

Leonard, Irving A. (trans. and ed.). *The Mercurio Volante of Don Carlos Sigüenza y Góngora: An Account of the First Expedition of Diego de Vargas into New Mexico, 1692 (The Quivira Society Publications*, III, ed by George P. Hammond). Los Angeles, The Quivira Society, 1932.

Pino, Pedro Bautista. *Exposición sucinta y sencilla de la provincia del Nuevo México.* Cádiz, Imprenta del Estado Mayor General, 1812.

Simpson, Lieutenant James H. *Navaho Expedition: Journal of a Military Reconnaissance from Santa Fé, New Mexico to the Navaho Country, Made in 1849.* Ed. and annotated by Frank McNitt. Norman, University of Oklahoma Press, 1964.

II. Secondary

A. *Guides, Catalogues, Manuals*

For any extensive use of manuscript materials in the Spanish Archives of New Mexico and the Archivo General de la Nación, preliminary research in two reference works is indispensable. Ralph E. Twitchell, *The Spanish Archives of New Mexico*, lists in two volumes the documents available in that collection housed in Santa Fe. Although his translations are sometimes untrustworthy, the author's organization of material and short summaries of major documents are of considerable aid in finding pertinent information on any given subject relating to the Spanish colonial period in New Mexico. Herbert E. Bolton's *Guide to Materials in the Archives of Mexico* is of similar value for the use of the Archivo General de la Nación and the Biblioteca Nacional de México. Charles E. Chapman, *Catalogue of Materials in the Archivo General de Indias*, is useful for that documentary collection in Spain, although it preserves the old numbering system and must be converted to the new one for actual finding of manuscripts. A very useful aid for the translator of Spanish documents is J. Villasana Haggard and Malcolm D. McLean, *Handbook for Translators of Spanish Historical Documents*, since it contains abbreviations, tables, and helpful suggestions in resolving problems of paleography.

Bolton, Herbert E. *Guide to Materials for the History of the United States in the Principal Archives of Mexico*. Washington, D. C., The Carnegie Institute, 1913.

Chapman, Charles E. *Catalogue of Materials in the Archivo General de Indias for the History of the Pacific Coast and the American Southwest*. Berkeley, University of California Press, 1919.

Haggard, J. Villasana, and McLean, Malcolm D. *Handbook for*

Translators of Spanish Historical Documents. Austin, University of Texas Archives Collections, 1941.

Twitchell, Ralph E. *The Spanish Archives of New Mexico.* 2 vols. Cedar Rapids, Iowa, The Torch Press, 1914.

B. *Major Studies*

Included in this category are comprehensive studies of the history of New Mexico, scholarly works, and important monographs. Hubert H. Bancroft's *History of Arizona and New Mexico*, although somewhat outdated now and superseded by three quarters of a century of research, is still a valuable study, providing not only continuity, but also occasional information not available elsewhere. Ralph E. Twitchell's *Leading Facts of New Mexican History* provides extensive coverage of the reconquest in Volume I, but the details on eighteenth century developments are limited to a pedestrian treatment, compressed into one chapter at the end of that volume. The same author's *Old Santa Fé* contains some additional information of note on the events of the reconquest. However, the most thorough, well-documented studies of the reconquest period are J. Manuel Espinosa's *First Expedition of Vargas* and *Crusaders of the Río Grande*, which deal with the entire era of reconquest from 1692 through 1697. Cleve Hallenbeck, *Land of the Conquistadores*, is a valuable survey of the major events of the reconquest and the following century. Jesse B. Bailey, *Diego de Vargas and the Reconquest of New Mexico*, must be examined critically as it is less accurate, but it does contain useful corroborating information on the reconquest. Most of the other works listed alphabetically below supply background information or concentrate upon other regions and subjects. Of unusual importance are Philip W. Powell's *Soldiers, Indians, and Silver*, for its chapter on and understanding of the role of Indian auxiliaries, and Edward H. Spicer, *Cycles of Conquest*, for its recognition of the importance of natives in the expansion of New Spain into present-day New Mexico, Arizona, Sonora, and Chihuahua.

Aiton, Arthur S. *Antonio de Mendoza: First Viceroy of New Spain*. Durham, North Carolina, Duke University Press, 1927.

Bailey, Jesse B. *Diego de Vargas and the Reconquest of New Mexico*. Albuquerque, University of New Mexico Press, 1940.

Bancroft, Hubert H. *History of Arizona and New Mexico, 1530–1888 (The Works of Hubert Howe Bancroft*, XVII). San Francisco, The History Company, 1889.

Bobb, Bernard E. *The Viceregency of Antonio María Bucareli in New Spain, 1771–1779*. Austin, University of Texas Press, 1962.

Bolton, Herbert E. *Texas in the Middle Eighteenth Century: Studies in Spanish Colonial History and Administration*. Berkeley, University of California Press, 1915.

Bolton, Herbert E., and Ross, Mary. *The Debatable Land: A Sketch of the Anglo-Spanish Contest for the Georgia Country*. Berkeley, University of California Press, 1925.

Bolton, Herbert E. *The Spanish Borderlands: A Chronicle of Old Florida and the Southwest (Chronicles of America Series*, XXIII, ed. by Allen Johnson). New Haven, Connecticut, Yale University Press, 1921.

Carmén Velázquez, María del. *El estado de la guerra en Nueva España, 1760–1808*. México, El Colegio de México, 1950.

Caughey, John W. *Bernardo de Gálvez in Louisiana, 1776–1783*. Berkeley, University of California Press, 1934.

Chamberlain, Robert S. *The Conquest and Colonization of Yucatán, 1517–1550*. Washington, D. C., Carnegie Institution, 1948.

Chapman, Charles E. *The Founding of Spanish California: The The Northwestward Expansion of New Spain, 1687–1783*. New York, The Macmillan Company, 1916.

DeVoto, Bernard. *The Course of Empire*. Boston, Houghton Mifflin Company, 1952.

Espinosa, J. Manuel. *Crusaders of the Río Grande*. Chicago, Institute of Jesuit History, 1942.

———. *First Expedition of Vargas into New Mexico, 1692* (*Coronado Cuarto Centennial Publications*, X, ed. by George P. Hammond). Albuquerque, University of New Mexico Press, 1940.

Folmer, Henry. *Franco-Spanish Rivalry in North America, 1524–1763*. Glendale, California, The Arthur H. Clark Company, 1953.

Forbes, Jack D. *Apache, Navaho, and Spaniard*. Norman, University of Oklahoma Press, 1960.

Ford, Lawrence C. *The Triangular Struggle for Spanish Pensacola, 1689–1739*. Washington, D. C., The Catholic University of America Press, 1939.

Gardiner, C. Harvey. *Naval Power in the Conquest of Mexico*. Austin, University of Texas Press, 1956.

Gibson, Charles. *Tlaxcala in the Sixteenth Century* (*Yale Historical Publications*, XXXIII). New Haven, Connecticut, Yale University Press, 1952.

Hallenbeck, Cleve. *Land of the Conquistadores*. Caldwell, Idaho, Caxton Printers, 1950.

Hammond, George P. (ed.). *New Spain and the Anglo-American West*. 2 vols. Lancaster, Pennsylvania, Lancaster Press, 1932.

Kirkpatrick, F. A. *The Spanish Conquistadores*. Cleveland and New York, The World Publishing Company, 1962. (Originally published in 1934.)

McAlister, Lyle N. *The "Fuero Militar" in New Spain, 1764–1800*. Gainesville, University of Florida Press, 1957.

Mecham, J. Lloyd. *Francisco de Ibarra and Nueva Vizcaya*. Durham, North Carolina, Duke University Press, 1927.

Newton, Arthur P. *The European Nations in the West Indies, 1493–1688.* London, A. & C. Black, Ltd., 1933.

Powell, Philip W. *Soldiers, Indians, and Silver: The Northward Advance of New Spain, 1550–1600.* Berkeley and Los Angeles, University of California Press, 1952.

Prescott, William H. *History of the Conquest of Mexico.* New York, Modern Library, n. d. (Originally published in 1843.)

Priestley, Herbert I. *José de Gálvez: Visitor-General of New Spain (1765–1771).* Berkeley, University of California Press, 1916.

Russell, Carl P. *Guns on the Early Frontiers: A History of Firearms from Colonial Times through the Years of the Western Fur Trade.* Berkeley and Los Angeles, University of California Press, 1957.

Simpson, Lesley B. *The Encomienda in New Spain: The Beginning of Spanish Mexico.* Berkeley, University of California Press, 1950.

Smith, Donald E. *The Viceroy of New Spain (University of California Publications in History,* I, No. 2). Berkeley, University of California Press, 1914.

Spicer, Edward H. *Cycles of Conquest: The Impact of Spain, Mexico, and the United States on the Indians of the Southwest, 1533–1960.* Tucson, University of Arizona Press, 1962.

Twitchell, Ralph E. *Old Santa Fé: The Story of New Mexico's Ancient Capital.* Santa Fe, New Mexican Publishing Corporation, 1925.

————. *The Leading Facts of New Mexican History.* 5 vols. Cedar Rapids, Iowa, The Torch Press, 1911.

Villa, Eduardo W. *Historia del estado de Sonora.* (2d ed.) Hermosillo, Sonora, Editorial Sonora, 1951.

Wedel, Waldo R. *An Introduction to Kansas Archeology (Smithsonian Institution Bureau of American Ethnology,* Bulletin 174). Washington, D. C., Government Printing Office, 1959.

Whitaker, Arthur P. *The Mississippi Question, 1795–1803: A Study in Trade, Politics, and Diplomacy.* New York, D. Appleton Century Company, 1934.

————. *The Spanish–American Frontier, 1783–1795: The Westward Movement and the Spanish Retreat in the Mississippi Valley.* Boston, Houghton Mifflin Company, 1927.

C. *Minor Studies*

Information on specialized subjects provides greater depth, in some instances, for the comprehension of the role of Pueblo and other Indian auxiliaries. Scholarly articles and short monographs are listed below alphabetically.

Adams, Richard N. "Social Change in Guatemala and U. S. Policy," *Social Change in Latin American Today* (New York, Vintage Books, 1961), 231–84.

Bloom, Lansing B. "A Campaign against the Moqui Pueblos under Governor Phelix [*sic*] Martínez, 1716," *New Mexico Historical Review*, Vol. VI, No. 2 (April, 1931), 158–226.

Bolton, Herbert E. "Defensive Expansion and the Significance of the Borderlands," *The Trans-Mississippi West: Papers Read at a Conference Held at the University of Colorado, June 18–June 21, 1929.* Ed. by James F. Willard and Colin B. Goodykoontz. Bolder, University of Colorado Press, 1930, 1–42.

Cháves, Amado. *The Defeat of the Comanches in 1717 (Historical Society of New Mexico Publications*, No. 8). Santa Fe, New Mexican Printing Company, 1906.

Espinosa, J. Manuel. "Governor Vargas in Colorado," *New Mexico Historical Review*, Vol. XI, No. 2 (April, 1936), 179–87.

Frazer, Robert W. "Governor Mendinueta's Post on the Cerro de San Antonio" (University Studies No. 49, University of Wichita *Bulletin*, Vol. XXXVI, No. 4 (November, 1961), 1–11.

Hagan, William T. *The Indian in American History* (Service Center for Teachers of History, Publication No. 50). New York, Macmillan Company, 1963.

Jenkins, Myra E. "The Baltasar Baca 'Grant': History of an Encroachment," *El Palacio*, Vol. LXVIII, No. 1 (Spring, 1961), 47–64.

Jones, Oakah L., Jr. "Pueblo Indian Auxiliaries in New Mexico, 1763–1821," *New Mexico Historical Review*, Vol. XXXVII, No. 2 (April, 1962), 81–109.

————. "Pueblo Indian Auxiliaries and the Reconquest of New Mexico, 1692–1704," *Journal of the West*, Vol. II, No. 3 (July, 1963), 257–80.

Kelly, Henry W. "Franciscan Missions of New Mexico, 1740–1760," *New Mexico Historical Review Vol.* XVI, No. 1 (January, 1941), 41–69.

McAlister, Lyle N. "The Reorganization of the Army of New Spain, 1763–1766," *The Hispanic American Historical Review*, Vol. XXXIII, No. 1 (February, 1953), 1–32.

Park, Joseph E. "Spanish Indian Policy in Northern Mexico, 1765–1810," *Arizona and the West*, Vol. IV, No. 4 (Winter, 1962), 325–44.

Reeve, Frank D. "Navaho-Spanish Diplomacy, 1770–1790," *New Mexico Historical Review*, Vol. XXXV, No. 3 (July, 1960), 200–35.

————. "Navaho-Spanish Wars, 1680–1720," *New Mexico Historical Review*, Vol. XXXIII, No. 3 (July, 1958), 205–31.

Scholes, France V. "Civil Government and Society in New Mexico in the Seventeenth Century," *New Mexico Historical Review*, Vol. X, No. 2 (April 1935), 71–111.

Thomas, Alfred B. "Antonio de Bonilla and Spanish Plans for the Defense of New Mexico," *New Spain and the Anglo-American West*, ed. George P. Hammond (2 vols., Lancaster, Pennsylvania, Lancaster Press, 1932), I, 183–209.

211

———— (ed.). *Documents Bearing on the Northern Frontier of New Mexico, 1818–1819*. Santa Fe, 1929.

————. "Governor Mendinueta's Proposals for the Defense of New Mexico, 1772–1778," *New Mexico Historical Review*, Vol. VI, No. 1 (January, 1931), 21–39.

Tompkins, Stuart R., and Moorhead, Max L. "Russia's Approach to America," *The British Columbia Historical Quarterly*, Vol. XIII, Nos. 2, 3, 4 (April and July–October, 1949), 55–66, 231–55.

Twitchell, Ralph E. "The Last Campaign of General de Vargas, 1704," *Old Santa Fé*, Vol. II, No. 1 (July, 1914), 66–72.

————. "The Pueblo Revolt of 1696—Extracts from the Journal of General de Vargas," *Old Santa Fé*, Vol. III, No. 2 (October, 1916), 333–73.

West, Elizabeth H. "The Indian Policy of Bernardo de Gálvez," *Proceedings of the Mississippi Valley Historical Association for the Year 1914–1915* (Cedar Rapids, Iowa, The Torch Press, 1916), 95–101.

Index

213

control and threats of, 31–32, 38, 134, 151, 152; Spanish policies against, 32n., 80, 151, 157; assistance to Pueblos in Revolt of 1680, 38n.; spies from, 43; capture of Picurís fugitives, 60, 73; erroneous use of term for Navahos, 65n.; hostilities toward Pueblos, 80; forced south by Comanches, 80, 140; alliances and services with Spaniards, 94n., 99, 132; Spanish treatment of, 111, 161; warfare against, 166, 168; resistance of ended, 187–88

"Apachería": *see* Apache country

"Apaches Gentiles": 86

"Apaches Navajos": 114n.

"Apaches Yutas": 114 & n.

Arizona: 30n., 60, 95, 156, 159, 187

Arizpe, Mexico: 25, 31

Arkansas River, Colorado: 74, 100, 125n., 139, 144

Asientos: 7

Athapascans: 38n.

Atrisco, New Mexico: 142

Audiencia: 18

Auto de remisión of Diego de Vargas: 55

Aztec Indians: 3–4, 15–17, 19, 22

Baja California: 34

"Bárbaros Cumanches": *see* Comanche Indians

Belén, New Mexico: 142, 166

Beltrán, Sergeant Antonio: 28

Bernalillo, New Mexico: 13, 47, 65, 70–71, 77, 86, 118, 142, 172; rendezvous for Sandía Mountain campaign, 66; death of Vargas at, 67

Bocas of Abó: *see* Abó

Bonilla, Antonio de: 152–53, 154n., 157

Brigantines used by Cortés: 17

Brito, Juan de León: 23n.

Bucareli y Ursua, Antonio de (viceroy of New Spain): 146

Bustamante, Bernardo de: 119

Bustamante, Juan Domingo de: 103

Cabildo of Santa Fe: 84

Caiquiro, Cristóbal: 95

California: 8, 148

Canadian River, New Mexico and Texas: 125n., 128

Canary Islands: 13, 18

Capitán mayor de la guerra: 54, 79, 80, 98, 135, 172–73, 180

Capitulaciones: 6

Caribbean Sea: 5n.

Carlana, Chief (of Sierra Blanca Apaches): 99

Carlana Apaches: 76, 126, 130; auxiliary services of, 101n., 122; requests of for a presidio, 102; *see also* Sierra Blanca Apaches

Castilian language: 28, 39 & n., 45, 50, 79, 120–21, 123, 176

Cempoala, Mexico: 14–15, 16n.

Cerro de San Antonio: *see* San Antonio Peak

Chacón, Fernando de: 166–67

Chama, New Mexico: 115

Chama River, New Mexico: 36n., 50, 87, 155

Charles I (king of Spain and Charles V of the Holy Roman Empire): 18

Charles II (king of Spain): 33, 47, 55, 62n.

Charles III (king of Spain): 148, 150

Chichimeca: frontier, 6–7, 19, 21–22; Indians, 7, 19–22

Chihuahua, Mexico: 24, 138; supply route to New Mexico, 32; council at to determine frontier Indian policy, 151–52, 154, 168

Chimayo, New Mexico: 77

Chiricahua Apaches: 188

Cholula, Mexico: 15, 16 & n.

Christian Indians: 57, 72, 77, 79, 84, 87–88, 124, 132, 136, 143, 145, 167, 172; observations of by Rivera, 104

Cíbola: 38

Cieneguilla, New Mexico: 62, 65

Cimarron Canyon, New Mexico: 74

Cimarron, New Mexico: 74, 99

Ciudades: 9

Coahuila, Mexico: 12, 30n., 140, 148

Coara, New Mexico: *see* Quarai

Cobían Busto, Don Antonio: 103

Cochiteños: *see* Cochití Pueblo

Cochití Pueblo: 40 & n., 42, 44, 46, 55, 62, 66, 71, 77, 81, 83–84, 85n., 89, 94, 96–98,

215

The text for *Pueblo Warriors and Spanish Conquest* has been set on the Linotype in 11-point Times Roman, a highly legible and contemporary face designed by Stanley Morison. The paper on which the book is printed bears the watermark of the University of Oklahoma Press and has an effective life of at least three hundred years.

Due